Literary Trials

Literary Trials

Exceptio Artis and Theories of Literature in Court

Edited by
Ralf Grüttemeier

Bloomsbury Academic
An imprint of Bloomsbury Publishing Inc

B L O O M S B U R Y
NEW YORK • LONDON • OXFORD • NEW DELHI • SYDNEY

Bloomsbury Academic
An imprint of Bloomsbury Publishing Inc

1385 Broadway
New York
NY 10018
USA

50 Bedford Square
London
WC1B 3DP
UK

www.bloomsbury.com

BLOOMSBURY and the Diana logo are trademarks of Bloomsbury Publishing Plc

First published 2016

Library of Congress Cataloging-in-Publication Data
Literary trials: exceptio artis and theories of literature in court/
edited by Ralf Grüttemeier.
pages cm
Papers from a conference held 21–22 March 2014 in Oldenburg in
North-Western Germany. – ECIP Acknowledgments.
Includes bibliographical references and index.
ISBN 978-1-5013-0317-3 (hardback)
1. Freedom of expression–Congresses. 2. Press law–Congresses.
3. Law and literature–Congresses. 4. Obscenity (Law)–Congresses.
5. Libel and slander–Congresses. I. Grüttemeier, Ralf, 1961- editor.
K3253.A6L58 2016
342.08'53–dc23
2015018670

ISBN: HB: 978-1-5013-0317-3
ePub: 978-1-5013-0318-0
ePDF: 978-1-5013-0319-7

Typeset by Integra Software Services Pvt. Ltd.
Printed and bound in the United States of America

Contents

Notes on Contributors

Klaus Beekman is a guest-researcher at the University of Amsterdam (UvA, Netherlands) where he was Associate Professor. In 2005 he published *De wet van de letter. Literatuur en rechtspraak* together with Ralf Grüttemeier. He edited *Avant-Garde Critical Studies*.

Ralf Grüttemeier is Professor of Dutch literature at the Carl von Ossietzky University of Oldenburg (Germany). He was research Fellow of the Netherlands Institute of Advanced Study (NIAS, Wassenaar) in 2008/9; was co-editor (2003–9) and editor in chief (2009–12) of the journal *Internationale Neerlandistiek*; and is co-editor of the journal *Spiegel der Letteren* since 2013.

Katharina Hupe studied Dutch and German Language and Literature at the Carl von Ossietzky University of Oldenburg (Germany) and is writing currently her PhD in a project funded by the German Research Foundation (DFG) about trials caused by literary texts in Belgium.

Martin A. Kayman is Professor at the School of English, Communication and Philosophy at Cardiff University (Wales), serving as Head of School from 2004 to 2014. He was the editor of the *European English Messenger* (1998–2003) and is co-editor of the *European Journal of English Studies* (from 2004).

Anton Kirchhofer is Professor of English Literature at the Carl von Ossietzky University of Oldenburg (Germany). He is, among others, co-author of *Religion, Secularity and Cultural Agency* (2010) and co-editor of *The Workings of the Anglosphere. Contributions to the Study of British and US-American Cultures* (2009).

Ted Laros is Assistant Professor at the Open University at Heerlen (Netherlands). He took his PhD at the Carl von Ossietzky University of Oldenburg (Germany) in March 2014 with a thesis entitled 'Long Walk to Artistic Freedom: Law and the Literary Field in South Africa, 1910–2010'.

Claudia Lieb is Assistant Professor at the University of Münster. She is co-editor of *Philologie als Literatur- und Rechtswissenschaft. Germanistik und Romanistik 1730–1870* (2013) and she recently finished her *Habilitation*-thesis 'Germanistiken: Zum Verhältnis von Literatur- und Rechtswissenschaft 1630-1900' (2014).

Peter D. McDonald is Professor in English and Related Literature at the University of Oxford. His major publication in the field of literature and law is *The Literature Police: Apartheid Censorship and Its Cultural Consequences* (2009).

Gisèle Sapiro is Research Director at the CNRS (Centre de sociologie européenne) at Paris (France). She is the author of *La Guerre des écrivains, 1940–1953* (1999; English translation forthcoming) and *La Responsabilité de l'écrivain. Littérature, droit et morale en France (19e-20e siècles)* (2011).

Sylvia Sasse is Professor for Slavonic literary studies at the University of Zurich (Switzerland). In 2013, she was co-organizer of the international conference 'Kunsturteile & Urteilskünste. Literatur und Kunst vor Gericht' in Zurich. Sasse is co-author of (amongst others) *Mystifikation, Autorschaft, Original* (2001) and *Kunst als Strafe. Zur Ästhetik der Disziplinierung* (2002).

Acknowledgements

First of all I would like to thank all contributors to this volume, not only for their readiness to come together on 21–22 March 2014 in Oldenburg in North-Western Germany but especially for their dedication and patience to embark together on the enterprise which finally led to this volume. The meeting could not have taken place without the generous financial support of the German Research Foundation (DFG) for a project on literary trials in Belgium and South Africa. Many thanks go out to the members of my DFG team: Ted Laros and Katharina Hupe, assisted by Fabian Nattkämper and Janka Wagner, for all the work and energy they put into this project, and of course to my home university, the *Carl von Ossietzky Universität Oldenburg*, which offered a most stimulating surrounding for such an interdisciplinary enterprise.

In cultures without good publishers, projects dry up, one could rephrase Foucault. I am therefore very grateful to Bloomsbury Publishers for their trust in this project and all the persons involved in the publishing process. Especially I would like to thank my editors, Haaris Naqvi and Mary Al-Sayed. Thanks go out to the two anonymous reviewers for their very constructive reports which greatly helped in shaping this volume and Dr. Katherine Bird for correcting the English of the non-natives.

Oldenburg, March 2015
Ralf Grüttemeier

Literary Trials as Mirrors. An Introduction

Ralf Grüttemeier

The history of literary trials may have started 2,500 years ago with a case reported by Herodotus (6.21), only one or two years after the destruction of the Ionian city of Miletus – a colony of Athens – and the deportation of its inhabitants by the Persians in 494 BC. The drama writer Phrynichus turned these events into a tragedy that was performed in Athens around 493/2 BC. Unfortunately, we do not know the text of this play. But what we do know is that the whole theatre burst into tears while watching. For this reason Phrynichus was fined and the drama was forbidden ever to be performed again, Herodotus tells us (cf. Wilson 2000: 115–16). In our sources, there is no evidence that Phrynichus was punished for an individual message, for example concerning politics against Persia. Phrynichus' reputation and position seem not to have suffered, if we go by the list of plays attributed to him after the trial: he was still asked to contribute to the feast of the Dionysia and did win the competition. Nor did he change his ideas about playwriting fundamentally, since some ten years later, he returned to the 'contemporary mode' in *Phoenician Women* – in opposition to the dominant mythological mode as of for example Sophocles' *Oedipus* (cf. Cartledge 1999: 24). Apparently Phrynichus had not been convicted for using real historical topics in his drama but for approaching too directly a specific aspect of historical reality, here: the still fresh Athenian trauma of the deportation of the closely related inhabitants of Miletus, thus making the public consider and emotionally respond to this event. Or, in the words of Herodotus, he was punished 'for reminding the Athenians of troubles close to home (*oikeia kaka*)' (cit. Wilson 2000: 115). Obviously, Phrynichus had neglected 'the safe distance' that makes intense emotion in a tragedy pleasurable and valuable for the audience (cf. Finkelberg 1998: 179; Wilson 2000: 115). What the trial in the end sanctioned was the disorder caused during the sacred ritual and public feast of the Dionysia to which the performance of the tragedy contributed. Through the sanctions imposed (heavy fine for Phrynichus, eternal ban on the drama), order was sufficiently restored – at least we do not know of any further consequences.

For *law and literature* scholars nowadays, this is a strange world: a whole theatre bursting out in tears of grief during a performance, and a court punishing exactly that, while after the verdict, author and theatre-world immediately back to business as usual. At the same time, this world is still close enough to ours to conceptualize the event, notably: as a trial in which the contemporary legal system negotiated what is societally acceptable in what we would now call art or literature. In this sense, a line of continuity can be drawn from fifth century BC Athens to our days concerning the long history of the phenomenon of literary trials.

More specifically, the Phrynichus trial can function as binoculars as well as a mirror – telling us something about the institutional status of literature and the theories about literature in times and places that are not ours, within and outside a legal context, some 2,500 years ago. At the same time, exactly because of the analogies and the differences, contrasting this legal conflict with present day literary trials we can see both sides of the comparison more clearly, including the possibility to re-think the corresponding practices in contemporary times and places. Trying to make use of these two heuristic functions of literary trials is, in a nutshell, what this book is about.

Let me specify this point with a reference to a trial that recently attracted international news coverage, i.e. the one against Antwain Steward, aka Twain Gotti, for double murder, in Virginia, USA, in May 2014. The widespread media attention was caused by a judicial practice in the preparation of the trial: the use of rap music lyrics as evidence. The use of this kind of evidence can be retraced to the 1990s. Lyrics like: 'B— made me mad and I had to take her life/My name is Dennis Greene and I ain't got no f—ing wife' or 'Key for Key, Pound for pound I'm the biggest Dope Dealer and I serve all over town' (cf. Dennis 2007: 6 *et passim*) have been read literally and as autobiographical statements by the prosecution. Similarly, in the 2014 Virginia case, parts of the preliminary investigation had been directed at Gotti's lines 'Everybody saw when I motherfuckin' choked him/ But nobody saw when I motherfuckin' smoked him.'

To the surprise of many, however, in the end, the prosecution avoided going into lyrics during the trial itself. This was probably not in the last place due to the fact that the scholar Erik Nielson was waiting in a hotel nearby ready to be called into court as an expert witness. Nielson's position in these cases is clear: for him and other expert witnesses, the present judicial use of rap lyrics is 'judicial abuse'

(Kubrin and Nielson 2014: 185), at least when the lines are read literally and autobiographically. Instead, rap music lyrics should be treated 'as an art form whose primary purpose is to entertain'. Rap requires from the 'aspiring artists to create a persona worthy of respect in the rap community', a process staged within 'record industry conditions that often push would-be artists toward violent themes' (Kubrin and Nielson 2014: 186, 195). Consequently, the debate about the judicial use of rap lyrics is seen by Kubrin and Nielson as a 'battle' between judicial practices on one side and lyrics on the other as an art form that is not adequately interpreted. From their perspective, the troops in this battle might be characterized as uninformed, uncomprehending judicial experts contributing to institutional racism, fought against by cultural experts with an affinity to new art forms. Or, more generally speaking, as a battle between law and art. There can be no doubt on which side Kubrin and Nielson stand in their fight for giving rap lyrics a special status within jurisprudence. Their effort is about making clear that this kind of lyrics needs trained experts for their interpretation, as for example Nielson himself – a teacher of courses on hip-hop culture at the university of Richmond.

Such an agenda directed against retarded legal structures and practices in the name of the arts can, on an institutional level, be seen as a fight for more autonomy of the arts and literature within the law. In this respect, Kubrin and Nielson are typical for what much scholarship in the field of (pre-publication) censorship and (post-publication) literary trials are working towards. One of the classical books in the field, Edward de Grazia's (1993) *Girls Lean Back Everywhere*, for example presents its author in exactly this way: 'he continues to work for the expansion of literary and artistic freedom'. That fighting for autonomy, however, is *not* at the core of the present book, neither as its starting point, nor as its aim. What *is* at the core of this book on the judicial dealings with literature in court rooms and other legal contexts is the idea that these conflicts can be used as an analytic tool to gain insights into the basic rules and conditions guiding these clashes around literature and art within the arena of the law at specific times and places.

The literary expertise on literary trials in the present volume will be used – *nota bene* by *literary* scholars – to address questions like: What is the institutional position of literature and the arts within a specific societal context at a specific moment? What theories of literature turn out to be dominating in the conflicts at specific moments, among literary as well as among non-literary experts? What conventions and poetic values can literary scholars detect in the verbal behaviour of legal experts – ideas the latter may or may not be aware of? And what institutional explanations can be given for scholars who do take sides in what they see as a battle for 'the expansion of literary and artistic freedom'?

As will be clear by now, the book is not aiming at juicy stories about sleeping judges and ridiculous prosecutors. Instead, the questions above will be used to establish a framework for the analysis of the discussions in and around literary trials between and within literary and legal scholarship – a framework directed too at explaining the open ridicule mentioned above, which can be found in quite some work on the matter by literary scholars. Following that route, a more adequate possibility of reflecting on the judicial clashes around literature might be within reach.

International comparison, history, institutions

The following essays together form a book that opens up a three-dimensional space along the axes of international comparison, history and institutions. Essential for the profile of the volume is, first of all, the *international dimension*: the book brings together specialists from different national traditions who have been working on literary trials. These scholars present a wide range of European countries, including some of the largest. The French case is treated by Gisèle Sapiro. A global picture of literary trials in Britain is drawn in three complementary essays by Anton Kirchhofer, Peter McDonald and Martin Kayman. Ralf Grüttemeier's and Claudia Lieb's contributions try the same for Germany, with Lieb also touching briefly on Austria and the European Court for Human Rights (ECHR). Sylvia Sasse deals with literary trials in the USSR, Czechoslovakia and today's Russia. In other contributions, smaller European nations are at the centre of the essays. Klaus Beekman addresses trials in the Netherlands and Katharina Hupe deals with the basically bilingual (Dutch and French) Belgium. The set of objects is completed with a non-European point of reference: Ted Laros looks at cases of South African literary trials.

Of course such a list of topics gives an arbitrary impression – as any list would do that does not involve all countries in the world republic of literature. Let me therefore stress again that the choice of contributions in the present volume has not been one along lines of languages or countries. It has been a choice for international specialists in the field of research on literary trials. By bringing together these specialists, the volume, as a whole and in its parts, is deliberately intended as an invitation to transfer the structural questions pursued here to countries that are not treated in this volume. In that sense, the contributions should be regarded as stimulating examples for further research elsewhere – which does not mean of course that the characterization of one country can be simply transferred to another. In fact, one conclusion of this volume is that research on literary trials can only yield results if the very different legal and literary traditions and practices in a specific national or supranational context are taken into consideration.

The *historical axis* is the second dimension of the picture of literary trials drawn here, providing the general context of a certain national tradition and historical specificity in and around the trials analysed. There are two contributions that give a more or less complete historical overview of literary trials in one country. There is the opening essay by Sapiro who tells the story of 200 years of trials in France. She uses the opening of a new liberal era for the book market by the Bourbon *Charte consitutionelle* of 1814 as a starting point and touches on, among others, the famous Flaubert and Baudelaire cases and the purge trials after 1945, up to the 2013 trial against Christine Angot, accused of defamation with her novel *Les Petits*. Laros does something similar for South Africa from 1910 to 2010, where only a very limited number of cases have been taken to court. Included are for example the English language case against Wilbur Smith, the Afrikaans language case against André Brink and the measures taken against Salman Rushdie's *Satanic Verses* in post-apartheid South Africa.

The other contributions generally focus on specific trials or shorter historical periods. These cases however are always put into a wider historical context, so the readers get at least a global idea of the history of literary trials in these countries over the last one or two centuries. Beekman focuses on Dutch legal actions against obscenity in literature, theatre and film in the 1960s and 1970s, framed by the most important Dutch literary trials from 1920 to 2001. Hupe deals with the recent 1999–2000 trial against the Flemish writer Herman Brusselmans for insulting the famous fashion designer Ann Demeulemeester in a novel, analysed against a background of trials that includes among others the 1900 trial in Bruges against Camille Lemonnier. The contribution by Sasse draws the picture of literary trials in what was called the Eastern Bloc with the focus on the 1960s and 1970s, showing their roots in post-revolutionary USSR and lines of continuity up to the 2012 Russian trials against Pussy Riot. The two contributions dealing with Germany depart from one specific case respectively:

Lieb analyses the 1895 Munich blasphemy trial against the writer Oskar Panizza and Grüttemeier the 2003–9 defamation case against Maxim Biller. Both papers taken together facilitate recognizing the first brushes of a general picture of the history of literary trials in Germany from the foundation of the *Deutsche Reich* in 1871 up until today.

In a similar way an overview is given by the three contributions dealing with the UK, stretching from the mid-nineteenth century (1843 Libel Act and 1857 Lord Campbell's Obscene Publications Act) via the famous 1960 *Lady Chatterley's Lover* trial to contemporary entanglements of law, literature and arts. In this triptych, Kirchhofer dives into the discussions leading to the 1959 Obscene Publications Act while McDonald takes a 2008 *Guardian* satire accused of defamation of Elton John as the focal point for his analysis taking him into the long history of libel. The essay by Kayman visits several signposts – the relative dearth of trials after the 1960 Lady Chatterley trial; *The Satanic Verses* as the most notable trial *not* to take place in the UK; the introduction of the Racial and Religious Hatred Act in 2006; and the abolition of the blasphemy laws in 2008 – which, taken together, point literary and legal scholars towards the contemporary diagnosis of 'secular law's nervous negotiation of its relations with the sacredness of religious belief in multicultural Britain' (Kayman, *infra*). Against the background of the protests and the terror related to Mohammad representations in literature or images, with the 2015 *Charlie Hebdo* attack fresh in mind, one can confirm that this 'nervous negotiation' is definitely not restricted to Britain nor is its possible ending in sight yet.

The final and third axis of the present volume is the *institutional dimension*. From this perspective, the national courts – from jury jurisdiction and lower courts up to the Supreme or Constitutional Courts – as well as supranational courts like the ECHR are the societal arena for literary trials in which one can recognize behaviour which is typical for certain groups of actors, bound together by shared practices and resources, and always acting in contradistinction to other groups of actors. These groups will be analysed as institutions, of which the most important for our enterprise are: in the legal field the prosecution, the defence counsels and the judges, and in the literary field the authors and their organizations, the publishers and literary criticism. The contribution by Sapiro starts with an explicit overview of these institutional agents and their behaviour and options in literary trials. Her notion of institution is based on a field theoretical model inspired by Pierre Bourdieu (2011), which also underlies most other contributions in this volume, though some engage to highlight the institutional dimension from a view inspired by Michel Foucault (Kirchhofer), Judith Butler (Sasse) and post-structuralism (Kayman).

Around this core of institutions in literary trials, other groups of actors are analysed. A closer look at the roles of the witnesses for example unravels a broad range of national and historical options, reaching from laypersons whose function is only to corroborate the devastating effect of literature (or art) on others as a kind of 'effect witness' in the Eastern Bloc (cf. Sasse, *infra*) to literary experts who at certain points in history may or may not be admitted to the court room, as for example in South Africa (cf. Laros, *infra*) or the UK (cf. Kirchhofer, *infra*). These literary experts make it especially interesting to have a closer look at the institution of academic literary criticism and its relevance to the other actors in literary trials (see the contributions by Kayman and Grüttemeier). Finally, the volume touches upon institutions related to the political field, for example semi-judicial pre-publication censorship committees (as dealt with by Laros for South Africa concerning literature and by Beekman concerning film in the Netherlands) but also including looks at legislation, as in the analysis by Kirchhofer of how the 1959 Obscene Publications Act came about.

The volume does not intend to deliver a systematic classification of all institutions involved in literary trials, across times and nations – it even raises serious doubts that such an approach would be possible, given the often incompatible judicial frameworks in which these conflicts take place. The idea that binds the institutional panorama of this volume together is that only by uncovering the institutional dimension can literary trials be adequately understood. As John R. Searle (2010: 90) put it in general terms: 'We live in a sea of human institutional facts. Much of this is invisible to us. Just as it is hard for the fish to see the water in which they swim, so it is hard for us to see the institutionality in which we swim.' More specifically, the present volume shows that literary trials cannot adequately be understood when they are looked at as individual victories, losses or dramatic events – which they are of course, too, but only from the involved individual's perspective, as one of the parties in the fight. It is the institutional dimension that allows us to leave the trenches and analyse trials in their structural relevance for the relationship of literature and law and the specific societal and historical constellation of which both are a part.

Within this three-dimensional space along the axes of international comparison, historical specificity and institutions, the reconstruction of the literary trials should function as a double mirror: for literary as well as for legal scholarship interested in the fundamental questions raised above, it stimulates the reflection of the role of law and literature in their work. In spite of all efforts – as outlined above – aiming at the coherence of an edited volume: it is a central generic feature of a collection of essays by different contributors, too, that such a collection will also float on the competent richness of different and not in all respects compatible work. Therefore it is impossible – and not intended – to coerce the ten paintings that follow into one painting, let alone one with a central perspective. However, it seems that at least some visual clusters come out of the analyses taken together. The insights the articles yield are most clearly visible around the two notions that form the subtitle of the present book: *exceptio artis* and literary theories.

Exceptio artis

A central feature of literary trials from the second half of the nineteenth century onwards is the judicial acceptance of a certain kind of autonomy for literature. The research on what one might call *literature in law* (as opposed to the established notions *law in literature* or *law as literature*, cf. Dolin 2007; Olson 2014) gathered in this volume could to a large extent be summarized as showing a codification of a certain degree of social esteem for literature in legal texts or legal practices in the context of a public judicial negotiation about the boundaries of what is allowed in literature and what not. At least in democracies, this double legal move – showing esteem and imposing restrictions – can be solidified into a specific legal figure in written law and/or in jurisdiction: from the second half of the nineteenth century onwards, a possible violation of the law by a text may be judged differently when the text is classified as a literary text. This figure is what is called in the following *exceptio artis*.

There are some misunderstandings about the term possible. First of all, it is a practice that does not necessarily need an explicit codification in written law, though there are quite some countries that do have a corresponding Article in their constitution. These Articles are basically aimed at guaranteeing the freedom of artistic creativity or artistic production or of art in general. Examples can be found in the constitutions of Austria (Art. 17a STGG), Germany (Art. 5 (3)), Italy (Art. 33), Portugal (Art. 42 (1)), South Africa (Section 16 (1c)), Spain (Art. 20 (1b)) or Switzerland (Art. 21 BV). Telling only from this list, it is hard to find an explanation why the freedom of art was explicitly incorporated in a constitution.

When adding the years of constitutional codification to the countries listed here, one might give as a rule of thumb that a more or less revolutionary democratic change, following a previous non-democratic regime, seems to improve the chances of finding such a paragraph in a constitution, especially when it is drafted after the Second World War: Italy in 1947, Germany in 1949, Portugal in 1976, Spain in 1978 and South Africa in 1996 might serve as cases in point. But a drastic political change is definitely not a necessary condition, as Austria (amendment of 1982) and Switzerland (amendment of 2000) show. Still one might claim that time is on the *exceptio artis*-side, apparently.

But there is more to be said when one sticks to the historical dimension a little longer: as far as I can see, the Constitution of the Weimar Republic in Germany of 1919 was the first one ever explicitly giving art a special status in a constitution (Art. 142). Again, this was a constitution generated by a democratic revolution. But what I want to point at is another aspect: in the constitutions after the democratic revolutions in 1848 in Germany, such a special status for art is absent. What can be found in the constitution of the *Paulskirche* of 1849 however was an exception for science (cf. Knies 1967: 185), which was taken over in all other German constitutions that would follow. Obviously, art followed historically, with quite some delay, in the slipstream of a special status for science in constitutional law. Both developments could be seen as indications for the emergence of a certain autonomy of the fields of science and arts/literature within the law between 1849 and today. From this perspective and concerning the arts, the increase of constitutional *exceptio artis* examples dating from after 1945 – when most nation states already had their constitutions: documents that do not easily lend themselves to changes – indicates a growing pressure on legislation to accept a special status for art and literature in the law. A growing institutional autonomy of the fields of art and literature can be inferred as underlying this pressure. The fact that Austria and Switzerland amended their constitutions – as mentioned before: a highly inert genre – could be seen as pointing into the same direction.

This assumption seems to hold, too, when we look at the legal systems of for example France, the Netherlands or Belgium where there is no such thing in the constitution (nor elsewhere in the law), or of course at the constitution of the United States, where art is protected on the constitutional level by the freedom of speech of the First Amendment. What is striking is that the absence or presence of an explicit *exceptio artis* in *written* law, be it constitutional or not, does not allow for significant distinctions concerning the way in which the judiciary deals with literature, neither in internal comparison (for example, German jurisdiction before and after 1919; cf. Grüttemeier 2007) nor in international legal comparison between states with and without an explicit *exceptio artis* in their constitution (cf. Hempel 1991: 453; Bünnigmann 2013: 452–78). In the Netherlands for example, in the most recent trials on literature before the Supreme Court (*Hoge Raad*) in 2001 dealing with Pieter Waterdrinker's novel *Danslessen* (cf. Beekman, *infra*), many quotes from the German Constitutional Court's legal rulings can be found – in spite of the lack of any explicit special status for art in Dutch law. Still, there is no doubt that German and Dutch jurisprudence guarantee literature a quite similar high degree of autonomy at the beginning of the twenty-first century (cf. Grüttemeier 2007).

Apparently, the *explicit* codification of *exceptio artis* is obviously only *one* possibility to indicate the acceptance of a certain kind of autonomy of literature in relation to the legal field – it is not what a logician would call a necessary condition for autonomy. The British Obscene Publications Act of 1959 is another case in point. It is the first act to introduce into UK law an explicit *exceptio artis* with the criterion of 'literary merit' and in that sense can be seen as making the *exceptio artis* 'more explicit and robust' (cf. McDonald, *infra*). At the same time, this explicit codification goes along with giving to the judiciary what could be described as a couple of other judicial tools that are now written into the law since there is: the necessity that a literary text must be read as a whole and not only in its possibly obscene parts, a restriction of the relevant readership must be taken into account (the 'likely reader' gives more autonomy to literature than the average reader, with vulnerable readers – for example youth – at the far end of this autonomy-heteronomy scale) and finally the admission of evidence given by literary experts in the courtroom. None of these judicial tools was invented by lawmakers around 1959 – parts of the arsenal had been in judicial use for quite some time in order to give some autonomy to literature, even in English-law dominated South Africa, as the contribution by Laros (*infra*) shows.

Consequently, the growth of the autonomy of literature in law must be described in terms of degrees. From this perspective, British legal history before 1959 already indicates a 'significant degree of literary autonomy', as Kirchhofer (*infra*) puts it. Reviewing this historical development from an institutional perspective, a growing robustness can be detected over the last 150 years. This process starts at the latest with the Campbell Act, which did not want to bother with classical, expensive books for the elite (cf. McDonald 2008: 298). It continues for example with the recommendation of a British Parliament Select

Committee in 1908 to add in a possible new Obscenity Act – which did not come into force – a provision 'to exempt from the operation of the Act any book or reputation or any genuine work of Art' (cit. Kirchhofer, *infra*). And a new degree of robustness of the *exceptio artis* is finally reached with the 1959 Obscene Publications Act and its explicit introduction of literary merit. In that sense the 1959 Act is not a decisive revolution but part of an overall gradual increase of institutional autonomy of literature within the judiciary.

Of course, this tendency of increasing autonomy for literature is not a general rule for all countries since it depends on specific constellations of state and market (cf. Sapiro 2003). For example, the developments in the communist Eastern Bloc and today's Russia show signs of autonomization only in what could be called 'a defiant subfield based on artistic merit and political disloyalty', as opposed to the dominance of political heteronomy in the official state-controlled and state-sponsored area of culture, including political interference in the judiciary, too (cf. Sasse, *infra*). But the other legal fields analysed in the present volume corroborate the tendency of growth and stability of the autonomy of literature and art during the last 150 years. As Sapiro summarizes regarding France: 'The French laws on the freedom of the press never recognized any *exceptio artis*. In practice, however, a process of progressive recognition of the relative autonomy of literature can be observed, starting under the Third Republic, in close relation to the autonomization of the literary field' (Sapiro, *infra*).

Again, several possible misunderstandings must be addressed. One is that this 'progressive recognition' is neither teleological, nor is it linear. It is the result of a societal institutional fight between legal, political and literary actors, the result of the relation between the field of power and the literary field, and its history is full of rollbacks, as Laros (*infra*) shows for certain periods in the South African apartheid system or as the German Nazi dictatorship of 1933–45 reminds us. Furthermore, as has been stressed before, the autonomy of literature within the judiciary is always a gradual phenomenon. It never was and has nowhere become a trumping value: play this card and any prosecution will stop. I do not know of any legal system that guarantees such a status to literature, nor, by the way, to science. All there is are claims demanding such a status, but they are generally strategic claims originating from the literary field (cf. Sapiro, *infra*). The autonomy of literature in the judicial field never was and never will be absolute, it will only be a *relative* autonomy.

This has two implications: one is that the judicial conviction of a specific literary text is always an option even under the most robust *exceptio artis* existing.

The other is that a verdict in which the literary side loses is not automatically an indication for the end of literature or autonomy as we know it. The relevance of a specific verdict can only be determined when the structural and institutional dimensions of the case are focussed. This institutional perspective must take into account that the law is aiming at predictability and stability – which however always seem to lay beyond the horizon, as the saying (and much *law as literature* research) reminds us: *coram iudice et in alto mari sumus in manu Dei* (before the court and on the high sea one is in God's hand). Furthermore, the institutional view urges scholars to reconstruct the degree of autonomy at any specific historical moment in the relationship between literature and the judiciary in order to understand literary trials better. This is what the volume will do with exemplary cases.

In this context it is interesting to point to the fact that in some states there is evidence for a temporal connection between the emergence of a literary field *sensu* Bourdieu and the consecration of a relatively high degree of *exceptio artis* in the legal field. This seems to be the case for example in the Netherlands (Grüttemeier and Laros 2013) and South Africa (Laros 2013). Obviously the introduction of significant tools of *exceptio artis* into jurisdiction – whether into positive law or not – can be seen as a kind of consecration of the literary field by the field of power, indicating a structural and conceptual homology between the elites in both fields. This homology however, is not only traceable on the institutional side – it may also be found on the level of theories of literature.

Theories of literature

The institutional autonomy given to literature within the judiciary depends in parts on what legal experts think of the nature and properties of literature and, in relation to that, of the specific incriminated text at trial. In other words, the judicial dealings with literature rely on judicial theories of literature – concerning form and content, ways of interpretation, effect and function – even when the legal field is usually very implicit and reluctant about its ideas of literature. Nevertheless, some general insights can be yielded, for example when looking at the British case.

As we heard before, 'literature' was not meant to be bothered by the Obscene Publications Act of 1857 in the view of its architect Lord Campbell. But what were 'works of literature' to him? Some of his remarks in Parliament give a clue to what he was thinking of: 'the classics, Rochester's poems, plays of Wycherley and Congreve and so on' (cit. Kirchhofer, *infra*). This normative preference for late seventeenth and early eighteenth century British classics to be exempted from the act went along with analogous preferences for writers of antiquity, as we can tell from other contextual sources. The contemporary leading journal *Pall Mall Gazette* for example argued in July in the context of the Hicklin test trial of 1867 that 'grossly obscene' matter could be found in medicine, law and 'many classical books – Ausonius, Juvenal, Aristophanes, and many others': 'but such publications are not criminal, because the interests of medicine, law and classical literature require it' (cit. McDonald 2008: 299). So it is canonical *classical* literature, both national and from antiquity, made for the elite and not for mass consumption, that should not be bothered by the act. Comparing this view with the Obscene Publications Act from 1959 and the Lady Chatterley trial one year later, it is clear that 100 years on there are other theories of literature at stake and there is other literature to be exempted. These theories now include from a legal perspective *contemporary* British literature, the extensive and serious dealing with sex and with the lower classes, and what is more, they include distributing this literature in cheap paperback versions for the masses. Another metonymic indication for changing theories of literature in the judiciary can be found in the quoted recommendation of the 1908 Select Committee, though the Committee did not give any explicit clues as to what it had in mind as being valuable literature. However, at least one can hold that their conception of literature must have been wider than that of Lord Campbell, since the adjective 'classic' is nowhere to be found in their deliberations.

As will be obvious by now is that a handicap of this kind of research is the very limited kind of empirical evidence it can use. Nevertheless, I hope that I could make plausible what is an important assumption of this volume: legal experts do rely on theories of literature, and these theories change over time in a way that can tell us something about the ideas on literature in non-literary circles and about the way the autonomization of the literary field was conceptually underpinned. The example given here allows at least to confirm that classical literature was the 'crack in the door' through which later on contemporary and erotic fiction could pass, as Felice Flanery Lewis (1976: 44–5) once put it.

This 'crack in the door' – I would add: the door giving way to institutional autonomy of literature in the legal field – is on the level of theories of literature closely connected to a version of a Platonic, idealist aesthetics, as already could be inferred from the names quoted above. As the judgement in the 1857 Flaubert trial for example elaborately explains, 'the mission of literature should be to beautify and enhance the spirit by elevating the intelligence and purifying morals' (cit. Ladenson 2007: 25). The 1857 version of 'beauty, goodness and truth' constitutes the dominating values underlying most legal dealings with literature from the nineteenth far into the twentieth century in many countries. Examples are, next to the UK, the United States (cf. Beisel 1993: 153), Germany (cf. Jauß 1991; Grüttemeier 2007: 183) or the Netherlands (cf. Beekman, *infra*). The shape that this modern version of idealist aesthetics usually receives in the courts is that of a transformation of the world of accidentals and contingencies into something essential and valuable. In literary trials, a prominent argument is that showing vice and what is ugly is transformed in literature into a respectable, moral view of the author. The line of this didactic inversion, often used by the defence, can be drawn from Balzac and Flaubert (cf. Sapiro, *infra*) via the Lady Chatterley trial and an argument for defending erotic movies in the 1970s (cf. Beekman, *infra*) up to the defence of *Lord Horror* around the end of the millennium (cf. Kayman, *infra*). However, the success of such a defence lies not in the argument itself, nor in how it is individually presented or received. Its success depends on the institutional and literary-conceptual context, as we have seen above and as the outcomes of the different trials show. On this level, Sapiro comes to the conclusion that the truth- and transformation-bound intentional conception of the writer's responsibility enacted in the arena of the courts 'contributed to the long-term process of "subjectivation" of responsibility' that the history of legal responsibility shows (cf. Sapiro, *infra*).

This process of subjectivation of responsibility is closely connected to the judicial (and literary) norm of interpreting the 'work as a whole' – one of the tools used for corroborating the relative autonomy of literature within the judiciary. But at the same time, this tool can be seen as part of a process that contributes to the societal negotiations of how to read literature. This becomes especially clear during the clashes of deviating theories of literature with the established idealist aesthetics in the 1960s and 1970s, when not only ideas about sexual liberties changed but many writers aimed at blurring the separation between high and low art (cf. Beekman, *infra*). In such a context it seems that the more the literary field splits up in opposing theories of literature, the more carefully the legal experts try to avoid making their own literary theories explicit. Still, Beekman plausibly argues in his contribution that 'there were changes on the level of theories of literature in the legal field, which seem to have been triggered by the rise of corresponding poetics becoming dominant among experts in the fields of literature and the arts'.

Apparently, the shaping of how to read literature through literary trials is not specific for political constellations based on a separation of powers and on a relatively autonomous judiciary dealing with actors from a relatively autonomous field. Something very similar is at stake in literary trials in systems where the state massively interferes with both kinds of autonomy as in the former communist Eastern Bloc and in contemporary Russia. Still, also in these cases literary trials can 'become the stage to create a valid understanding of literature': in the Russian case one 'in which the belief in a word's performativity is paramount' (Sasse, *infra*). This belief in performativity and the word or image 'as deed' can be related to Socialist Realism and writers like Gorky. Its traces reach even further back to Tolstoy, to an understanding of images 'which is at the same time religious and iconic', and to Russia's legal history of the seventeenth century (cf. Sasse, *infra*).

What binds together these two very different cases analysed by Beekman and Sasse is that the process of literary theories dripping into the legal field can apparently be detected in a close analysis of the arguments exchanged in and around the trials in both the fields of literature and the judiciary. At the same time, it seems that the judicial preference for a certain aesthetics or a theory of literature can be explained by preferences of relevant authorities in the field of literature, art and aesthetics – relevant in the eyes of the judiciary. Those authorities are in western countries usually sought in the academic community (cf. Grüttemeier and Laros 2013: 212–16; Grüttemeier, *infra*). Against this background, one might conclude that the legal and the literary elites are bound together, too, by homology on the level of literary theories.

There is also an indirect indication for this homology – that is, the threat that legal experts might become a laughing stock when they appear to be out of touch with what at a certain moment are regarded as legitimate theories of art and literature. The idea of courts making themselves ridiculous runs like a thread through art trials from the nineteenth century onwards. In 1880 for example, Flaubert wrote a letter as a public statement in support of Maupassant, anticipating what would happen if the prosecution continued: 'it will look ridiculous', and Maupassant will win notoriety (cf. Ladenson 2007: 8). Similarly, after Anthony Comstock had instigated the arrest of the respected art dealer Roland Knoedler in New York in 1887 the *New York Herald* titled: 'How Paris Will Laugh!' (cf. Beisel 1993: 155). Nearly a century later, a similar threat is diagnosed by M. Jarvis to have fed the motivation of the Conservative government to agree on the 1959 Obscene Publications Act, that is, the fear of appearing 'ridiculous to a highly articulate section of the public' (cit. Kirchhofer, *infra*). Apart from the fear of actors, the very problem of the judiciary becoming a laughing stock indicates something fundamental about legal and aesthetic discourse in general, which Kayman (*infra*) puts in a nutshell: 'While law must not take itself too seriously, it is of course, no laughing matter. An anxiety about humour is thus fundamental to its negotiations with aesthetics.'

The homology described here can be summarized as translating into legal discourse what the literary field considers legitimate ideas about reading. And because it is a translation, an analysis of legal discourse (the target language, so to speak) by literary scholars (as literary native speakers) promises to be fruitful for a better understanding of the translation and what is done with it. As has been argued above, this analysis can work both ways: it helps to make explicit what legal scholars seem to think about properties, functions and the nature of literature, but it also may help literary scholars to gain a clearer idea on what kind of literary theories do find acceptance outside the literary field and crystallize there in the efforts of the judiciary to develop more or less systematic dealings with literature and art.

This is especially relevant when considering 'the fact that there is no way of telling how to distinguish literature from other kinds of writing', as McDonald (*infra*) compellingly states. It is exactly here that the heuristic possibility of literary trials comes into play to get an indication of which ideas from the literary battlefields on literary theories actually did manifest themselves outside the literary field – not in search of an arbiter, of course, but as an extra possibility for historical diagnosis. Research on the more or less systematic judicial efforts to come to terms with literature can indicate which literary theories are regarded as societally (in the sense of: outside the field of literature) more compelling and authoritative than others at a specific historical point. The comparison of these preferences with the existing accounts of literary history by literary scholars should enable us to more precisely determine the interaction between the legal and the literary field and the constellations of temporary dominance of literary theories within both at different historical moments. However, the relevance of this approach lies not only in the historical perspective but can be taken into our present time. Research into the most recent trials could tell us something about cultural and literary changes that are on their way, and that may not yet, or not yet as sharply, have been detected by research focussed only on literature and/or the literary field.

Taking into account this double relevance of historical and contemporary diagnosis, the volume presents itself with a bipartite structure. The first part offers the reconstruction of an international, institutional and historical framework of literary trials over the last two centuries in six essays (Sapiro, Kirchhofer, Laros, Beekman, Lieb and Sasse). The second part contains four essays which are based on the multifaceted matrix of the first part, taking very recent trials (or the dearth of them) as a point of departure to address what seem to be recent changes on an institutional and conceptual level in law, literature and their interaction, in and around the arena of literary trials (Grüttemeier, Hupe, McDonald and Kayman).

References

Beisel, N. (1993), 'Morals Versus Art: Censorship, the Politics of Interpretation, and the Victorian Nude', *American Sociological Review* 58(2): 145–62.

Bourdieu, P. (2011), *The Rules of Art. Genesis and Structure of the Literary Field*, trans. S. Emanuel, Cambridge etc.: Polity Press.

Bünnigmann, K. (2013), *Die 'Esra'-Entscheidung als Ausgleich zwischen Persönlichkeitsschutz und Kunstfreiheit. Rechtsprechung im Labyrinth der Literatur*, Tübingen: Mohr Siebeck.

Cartledge, P. (1999), '"Deep Plays": Theatre as Process in Greek Civic Life', in P.E. Eeasterling (ed.), *The Cambridge Companion to Greek Tragedy*, 3–35, Cambridge: Cambridge University Press.

De Grazia, E. (1993), *Girls Lean Back Everywhere. The Law of Obscenity and the Assault on Genius*, New York, NY: Vintage Books.

Dennis, A.L. (2007), 'Poetic (In)Justice? Rap Music Lyrics as Art, Life, and Criminal Evidence', *Columbia Journal of Law & The Arts* 31(1): 1–41.

Dolin, K. (2007), *A Critical Introduction to Law and Literature*, Cambridge: Cambridge University Press.

Finkelberg, M. (1998), *The Birth of Literary Fiction in Ancient Greece*, Oxford: Clarendon Press.

Grüttemeier, R. (2007), 'Law and the Autonomy of Literature', in G.J. Dorleijn, R. Grüttemeier and L. Korthals Altes (eds), *The Autonomy of Literature at the* fins de siècles *(1900 and 2000)*, 175–92, Leuven: Peeters.

Grüttemeier, R. and T. Laros (2013), 'Literature in Law: *Exceptio Artis* and the Emergence of Literary Fields', *Law and Humanities* 7(2): 204–17.

Hempel, H. (1991), *Die Freiheit der Kunst. Eine Darstellung des schweizerischen, deutschen und amerikanischen Rechts*, Zürich: Schulthess Polygraphischer Verlag.

Jauß, H.R., ed. (1991), *Die nicht mehr schönen Künste. Grenzphänomene des Ästhetischen*, München: Fink.

Knies, W. (1967), *Schranken der Kunstfreiheit als verfassungsrechtliches Problem*, München: Beck.

Kubrin, Ch.E. and E. Nielson (2014), 'Rap on Trial', *Race and Justice* 4(3): 185–211.

Ladenson, E. (2007), *Dirt for Art's Sake. Books on Trial from* Madame Bovary *to* Lolita, Ithaca, NY etc.: Cornell University Press.

Laros, T. (2013), 'Long Walk to Artistic Freedom: Law and the Literary Field in South Africa, 1910–2010', diss., Faculty III: Language and Cultural Studies, Carl von Ossietzky University of Oldenburg.

Lewis, F.F. (1976), *Literature, Obscenity, and Law*, Carbondale: Southern Illinois University Press.

McDonald, P.D. (2008), 'Old Phrases and Great Obscenities: The Strange Afterlife of Two Victorian Anxieties', *Journal of Victorian Culture* 13(2): 294–302.

Olson, G. (2014), 'Narration and Narrative in Legal Discourse', in P. Hühn et al. (eds), *The Living Handbook of Narratology*, available online: http://www.lhn.uni-hamburg.de/article/narration-and-narrative-legal-discourse (accessed 16 February 2015)

Sapiro, G. (2003), 'The Literary Field between the State and the Market', *Poetics* 31: 441–61.

Searle, J.R. (2010), *Making the Social World*, Oxford: Oxford University Press.

Wilson, P. (2000), 'Powers of Horror and Laughter', in O. Taplin (ed.), *Literature in the Greek and Roman Worlds. A New Perspective*, 88–132, Oxford: Oxford University Press.

Part One

Towards More Autonomy of Literature. Histories of Literary Trials

1

The Legal Responsibility of the Writer Between Objectivity and Subjectivity: The French Case (Nineteenth to Twenty-First Century)

Gisèle Sapiro

The regime of free press in France was adopted during the Revolution to be immediately suppressed and was not revived until the Bourbon Restoration. The *Charte constitutionnelle* of 1814 and the *lois de Serre* of 1819 opened a new liberal era for the book market: in contrast to the periodical press, censorship was not restored for books except in wartime. In theatre, censorship was maintained until 1904. But this newfound freedom of expression was restricted on both moral and political levels. At a moment when publishing was becoming an industry (and the political liberalization of print a way to encourage the book trade), the printed word appeared in the law, under the notion of 'moral complicity' (*complicité morale*), as one of the means of incitement to crime – for instance, incitement to murder or to rebellion – or, as a crime in itself, like in the case of offence to 'public morality' (*offense à la morale publique et aux bonnes moeurs*). The regime of free press, which was more or less free according to the governments, replaced censorship before publication by prosecutions after publication. Many authors were prosecuted during the nineteenth century, including under the Republican regime which liberalized printing with the laws passed in 1881 and that are still in force.

In *La Responsabilité*, the Durkheimian sociologist of law Paul Fauconnet demonstrates that, historically, the definitions of legal responsibility (or liability) oscillate between objectivity and subjectivity (Fauconnet 1920). Pure objective responsibility – in which the relation between agent and crime is exterior – may be illustrated by ritual expiation, while pure subjective responsibility – represented by religious morality – condemns culpable thoughts and intentions. Modern juridical responsibility is a compromise between these two opposing tendencies.

Infractions are registered on the basis of an external fact, which constitutes their material element and which is the product of an action imputable to a perpetrator, with respect to which one then examines the voluntary character, to wit, the intention – and this is the moral or subjective element of the infraction.

This frame of analysis proves to be heuristic when applied to the case of literary trials, as I argued in my book on the responsibility of the writer (Sapiro 2011).[1] Legal responsibility always implies an objective (material) element and a subjective one (intention). A close reading of the 1819 French law on the freedom of the press and the debates which surrounded it in Parliament reveals that the objective element is in the case of literary trials the publication, conceived of as an act, while the subjective one is the intention underlying this act, on the part of all the persons involved in it, especially the publisher, the writer and the printer (Maiseau 1819). In the present paper, I will use this frame in order to study the evolution of the conception of the writer's legal responsibility in France from the nineteenth century to the twenty-first and the writer's response, which contributed to the construction of a professional ethics based on an autonomous conception of their rights and duties.

Although Fauconnet never mentions them, the writers contributed highly to the long-term process of 'subjectivation' of responsibility that he describes in his book. Subjective responsibility emerged, according to him, as a result of a historical process by which responsibility became spiritualized and individualized, a process closely tied to an evolution in the religious conception of sin. As the French historian Jacques Le Goff (1977: 169–70) argues, in the twelfth century, Catholic religious morality displaced attention from the sin to the sinner, from the fault to the intention. This new conception of action and of culpability broke with magical interpretations of the connection between event and agent: an event can only be characterized as an act if an internal causal relation – that is to say, an intention – links it to the agent. Such a causality presupposes the notion of free will, upon which is founded the subjective conception of responsibility; by this fact, it may exempt beings who are deprived of it – like animals, children and the insane – who are deemed to be irresponsible. This conception of responsibility was reinforced by the eighteenth-century philosophers who secularized morality by putting forward the autonomy of reason. Kantian morality appears in this respect as a secular version of radical subjectivism. The imputation of an act – that is to say, liability for it – has freedom as its condition (Fauconnet 1920: 96–7).

The subjective conception of the author's responsibility culminated with romanticism but also with the eighteenth-century representation of the author as a rational actor, as illustrated by the trials of Béranger and Courier under the Bourbon Restoration. This conception still prevailed during the Second Empire: the court which tried Flaubert for *Madame Bovary* decided not to convict him, after having recognized that his intention was 'pure'. However, under the Third Republic, a more objective conception of the writer's responsibility appeared with the notion of 'obscenity' (*obscénité*). After the Second World War, the 'purge trials' (*épuration*), in which intellectuals who had collaborated with the Nazi occupying forces were prosecuted for 'intelligence with the enemy' – a crime referring to national treason – and some of them sentenced to death, indicated that the subjective conception of responsibility still prevailed for political crimes. In contrast, regarding offence to high morality, the objective conception was reinforced in the same period with the 1949 laws on the protection of youth, which allowed the government to ban any 'pornographic' book that could fall in the hands of minors. Subjective responsibility is however still determining when real persons are concerned, in cases of defamation or of infringement of privacy, as can be observed in some recent lawsuits.

The French laws on the freedom of the press never recognized any *exceptio artis*. In practice, however, a process of progressive recognition of the relative autonomy of literature can be observed, starting under the Third Republic (Sapiro 2011), in close relation to the autonomization of the literary field (Bourdieu 1992). Moreover, it can be argued that the conquest of literary autonomy was in large part a result of the struggle against the moral and political expectations from literature: in response to the accusations some of them had to confront, writers invoked specific values which grounded their claim for autonomy, such as artistic license, disinterestedness, objectivity and truthfulness in the representation of reality (Sapiro 2011).

The writer as a paradigmatic figure of subjective responsibility

As already mentioned, it is the act of publishing which is punished when infringing the limits of freedom of speech: thoughts are free, but when they are made public, one is liable for their consequences (objective responsibility). This is why the publisher is considered as the main liable person for literary crimes, the author being only party in the crime (the accomplice). This conception is not just an expression of liberalism: it ensures a better control of publication, since publishers can be prosecuted for reprinting provocative works of dead authors, like the Marquis de Sade.

In practice, however, when the author is alive, he always gets the highest punishment in the case of prosecution for a book. In the case of an article in a periodical, the sanction is usually the same for the author and for the editor. This means that the author is considered as the first person liable for his output. It reflects the high identification between the author and his writings in common representations – an identification based on a triple relation of metonymy, resemblance and causality:

(1) Metonymy: the author is defined by his works, as suggested by Foucault (1969), his name functions as a metonymy for his works (Flaubert is the author of *Madame Bovary*, who is also the author of *L'Éducation sentimentale*).
(2) Resemblance: an author is believed to paint himself in his works. Thus there is a supposed relation between the morality of the work and the morality of the author. This belief is so strong that Baudelaire was assumed to have committed the 'sins' he describes in *Les Fleurs du mal*. Following Foucault's approach, we can consider that the French personalist conception of 'author's right' (*droit d'auteur*) is based on this identification, as it was famously put by Diderot (1976: 509–10) in 1763 in his *Lettre sur le commerce de la librairie*. This personalist conception also implies that the moral rights can never be sold, in contrast to the Anglo-American law on copyright.
(3) Causality: the author embodies the paradigmatic conception of subjective responsibility in the sense that writings appear as the material proof of intentionality (or 'agency') and as the supreme product of rational action, as Sartre theorized after the Second World War (Sapiro 2006b, 2007). This conception which prevails in modern culture is not the only one possible: the antique poet acts out of inspiration, he is not the cause of his poetry. Moreover, the modern figure of the insane poet embodied by Hölderlin and Gérard de Nerval at the very moment when psychiatry established itself as a recognized speciality and when insanity became an extenuating circumstance in trials, appears to be the counterpart of the dominant conception of authorship as rational action. This figure of the insane was used for instance in defence of Céline, who was prosecuted after the Second World War for collaboration during the German Occupation in France (Sapiro, forthcoming).

What is dangerous about a literary work?

Defining objective responsibility requires to state in what respect writings are considered to be 'dangerous'. The ideas about 'dangerousness' of writings rely on shared and more or less theorized beliefs on literature and reception that can be reconstructed through a close reading of the parliamentary debates on the freedom of speech, the arguments of the prosecution in the trials, the critical reception of the prosecuted works and general essays on literature and morality published during the period under consideration. These beliefs concern not only their message (content) but also their form and style, the public they address and their alleged effects. These various aspects of writing have implications for the writer's responsibility and social role.

Regarding content, the reasons for prosecuting writers were both political and moral (the charge for offence to high morality being often a cover for ideological motives), but according to the regime there was more or less emphasis on certain values like religion, family and national interest. These differences are revelatory of the changing conceptions of public morality. Since the defence usually denied the accusation, many of the debates focused on the interpretation of the texts and on the author's and the publisher's intentions in publishing it. The debate on interpretation was all the more crucial considering that the question of direct or indirect statement was a major issue in the parliamentary debates on the laws on free press and in the literary trials: the promoters of a free press argued that only direct incitements to crimes (*provocation directe*) or crude pornography should be condemned. As a consequence, allusions, coded devices, metaphors and the introduction of material contradicting the main thesis were a means for authors to overturn censorship. These means applied to both fiction and non-fiction, that were not clearly delimited at the beginning of the nineteenth century (for instance, historical essays often displaced the settings in place and time in order to avoid prosecution). Thus fiction was mainly a means to get round the limits of freedom of speech.

For these reasons, the form of the publication, its genre and style were also relevant, since they indicated the writer's intent. They could be either taken as a sign of noxious intentions or of the seriousness of the work and of the commitment of the author to literature or to some high purpose. Whereas the *chanson* was considered a superficial genre that should not be taken too seriously, the lampoon (pamphlet) manifested a political intention. Literary devices such as free indirect style introduced by Flaubert were a source of ambiguity as we will see below.

The genre, the length, the style of the work, the kind of publication (book or newspaper), its price, were also important as indicators of the audience targeted by the author and the publisher. During the whole nineteenth century, the thesis of the two readerships prevailed, characterized by their different reading practices: the learned readership, trained to read with a critical distance, was believed to have a disinterested approach, whereas the new readers were considered as vulnerable and more susceptible to influence, both by non-fiction and by fiction, through identification with fictional characters. The expansion of literacy thus enhanced the writers' objective responsibility: they were liable for the effects independently of their intention. The authors had either to deny the fact that their writings addressed a large audience, by invoking the length and high price of the book, or they had to deny the influence of literature at all. The realist writers claimed that literature was a reflection of reality, they could not be held responsible for the mores they were just reproducing; moreover, they argued, after Balzac, that the true description of reality, including depravation, was a means of warning the readers of the consequences of such deviations from social norms.

How could writings have effects on readers? The effects of writings on the readers, which were first theorized by Plato, were represented through two main metaphors: poison and contagion. Poison was a metaphor commonly used by the Church. In the eighteenth century, medical discourse forged the notion of 'moral contagion'; it was through this notion that physicians achieved recognition as a profession (Goldstein 1984). The printing industry appeared to be a prominent conveyor of moral contagion. Thus the prosecutors emphasized the 'performative' character of discourse, to use the concept theorized by Austin (1962): from the standpoint of law, discourse was considered as an act, as noted by Foucault (1994); immoral writings led women to adultery, subversive writings armed the rebels, writings represented thus a danger for the social order. The defenders of the prosecuted writers usually denied this performative character of their writings: they denied any causal relation to concrete acts, be they individual behaviour or collective upheaval. Causality was indeed the most difficult thing to prove, since such a causal relation is very hard to establish.

Subjective responsibility has to do with the author's motives. From the legal point of view, personal reasons are the motives of a crime. For writers, generally assumed to have been acting rationally, reasons are of roughly four main kinds: personal conviction, desire for fame, desire for reward, desire to do harm. There are degrees of difference between the four, depending on the aim of the act of publication. These very general motives have specific meaning in the intellectual domain, because of its particular values. Personal conviction can be an extenuating circumstance in so far as it is linked both to freedom of thought and freedom of philosophical discussion, or to the particular rules of literature (its autonomy), and if it can be considered rational in terms of particular values, following the classification proposed by Max Weber (1995: 55–6). Being free to develop and publish his own system of thought, the author who acts out of personal conviction and the writer bound by the constraints of his art are deemed to have acted in good faith, not necessarily intending to do harm, and not having realized the consequences of their acts. Sincerity and good faith are extenuating circumstances. The accused is thought of as having made a mistake. Against this 'ethics of conviction' the prosecution usually sets the 'ethics of responsibility', to borrow the terms in which Max Weber (1991) formulated that opposition in his talk on 'Politik als Beruf'.

The prosecution also tries to prove that the act of publication has not been determined by moral factors alone but also by less pure ends. Desire for fame and desire for reward are aggravating circumstances, because in this case the author has acted out of self-interest without thought for the consequences of his actions. The metaphor commonly used to designate this kind of act is 'prostitution', with the underlying analogy between selling one's body and selling one's pen, which refers to the personalization of the idea of the 'author', and the identification of the man and his work. The quest for fame can lead ambitious authors to break the law solely to get talked about, and by that means become famous. The desire to acquire a reputation, however dubious, figures in the social imaginary as one of the commonest 'sins' of the ambitious writer, as portrayed by Balzac in *Illusions perdues*. The expedient is equally despised by writers who condemn easily-won success and have no confidence in reputations built on scandal. The defence then has to bring evidence of the good morality of the author and of his intellectual convictions, and to prove he didn't earn much money.

These different aspects of an author's legal responsibility were discussed in literary trials and can serve as an analytical framework to observe the evolution of the beliefs about literature and of the conceptions of a writer's rights and duties across different periods and regimes.

The Bourbon Restoration: The lampoon as a public danger

Religion and monarchy were the most sacred values during the Bourbon Restoration, which was still fighting the eighteenth century materialist doctrine. These values were protected by the laws limiting a free press. Writers used to get round the law by attacking priests or aristocrats rather than the religion and the monarchy as a regime, but it was not always sufficient to avoid prosecution, as the cases of two liberal authors, the lampooner Paul-Louis Courier and the *chansonnier* Béranger, illustrate. They were both charged for offence to high morality in 1821 and condemned to prison in addition to a fine. Béranger would be prosecuted again in 1822 and 1828. The defendants usually contested the restrictive interpretation of the laws on free press by the prosecutors, trying to extend the limits imposed upon the freedom of speech. They also contested the interpretation of the texts, often denying the political allusions or real meaning.

The genre was at stake in both trials. *Chanson* and lampoon were both popular genres, at the margins of literature, that were ennobled by Béranger and Courier. Being popular genres made them dangerous since they could reach a large public. Béranger was prosecuted for offence to high morality, offence to public and religious morality, offence to the king's person, and a fourth accusation which was abandoned because it was not defined legally as a crime: 'provocation to carry a prohibited rallying sign' (*provocation au port d'un signe de ralliement prohibé*).

Paradoxically, since Béranger decided to print his *chansons*, they acquired, according to the prosecutor, the status of poetry (he compared them to 'odes') and were therefore taken more seriously. The prosecutor also denounced them as 'manifestos', in order to underscore Béranger's political intention. Being printed also secured them a larger distribution, argued the prosecutor, thus increasing the *chansonnier*'s objective responsibility. The print-run of the volume was 10,000 copies, a very large distribution at that time (Stendhal sold 750 copies of *Le Rouge et le noir*, published in 1830). The irony is that the press reproduced the list of charges which included the banned verses, giving them a much larger distribution (100,000 copies) than the printed volume. Béranger was honoured for being recognized as a poet, and was unsatisfied with his counsel who built his defence on the fact that *chansons* were a light genre with no impact since they were not taken seriously.

Finally, the court declared Béranger guilty of the second charge, offence to public and religious morality. It concerned eight *chansons* – '*Deo gratias* d'un épicurien', 'La descente aux enfers', 'Mon curé', 'Les capucins', 'Les chantres de paroisse', 'Les missionnaires', 'Le Bon Dieu', and 'La mort du roi Christophe' – that combined a critique of the church and a more general social critic (poverty, famine), opposing the priest to the '*philosophe*' – the figure of the eighteenth century French philosopher embodied by Voltaire and Rousseau. He was sentenced to three months in prison and to a fine. His second prosecution occurred during his term in jail, because his counsel had printed his plea, infringing the law which did not allow making defence arguments public. The counsel argued that the public needed to understand why most of the charges against Béranger were abandoned, an argument supported by a petition signed by twenty lawyers. He won. This second trial thus marked a crucial step in the conquest of the freedom of expression in France.

In 1828, Béranger was prosecuted again for a new collection of *chansons*, some of which were accused once more of committing an offence to public and religious morality and to the State religion, an offence against the king's person and an attack against royal dignity, incitement to hatred and contempt against the government. Again the prosecutor tried to worsen Béranger's subjective responsibility by characterizing his *chansons* as 'rhymed lampoons' ('libelles rimés'; *Procès fait* 1828). The *chansonnier* was sentenced this time to nine months in prison and a fine of 10,000 francs, his case being aggravated because it was a repeat offence, which confirmed his political intentions. During his two terms in jail, Béranger received visits from many other writers expressing solidarity, including, during the second term, Victor Hugo who was just beginning to give up his royalist convictions. Thus, a network of authors defending the autonomy of the writer was forming. In the entry *gens de lettres* of the *Encyclopédie* (1751), Voltaire had presented sincerity, disinterestedness and courage as the most typical characteristics of isolated writers and scientists, who do not belong to institutions like the University, and who expose themselves to persecution by the government for telling the truth or expressing their ideas. In the light of these values, we can understand why being imprisoned twice for several months helped Béranger to achieve the status of a poet: under the July Monarchy, he would be celebrated as the 'national poet'.

The lampoon was characterized first by its short length, second by its political message, two features which made it suspect for the government. For Paul-Louis Courier (1964), the choice of this genre was, on the contrary, an embodiment of his conception of the writer's responsibility in a parliamentary regime. In contrast with the figure of the courtesan writer, whose social function was to entertain idle aristocrats, the role of the responsible writer was to spread the truth among the people, an argument he borrowed from Jonathan Swift, his mentor. As he explained, he wrote lampoons because the working people had no leisure to read long books.

For both Béranger and Courier, their large audience was the sign of their legitimacy and confirmed their prophecy. While the prosecutors tried to argue that they published out of greed, their poverty, the fact they did not earn any money for their works, the fact they took risks to spread the truth were proofs of their disinterestedness. In this sense, they embodied the modern figure of the prophet, according to Max Weber's idealtype (Weber 1968, 1995: 320f.). They contributed in this way to the transfer of the subversive function from the eighteenth century French '*philosophes*' to the writers, at a time when philosophy had been depoliticized as a result of its integration into the Napoleonic University.

The Second Empire: Realism on trial

Under the Second Empire, property and family became the pillars of social order, as illustrated by Flaubert's trial for *Madame Bovary* in 1857. More works were prosecuted for offence to high morality than in the former periods. Even poetry could be brought to court: Baudelaire was prosecuted for *Les Fleurs du mal* a few months later in the same year.

According to Dominick LaCapra (1982), Flaubert was in fact prosecuted for an ideological crime, since the novel was putting into question the very social norms for which it was charged. However pertinent, this reading of the trial does not explain why Flaubert was finally not convicted: in its judgement, the court blamed Flaubert for his use of the realistic device but considered that it was just an error, and that Flaubert's intention was 'pure' (Flaubert 1951: 681–3). Although he was objectively guilty, he was judged innocent from the standpoint of subjective responsibility. How did that happen?

While the prosecutor Pinard presented *Madame Bovary* as an apology for adultery, the writer's counsel, M[e] Senard, succeeded in convincing the jury that the novel was highly moral in its intent, since it described what happened to a woman coming from a modest background, who was corrupted by the reading of novels which gave her ambitions and expectations beyond her social condition. This interpretation of the novel as what would be called later a 'roman à thèse' (an ideological novel) is a kind of *mise en abyme* of the trial which itself was about the noxious effects of novels, especially on young women. Interpreting the novel this way was certainly excessive, in the sense that the novel is far more ambiguous, allowing for two contradictory interpretations, as the trial itself illustrated.

This ambiguity stemmed from the form, in particular from two devices that Flaubert borrowed from Goethe and introduced in France: the impersonal narrator and free indirect speech. The prosecutor, Pinard, reproached Flaubert for not judging Emma. Her suicide in the end was not a sufficient punishment in his eyes, since she chose it. Moreover, as already said, he argued that Flaubert praised adultery. But the quotations he brought in support were those where the narrator spoke from the standpoint of Emma, using free indirect speech, like the scene describing her looking at her image in the mirror after her first encounter with her lover: it is said that she had never been so beautiful; was it the narrator speaking or was he just reproducing Emma's thoughts? As argued by Hans Robert Jauß (1990: 86), it was this new literary device which induced the prosecutor's error. Senard had to explain in Flaubert's defence that this was not the author's point of view but Emma's. This debate contributed to establish the distinction between author and narrator, which since then has become a convention in modern novels. Flaubert was also blamed for his crude descriptions, for his 'realism', which challenged the classical convention of the 'Beau ideal', that is, idealizing reality. Baudelaire was also blamed for his realism and crude descriptions. He had even gone further in the '*détournement*' of the lyrical tradition, using the lyrical 'I' for corrupted characters, or providing realistic descriptions of death, including the scent, as pointed out by Elisabeth Ladenson (2007: 61–5).

In his prosecution speech against Flaubert, Pinard argued that *Madame Bovary* could fall into the hands of a vulnerable woman, who might identify with Emma and take her as a model. The expansion of literacy, especially among women, who were assumed to have less self-control and to be more threatened by the influence of emotions and imagination, was a major source of concern for moralists. Emma Bovary's fate precisely embodied this fear.

The defence replied that the writer was merely describing the real world, it was not his fault if there was evil in the world. As for the liberal authors of the beginning of the nineteenth century, 'truth' was an intellectual value founding the professional ethics of the writer. But, in the present case, the notion of 'truth' was borrowed from science: the narrator adopted the same objective posture as the scientist. This distanced narrative posture, that would redefine the space of possibilities constituting the literary field, was partly the expression of Flaubert's habitus: as the son of a physician whom he had accompanied on his visits to his patients and from whom he learned to observe and describe in a neutral, objective manner, he was predisposed to import scientific values into the realm of literature.

Two different options derived from this posture. Either the writers denied responsibility for the content of their work, following Flaubert and Baudelaire who considered they were liable only for the form and style of their work, and not for their appropriations by readers. This position had been theorized under the concept of art for art's sake, which contended that literature should be distinct from morality and submitted only to aesthetic criteria of judgement (Cassagne 1997). Oscar Wilde will take this position further in suggesting, in his *Portrait of Dorian Gray*, a theory of reception making the audience responsible for what they perceive in art works (nobody knows what Dorian's sins are, the reader imagines them).

Or, following Balzac, would they argue, like Flaubert's lawyer, Senard, that describing reality as it was, crudely, was the best way of preventing evil: the fate of Emma would prevent many women from adultery by displaying its delusive aspects and terrible consequences. Nevertheless, contrary to Balzac who did not hesitate to judge his characters, Flaubert refused to conclude, to take a stand: the reader had to do the job himself. This scientific posture will be taken over by Zola and the naturalists.

Thus Flaubert combined art for art's sake and the scientific ethos to define a new professional ethics of the writer. These two postures will develop separately in the next period, with, on one hand, the naturalists, and on the other, the symbolists and decadents. While they both expressed the claims for literary autonomy against attempts to subordinate literature to high morality and ideological objectives, they embodied different conceptions of the literary craft and of the writer's social role and responsibility.

National moralism: The redefinition of objective responsibility under the Third Republic

In 1881, the young Third Republic passed a liberal law on the press which privatized religion. In order to foster the secularization process which would lead to the separation of the State from the Church in 1905, public morality was 'nationalized'. As the trials of the naturalist writers illustrate, national interest became the main reason for defending high morality and institutions like the army, which were sacralized.

Lucien Descaves, for instance, was tried in 1889 for insulting the army and offending high morality in his satirical novel *Sous-Offs* which described life in the army. Military service had become compulsory in 1872, opening the experience of life in barracks to all citizens, including writers to whom it provided a new fictional framework. And fiction could be used, as in this case, to criticize the military system, which could not be denounced openly, because the humiliation of the military defeat that put an end to the Franco-Prussian War in 1871 was still alive in collective memory. Since fiction could easily escape the accusation of insult, the prosecutor tried to redefine Descaves' novel as a lampoon – he characterized it as a 'heinous lampoon' ('infâme libelle') – because it pretended to tell the 'truth'; in a parallel way, he described the author and the publisher as 'malefactors of the pen' (*malfaiteurs de la plume*), who were pursuing only publicity and mercantile interests (Descaves 1980: 448–9).

In response, Descaves' and his publisher's counsels all stressed the differences between a novel and a lampoon, between a book and a newspaper, between serious literature and popular fiction. The form of *Sous-Offs*, written in a difficult, dense style, as well as its format – its length, its high price (3.50 francs) as compared to cheap popular novels (10–50 cents), its publication directly as a book and not first as a magazine serial – all served to indicate that this work did not address a large audience but a small elite. This claim was aimed at reducing the objective responsibility of the author and of his publisher, as well as at dismissing the accusation concerning their supposed noxious intentions. Neither the author nor the publisher, they argued, sought a *succès de scandale* or commercial profit. Their intentions were pure. The author wanted only to reveal the truth, to denounce bad conditions and identify abuses that could be redressed; his counsel, Me Tézenas, provided evidence from the press and war councils which confirmed that the facts described in the novel were true. Tézenas compared *Sous-Offs* to a scientific treatise, the function of which was to inform the public.

Offence to high morality was in this case a pretext for political charges, which could not be brought within a liberal regime of freedom of the press. Like Flaubert, Descaves was finally not convicted. The prosecutor was not able to prove that Descaves had infringed the law. The evidence from the war councils had dismissed the accusation of insult, and the passages defined as obscene by the prosecutor appeared to be inoffensive compared to novels by Descaves' master Zola, against whom no legal proceedings had been brought. However, other naturalists were condemned for obscenity in this period, because the struggle against pornography had become instrumental in the building of a secular republican morality and in establishing the respectability of the young French Republic in the international competition between nations. This struggle against pornography was undertaken by morality leagues and became international at the turn of the century (Stora-Lamarre 1990). At a moment when the moral opposition between good and evil was being replaced by the medical opposition between normal and pathological, a more objective conception of the writer's responsibility appeared with the notion of 'obscenity', probably imported from the British legal vocabulary, and in relation to the biological paradigm of heredity and degeneration. This conception could also be applied to political writings, as illustrated by the laws on anarchy passed in the 1890s.

During this period, the thesis of hereditary dispositions to criminality, developed by Cesare Lombroso and Italian criminologists, was imported into France and challenged the prevailing conception of subjective responsibility: if the criminal was predisposed to crime and if it was of pathological nature, what was the role of his free will? Yet these criminals were still dangerous to society, so they should be punished not according to their intentions but according to their dangerousness. This is a paradigmatic illustration of the conception of objective responsibility. In France, however, heredity was never considered as acting alone: the environment could activate it or prevent its manifestations. The role of the environment left some room for manoeuvre for free will. Although the hereditary paradigm did not succeed in imposing itself in French law, there are some traces of this inspiration in the approach to repeat offences. Note that it is in this context that Paul Fauconnet wrote his doctoral dissertation on responsibility.

Drawing from the hereditary paradigm, Max Nordau, a Hungarian Jewish thinker who will become a Zionist leader, popularized in a book titled *Degeneration*, published in 1892 in German and translated into French in 1894, the idea that modern artists and writers were degenerates who suffered from mental pathology and represented a danger to society. He analysed the cases of symbolists and decadents, and dedicated a chapter to Oscar Wilde (it was just after the latter's trial for act of 'gross indecency', referring to his relations with men). In Nordau's eyes, art for art's sake was a sign of this pathology.

This attack brought discredit on art for art's sake. In a parallel way, the trials of the naturalists delegitimized Zola and the naturalists' pretension to elevate literature to the status of science. In his trial for his novel *Autour d'un clocher*, which described in a Rabelaisian style the love story of a Catholic priest with a school teacher in a small French village, Louis Desprez, one of the young naturalist writers who chose to defend himself, argued that the jury had no authority to judge his work. He wanted to be judged by his peers, writers like Zola, Daudet and others (Desprez 1992). Some of them had signed a petition to support him: it was the first public petition of intellectuals before the Dreyfus Affair. Desprez's claim can be read as a plea for assimilating the writing profession into the other organized professions. Yet, in contrast with the latter which adopted a specialized language, literature uses common language. In a context which made language a sacred issue at stake in the construction of national identity, the introduction into the novel of low-brow style and expressions by the naturalist writers in their attempt to reproduce the way their characters from lower social status talked was held against them: they were likewise contaminated by the 'vulgarity' of this style. This is one of the reasons that could account for their failure to achieve recognition as 'professionals', and for the fact they were not granted, like physicians, any 'immunity' before the law.

This lack of professionalization partly explains the politicization of the literary field in the 1890s. Writers played a leading role in the mobilization of intellectuals in favour of and against Captain Dreyfus who was prosecuted for treason. Relying on the symbolic capital he had accumulated as a writer, Zola wrote his famous piece 'J'accuse', denouncing the plot that led to the condemnation of an innocent. This accusation brought upon him a trial for defamation, in which he hoped to demonstrate the truth, but he failed to do so and was himself convicted. However, his symbolic act, which reminded of Voltaire's in the Affaire Calas one century earlier, became a reference and a model of the political commitment of the writer. He embodied the figure of the 'public intellectual' who takes a political stand on public matters in the name of 'truth' and 'justice'. Like art for art's sake, this professional ethics was based on the writer's autonomy from temporal powers (political, religious, economic). His commitment was not answering a demand from these powers like experts or intellectuals linked to a political party. His commitment was sincere, disinterested and courageous, embodying a prophetic posture.

National treason: The purge trials

In 1944, after the German Occupation during the Second World War, the provisional government organized a purge (épuration) of French society from those who had collaborated with the German occupying forces. The crime they were prosecuted for was treason: 'intelligence with the enemy', according to Articles 75–83 of the Penal Code, and 'national indignity' for more minor cases of collaboration (Novick 1968; Bancaud 2003: 73; Simonin 2008). I will focus here on the crime of 'intelligence with the enemy'. It was the crime for which Captain Dreyfus had been tried fifty years earlier – and it was because of Dreyfus that General Mercier requested the re-establishment of the death penalty for this crime, which happened in 1939.

Out of thirty-two cases of writers and journalists tried in the period of the *épuration* by the Cour de Justice de la Seine, a department whose jurisdiction over Paris encompassed a high concentration of intellectuals, twelve were sentenced to death, thirteen to penal servitude and six to prison. Only one was acquitted. Of the dozen authors condemned to death, seven were shot. The rate of execution for intellectuals was thus much higher than the national average of 11 per cent (767 executions out of 6,763 death sentences during the *épuration*).

The gravity of the punishment to which intellectuals were exposed – death – provoked an acute surge of emotion in the literary world. Justice seemed to be more severe for authors than for economic or political traitors who provided the material means for collaboration. To many it seemed that intellectuals served as scapegoats for a whole society. According to Fauconnet, treason is the modern equivalent of sacrilege, for which the sanction is collective. The *épuration* can be seen as such a collective punishment, aiming at expiation rather than prevention. On the other hand, the fact that daily collaboration was structurally imposed by the presence of the occupiers created objective rather than subjective responsibility.

The symbolic value of the punishment of intellectuals was that it allowed the transfer of the collective and objective responsibility of French society to individual and subjective responsibility: these individuals had a name well-known to the public, they expressed their ideas and beliefs in public, they were assumed to have acted rationally, they embodied ideological collaboration out of agency. Charges could be brought quickly, since evidence against authors was easy to gather and unequivocal when their writings had overtly served enemy propaganda. As the prosecutor said in journalist Herold-Paquis' trial, 'the writings are the only witnesses here, we do not need any other'.[2] In a memoir he wrote for his defence, the writer and journalist Henri Béraud argued, on the contrary, that since he was prosecuted for his writings, he was tried not for deeds but for ideas, for his 'opinions'.[3]

The purge trials were clearly a case of political justice. Does it mean that the accused were condemned for their opinions (which would, of course, contradict the democratic principle of free speech)? The answer is no, at least not in principle. Writers were prosecuted not for their ideas but for what was defined as acts of treason. Helping to formulate and disseminate the enemy's arguments was an act of treason, and so was denouncing French citizens. The prosecutors tried to prove that words entailed deeds, that they were 'performative', that they constituted a concrete act. Collective denunciations of Jews, Gaullists, Communists were defined as such. For instance, some of them, like Brasillach, had called on the government to shoot the 'traitors', i.e. the Gaullists and Communists. Others, like Charles Maurras or Lucien Rebatet, even urged the government to execute hostages. On 25 September 1942, in the context of the roundups and deportation of Jews, he wrote: 'We must separate from the Jews en bloc, and not keep the kids.' Nevertheless, it was difficult to demonstrate a causal relation between these writings and actual acts of violence. Yet this 'performative' dimension stemmed mainly from the fact that these intellectuals were supported by the political power and enjoyed a monopoly since their adversaries were not able to contradict them in public.

In the purge trials, all of the usual signs of a writer's success were taken as evidence for the potential power of his words (Sapiro 2006a): the writer's audience (especially when he wrote for presses with large circulation), the breadth of his talent, which increased his persuasive power and the efficacy of his propaganda, particularly among the young. As the prosecutors argued, even his literary style, colourful or violent, could have served the enemy's interest.

The defence also invoked literary arguments and scholarly references in what appeared as a parody of the literary trials of the nineteenth century. In the course of questioning, old writer Abel Hermant, a member of the *Académie française*, denied his subjective responsibility by arguing that one article was literary criticism and another 'just literary knockabout'. He invoked psychology, and comic effect, explaining: 'This article proves that when a man of letters tries his hand at politics he always lapses into literature. The writer in me was struck by the comic side to the way the young Bolsheviks were received in England.'[4]

Similarly, fascist writer Lucien Rebatet argued that his virulent anti-republican and anti-Semitic pamphlet *Les Décombres* was a 'confession', not a piece of propaganda. The aim of the confession was to rid him of political issues, and 'free him from some of the things that made him angry', so that he could devote his attention to literature. Justifying his style by reference to the playwright and satirist Courteline, he noted that 'an author is much more concerned with producing a colourful effect, or painting particular types or characters, than with setting out and propagating a political thesis'. Such an author will answer polemically when attacked. But, he added, denying now objective responsibility, 'Isn't the polemicist's bark always worse than his bite?'[5]

Robert Brasillach's defence counsel, Jacques Isorni, referred to Renan to explain his client's infamous remark: 'During those years, thinking Frenchmen effectively got into bed with Germany, with a few arguments, and the experience will have left them with happy memories.' Had not Renan written in the preface to his book *La Réforme intellectuelle et morale*: 'Germany was my mistress'? Just as in the nineteenth century the arguments of 'art for art's sake' were developed to exculpate writers accused of offences against morality and society, literature was now brandished to justify the works that stood accused, though these were no longer fiction.

While the defence brought talent as an extenuating circumstance, in most of the purge trials the prosecutor argued that the defendant had misused his talent and his influence for political or propaganda purposes and to serve the enemy. Talent thus appeared from the prosecution's standpoint as an aggravating circumstance. In Brasillach's trial, the *Commissaire du gouvernement* (equivalent to Prosecutor general) Reboul specified that Brasillach's treason was a 'clerk's treason', an expression referring to Julien Benda's essay, *La Trahison des clercs* (1924), which denounced the political commitment of intellectuals as a betrayal of their universal vocation and mission. He argued that Brasillach betrayed the ethics of every aspect of his profession: he was the writer who abandoned pure literature out of his ambition to enlarge his audience and gain political influence; he was the intellectual who misused his authority and his power of persuasion among young people to incite to denunciation and crime; he was the critic who abandoned dispassionate analysis for treasonous propaganda and collective denunciations of Communists, Jews, and civil servants; and he was the academic who called for the suppression of freedom of speech within the University. These accusations prove that the writers' claims for autonomy and the right to criticize society had become admitted in society to the point that they were now blamed for not having been more critical of the Vichy government's collaborationist policy.

The prosecution also blamed the accused for their servility to the enemy and lack of independence, which is associated with weakness of character – a typically 'feminine' feature, opposed to the strength of character and independence of 'superior' men. Servility is a primary moral characteristic of the traitor. The portrait of the servile feminine and irresponsible intellectual traitor (with an allusion to homosexuality in the case of Brasillach; see Kaplan 2000) was set in contrast to the resistant virile hero.

By denying subjective responsibility, the arguments of the defence corroborated this image of the intellectual traitor. They generally consisted in pleas for the good faith, sincerity, and disinterestedness of the accused: he was not motivated by base financial interest; he acted out of conviction. Making a contrast between doctrine and politics, young writer Lucien Combelle invoked his socialist ideals. Similarly, Robert Brasillach could plausibly argue that his fascist anti-Semitic views were rooted in a thoroughly French tradition. They all swore they had defended these ideas and principles in the interests of France, out of patriotism. Admittedly, some of them acknowledged, their pens had sometimes run beyond what they really thought, but such remarks had been written 'polemically'.

In any case, they said, they had only been following the official Collaboration policy of the French government and its representative, Marshal Pétain. Many of them denied their subjective responsibility, trying to transfer it to others further up the hierarchy: a leader, a superior, or a mentor. Béraud, who was a renowned writer, winner of the Goncourt prize in 1922, and a famous lampoonist who published in the extreme right weekly *Gringoire*, which had reached a print-run of 500,000 in the 1930s and maintained it at around 300,000 during the occupation, passed the blame on to Marshal Pétain: 'How could a simple citizen like myself, commanded by the Marshal at Verdun, helped by him in his literary career, and treated by him like a son, have doubted the Marshal's authority? I followed him.'[6] The young critic Lucien Combelle deflected his responsibility onto the writer Pierre Drieu La Rochelle, denouncing his elder's influence. Abel Hermant pretended he had been deceived by journalistic sources. With the benefit of hindsight, they recognized that they were wrong, but could an error be punished by death?

In contrast to Béraud and Combelle before him, Brasillach was the only writer who assumed sole responsibility, without however admitting his guilt.

Brasillach was shot on 6 February 1945, at the age of 35. This execution was, paradoxically, a form of recognition of the writers' symbolic power, which helped them preserve their symbolic capital (Rubinstein 1993). A few weeks later, fascist writer Pierre Drieu La Rochelle committed suicide. In an 'exordium' he left, Drieu, like Brasillach, claimed full responsibility for his actions as an intellectual. According to Drieu (1992: 502–3), 'The intellectual, the clerk, the artist is not a citizen like anyone. He has duties and rights superior to others'.

Soon after, Sartre developed a very similar idea, which he theorized with the concept of 'committed literature'. Sartre conceives of the responsibility of the writer as unlimited, in contrast to that of the physician or other professionals, because 'to name or to designate is to give meaning to acts, to make them exist in the general consciousness' (Sartre 1998: 21). To the co-founder of the main underground literary organization, Jean Paulhan, who contended that the crime resides in deeds and not in words, reproaching the government for sentencing intellectuals more severely than the political and economic collaborators (Paulhan 1948: 98), Sartre answered that writing was an act, it was in his eyes the supreme form of action (Sartre 1975: 260). Collapsing the traditional opposition between thought and action, Sartre's position compensated for the inferiority complex of the intellectual Resistance vis-à-vis the armed Resistance. The engaged writer is the virile public intellectual, in contrast to the servile traitor.

But the writer's responsibility extends, according to Sartre, beyond the national framework that determines legal responsibility. While writers were being judged as traitors to the nation, Sartre was de-nationalizing the concept of responsibility so as to give it a more universal bearing and thus reaffirming their autonomy vis-à-vis the political powers. The context of growing awareness that the Nazi crimes, especially the massacre of Jews, exceeded war crimes supplied him with the grounds (the notion of crimes against humanity became official in the Nuremberg trial but did not apply in France yet). In her article 'Oeil pour oeil' ('Eye for an Eye'), Simone de Beauvoir (1946: 816–7, 828) accused Brasillach not of having committed treason but of having committed a 'sin against man' in endeavouring to 'degrad[e] man into a thing'.

Sartre's concept of responsibility was founded on his philosophy of freedom. It was because the writer represented the highest expression of freedom that his responsibility was unlimited and that his task was to defend freedom everywhere in the world (Sapiro 2006b). Referring to Zola as a model, Sartre's conception is the most extreme and the most paradigmatic embodiment of subjective responsibility, in its autonomous version.

Freedom of expression and democracy in contemporary France

The opposite position was developed by Roland Barthes, starting in the 1950s, with his objective conception of '*l'écriture*', which led him to decree in his famous 1969 article the 'death of the author' (Barthes 1984). Barthes' approach was strongly related to the *nouveau roman*, which renewed art for art's sake, against the existentialist committed literature. For the leader of the *nouveau roman*, Robbe-Grillet, like for Barthes, the author engages only with problems in language.

In the legal settings, the 1939 law which created a committee for examining literary texts composed of representatives of morality leagues, of the state and of the *Société des gens de lettres* (the main literary society in France) introduced in practice a distinction between texts with a literary value and those with no such value. Ironically, it was the representative of the *Société des gens de lettres* who decided in 1946 to prosecute the French translations of Henry Miller's novels *Tropic of Cancer* and *Tropic of Capricorn*.

Furthermore, despite this apparent recognition of literary autonomy, this autonomy was menaced by the development of the practice of the administrative ban. The banning of writings was a common practice in wartime. During the Algerian war, the government banned writings criticizing the French government and army, like *La Question* by Henri Alleg. But banning was not limited to wartime. The 1949 law protecting youth, which is still in force, indeed allows the banning of any book considered as pornographic from the public space. Youth protection replaced national interest as a justification for censorship. The objective conception of responsibility, independent of the author's intentions, proved more efficacious, since it avoided any public debate.

Among the most famous trials that still took place during this period was that against Jean-Jacques Pauvert in 1956, for having published the Marquis de Sade's complete works. Pauvert was supported by many writers who argued that Sade's work had a philosophical value, beyond its obscenity. Though it recognized its literary merits, the court considered it to be still offensive and dangerous. In the appeal trial which was held two years later, the prosecuting attorney denounced the court's error in condemning Sade's nihilist philosophy and made a plea in favour of a literary exemption (*franchise littéraire*) comparable to scientific freedom. However, the court did not confirm this idea. On the contrary, the judgement reaffirmed the distinction between on the one hand, medical works, which enjoy immunity when they address a small circle of peers and students, and on the other hand, literary or art works, which do not escape the legal restrictions to freedom of expression (cf. Simonin 2008: 658–69).

The growing focus on an objective conception of responsibility in a context of extended liberalization of print (especially since the 1970s) can be interpreted as a way to reconcile the democratic principle of freedom of expression and the protection of public interest (youth protection, protection of minorities from racist attacks) and individual rights. Moreover, it allows to overturn the distinction between representation of and apology for crime put forward by the defence, as illustrated by the agreement between the government and the publisher in the recent case of Nicolas Johns-Gorlin's novel *Rose Bonbon* (2005), which stages a paedophile speaking in first person: it was distributed wrapped in cellophane packaging to prevent teenagers consulting it on the bookstore shelves.

The same year, another debut author Éric Bénier-Burckel and his publisher Flammarion were sued for incitement to racial and religious hatred, public insult with a racial dimension, offence to human dignity and distribution of a pornographic message that could be seen by minors in his novel *Pogrom*, which stages an anti-Semitic protagonist also speaking in first person. In this case, the court clearly established a distinction between apology and representation, considering that 'artistic creation requires an accrued freedom of the author which can express himself on consensual themes as well as on topics that upset, shock or worry' (cit. Tricoire 2007: 7).

However, the subjective conception of the writer's responsibility resurfaces when real people are concerned, as can be observed in the recent cases of prosecution for defamation and for violation of privacy. A famous recent case of defamation is the trial of the writer Mathieu Lindon and the publisher Paul Otchakovski-Laurens. They were sued for libel by Jean-Marie Le Pen, the National Front leader, for the novel ironically titled *Le Procès de Jean-Marie Le Pen* (1998). In this novel, which confronts the anti-racist camp and the National Front militants, Le Pen is compared, by fictional characters belonging to the first camp, to the 'chief of a gang of killers' and a 'vampire' who drinks the 'blood of his voters'. He is accused of being the real person responsible for the murder committed by a young National Front militant, because of his influence and indoctrination. The author and the publisher were convicted twice – once in 1999, by the *Tribunal de Grande Instance de Paris*, and once in 2007, by the European Court of Human Rights, to which they appealed. However, four of the magistrates of the European Court published dissenting opinions with regards to the verdict. They considered, among other things, that the fictional dimension was not sufficiently taken into account by the court. Thus in this case, contrary to the previous one, the distinctions between apology and representation and between the author and the characters was not considered relevant.

Freedom of expression can also be in contradiction with another democratic principle: the respect for privacy, which is an individual right (Article 9 in the Civil Code). With the development of the genre of autofiction, the number of prosecutions seems to have increased. I shall briefly compare two lawsuit cases: that of Camille Laurens and that of Christine Angot.

Camille Laurens was sued by her ex-husband for not respecting his privacy after she published *L'Amour, roman* (2003), which is about their separation. The *Tribunal de Grande Instance de Paris* dismissed his case, considering that 'Camille Laurens did not infringe on her husband's privacy' and that the use of a real first name does not suffice to remove from this work (*oeuvre*) the 'fictional character that the aesthetic dimension confers upon all art works, which certainly draws from the author's life-experience, but was also processed through the prism of memory and, in literary matter, of writing' (cit. Audran 2003).

In contrast, Christine Angot and her publisher Flammarion were convicted in May 2013 for having severely infringed on the privacy of the former partner of Angot's companion, Elise Bidoit, in the novel titled *Les Petits*. This infringement was considered peculiarly prejudicial to Elise Bidoit who was painted by Angot as a 'manipulative person' in a 'Manichean manner'. This painting could not be detached from Angot's personal interest (Robert-Diard 2013).

In these cases, fiction could not be invoked as such in defence of the writers, since they claim the veracity of the narrative (albeit not in all its details). However, the arguments put forward in the two cases underscore the capacity or the incapacity of the author to transform the materials borrowed from life experience through writing and stylization and to elevate them to a level of generality and exemplarity which transcends individual experience. Such a capacity was recognized for Camille Laurens but not for Christine Angot. During Angot's trial, the judges insisted on the fact that the litigants for infringement of privacy could hinder freedom of creation only if the infringement was very serious, which proves their will to find a compromise between the two democratic principles, and to avoid that the judgement set a precedent for all future cases. The judgement against Angot explained that the author could not pretend 'having transformed this real person into a character expressing a "truth" which belongs only to him [the author] as the product of his "work of writing", since this certainly imaginary representation was grafted on numerous elements of the reality of Elise Bidoit's private life that are given away to the public'. Fictionalization is thus not, in itself, a necessary nor a sufficient condition for getting round the law protecting privacy.

Another fact played a part in these decisions: the former behaviour of the litigants. Whereas Camille Laurens' counsel, Me Roland Rappaport, was able to demonstrate that her ex-husband had until that moment accepted to be named in his wife's works, and even appeared as such in the media, Elise Bidoit had already sued Christine Angot in 2009 for her previous book, *Le Marché des amants*; an agreement had finally been found between the author and the litigant. Consequently, the new case was judged as a repeat offence (AFP 2013; Ferrand 2013).

All these contemporary cases demonstrate the importance of the author's intentions, that is, of subjective responsibility. They also show the new limits of freedom of expression and of creation in democracy, as well as the limits of literary autonomy. The justification of these limits moved, historically, from the defence of religion and monarchy under the Bourbon Restoration to the defence of property and family during the Second Empire, then to national interest under the Third Republic, and to the protection of youth and of individual rights in the contemporary period. During this last period, the press was progressively liberalized and the autonomy of literature at least partly recognized by the government. The conception of the two readerships disappeared (though it is still in force in scholarship on reading) and was replaced by the distinction between youth and adult readers, which was and still is used for similar purposes. During the Third Republic, in the context of the growth of the readership, subjective responsibility became less important than objective responsibility thanks to the paradigm of degeneration and to the introduction of the concept of 'obscenity'. While the purge trials reaffirmed after the war the primacy of subjective responsibility for the crime of treason, conceived of as rational action, the banning practice developed as an objective approach to responsibility avoided any debate thanks to the 1949 Act on the protection of youth. The writer's existentialism and the *nouveau roman* embodied the two opposite conceptions of the professional ethics of the writer which redefined the responsibility of the author in an autonomous way, distinct from legal responsibility: the first represents the most paradigmatic example of the subjective definition, while the second focused on the objective aspects of writing. Subjective responsibility has resurfaced since the 1990s in the context of lawsuits brought against writers by litigants who recognized themselves in a literary work, displaying the tension between freedom of expression and individual rights in a democratic regime. Freedom of creation (and thus literary autonomy) is not considered in France as distinct from freedom of expression despite attempts to claim specific rights for creation (Tricoire 2011). However, as a result of the struggle of writers and artists for the recognition of literary autonomy, in practice, literary quality has been taken into account by the judges since 1945, less as an attenuating circumstance than as justifying a specific approach to texts, without avoiding ambiguities about what can be considered an artwork and what not.

Notes

1 This chapter is a synthesis of Sapiro (2011), apart from the last section which brings new materials. All translations from French are mine, unless indicated otherwise.
2 Stenography of Herold-Paquis' trial, 17 September 1945, Archives René Bluet, AN: 334 AP 15, p. 39.
3 Henri Béraud, 'Mémoire à l'intention du juge d'instruction', 4 November 1944, Dossier Henri Béraud. Archives Nationales.
4 'Procès-verbal de l'interrogatoire', 6 July 1945, Dossier Abel Hermant. Archives Nationales.
5 'Note de Lucien Rebatet sur *Les Décombres*'. Dossier Lucien Rebatet. Archives Nationales.
6 Henri Béraud, 'Mémoire à l'intention du juge d'instruction', 4 November 1944, Dossier Henri Béraud. Archive Nationales.

References

AFP (2013), 'Christine Angot a-t-elle "pillé" la vie privée d'Élise Bidoit?', *Le Point*, 27 May 2013, available online: http://www.lepoint.fr/culture/christine-angot-condamnee-pour-atteinte-a-la-vie-privee-27-05-2013-1672791_3.php.

Audran, M. (2003), 'Sa vie est un roman', *Le Point*, 11 April 2003.

Austin, J. (1962), *How to Do Things with Words*, Oxford: Oxford UP.

Bancaud, A. (2003), 'La construction de l'appareil juridique', in M.-O. Baruch (ed.), *Une poignée de misérables. L'épuration de la société française après la Seconde Guerre mondiale*, 61–97, Paris: Fayard.

Barthes, R. (1984), 'La mort de l'Auteur' in *Le Bruissement de la langue*, 61–7, Paris: Seuil.

Beauvoir, S. de (1946), 'Œil pour œil', *Les Temps modernes* (February): 813–30.

Bourdieu, P. (1992), *Les Règles de l'art. Genèse et structure du champ littéraire*, Paris: Seuil.

Cassagne, A. (1997), *La Théorie de l'art pour l'art en France chez les derniers romantiques et les premiers réalistes*, Paris: Champ Vallon.

Courier, P.-L. (1964), *Œuvres complètes*, Paris: Gallimard.

Descaves, L. (1980), *Sous-offs. Roman militaire*, ed. H. Mitterand, Geneva: Slatkine.

Desprez, L. (1992), '*Pour la liberté d'écrire*', in R.-P. Colin and J.-F. Nivet, *Louis Desprez (1861–1885). Pour la liberté d'écrire*, biography followed by *Pour la liberté d'écrire et de Mes prisons, par un naturaliste*, Tusson: Éditions du Lérot.

Diderot, D. (1976), '*Lettre sur le commerce de la librairie*', in *Œuvres complètes*, vol. VIII, Paris: Hermann.

Drieu La Rochelle, P. (1992), 'Exorde', in *Journal 1939–1945*, 502–3, Paris: Gallimard.

Fauconnet, P. (1920), *La Responsabilité. Étude de sociologie*, Paris: Alcan.

Ferrand, C. (2013), 'L'autofiction en procès', *Livres-Hebdo*.

Flaubert, G. (1951), *Œuvres*, vol. I, Paris: Gallimard.

Foucault, M. (1994), 'Qu'est-ce qu'un auteur?', in *Dits et écrits*, vol. I, *1954–1988*, 789–820, Paris: Gallimard.

Goldstein, J. (1984), ' "Moral Contagion": A Professional Ideology of Medicine and Psychiatry in Eighteenth- and Nineteenth-Century France', in G. L. Geison (ed.), *Professions and the French State 1700–1900*, 181–222, Philadelphia: University of Pennsylvania Press.

Jauß, H.-R. (1990), *Pour une esthétique de la réception*, trans., Paris: Gallimard.

Kaplan, A. (2000), *The Collaborator. The Trial and Execution of Robert Brasillach*, Chicago, IL: University of Chicago Press.

LaCapra, D. (1982), '*Madame Bovary' on Trial*, Ithaca, NY: Cornell UP.

Ladenson, E. (2007), *Dirt for Art's Sake. Books on Trial from* Madame Bovary *to* Lolita, Ithaca, NY: Cornell University Press.

Le Goff, J. (1977), *Pour un autre Moyen Âge. Temps, travail et culture en Occident: 18 essais*, Paris: Gallimard.

Maiseau, L.-R.-B. (1819), *Manuel de la liberté de la presse. Analyse des discussions législatives sur les trois lois relatives à la presse et aux journaux et écrits périodiques*, Paris: Pillet aîné.

Nordau, M. (1894), *Dégénérescence*, vol. II, *L'Égotisme*, trans., Paris: Alcan.

Novick, P. (1968), *The Purge of Collaborators in Liberated France*, New York: Columbia UP.

Paulhan, J. (1948), *De la paille et du grain*, Paris: Gallimard.

Procès fait aux chansons de P.-J. Béranger (1828), Paris: Baudouin frères.

Robert-Diard, P. (2013), 'Le jugement qui condamne Christine Angot pour atteinte à la vie privée', Blogs, Chroniques judiciaire, *Le Monde*, 28 May 2013, available online: http://prdchroniques.blog.lemonde.fr/2013/05/28/christine-angot-condamnee-a-40-000-euros-de-dommages-et-interets-pour-atteinte-a-la-vie-privee/

Rubinstein, D. (1993), 'Publish and Perish: The *épuration* of French Intellectuals', *Journal of European Studies* 89–90 (23): 71–99.

Sapiro, G. (2006a), 'Portrait of the Writer as a Traitor: The French Purge Trials (1944–1953)', *EREA* 4(2), available online: http://www.e-rea.org/.

Sapiro, G. (2006b), 'Responsibility and Freedom: Foundations of Sartre's Concept of Intellectual Engagement', *Journal of Romance Studies* 6(1–2): 31–48.

Sapiro, G. (2007), 'The Writer's Responsibility in France: From Flaubert to Sartre', *French Politics, Culture and Society* 25(1): 1–29.

Sapiro, G. (2011), *La Responsabilité de l'écrivain. Littérature, droit et morale en France (19e-21e siècle)*, Paris: Seuil.

Sapiro, G. (forthcoming), 'Figure de l'écrivain irresponsable: le procès de Céline', in Ph. Roussin and R. Tettamanzi (eds), *Céline à l'épreuve*, Paris: Presses de la Sorbonne nouvelle.

Sartre, J.-P. (1975), *Qu'est-ce que la littérature?*, Paris: Gallimard.

Sartre, J.-P. (1998), *La Responsabilité de l'écrivain*, Paris: Verdier.

Simonin, A. (2008), *Le Déshonneur dans la République. Une histoire de l'indignité 1791–1958*, Paris: Grasset.

Stora-Lamarre, A. (1990), *L'Enfer de la IIIe République. Censeurs et pornographes 1881–1914*, Paris: Imago.

Tricoire, A. (2007), '"Quand la fiction exclut le délit", comment on TGI Paris 17e ch. 16/11/2006, affaire: MP c/ Bénier-Bürckel', *Légipresse* nr. 240 (April): 7.

Tricoire, A. (2011), *Petit Traité de la liberté de création*, Paris: La Découverte.

Weber, M. (1968), *On Charisma and Institution Building. Selected Papers*, ed. S.N. Eisenstadt, Chicago, IL: The University of Chicago Press.

Weber, M. (1991), 'Le métier et la vocation d'homme politique', in *Le Savant et le Politique*, trans., reprint, 99–185, Paris: Plon.

Weber, M. (1995), *Économie et société*, vol. I, trans., reprint, Paris: Plon.

2

The Making of the 1959 Obscene Publications Act: Trials and Debates on Literary Obscenity in Britain Before the Case of Lady Chatterley

Anton Kirchhofer

1954 was a remarkable year for literature in UK courts. From provincial magistrates to the Central Criminal Court at the Old Bailey, a series of literary trials on charges of obscenity worried publishers and booksellers alike. The opposition suspected the conservative government of running a campaign against modern avant-garde literature, but this was repeatedly and resolutely denied. The Society of Authors started a campaign of its own, seeking to obtain better legal protection for the freedom of literary expression, and instituted a committee consisting of sixteen authors, public figures and politicians (cf. Herbert 1956: xi). The result of these efforts was a draft bill to amend the Obscene Publications Act of 1857, widely known as Lord Campbell's Act, so that literary works – past and present – as well as their publishers might be safe from the risk of being prosecuted alongside the large quantities of so called 'pure pornography' or 'mere pornography' which were regularly seized and destroyed by the authorities. The need for revised legislation was first suggested to the House of Commons in November 1954, but it took five years and a lengthy and tortuous process, before the 'Act to amend the law relating to the publication of obscene matter; to provide for the protection of literature; and to strengthen the law concerning pornography' was enacted (cf. Obscene Publications Act 1959).

The enactment of the new law has widely been described as the belated advent of literary autonomy in England, the formal recognition of an *exceptio artis*, permitting a defence on the plea of literary merit as well as the inclusion of 'evidence…from experts to support arguments of literary merit' (Dolin 2007: 49). The new law was immediately put to the test in the case of *Lady Chatterley's Lover*, and the ruling which cleared the novel from the verdict of obscenity has been seen as the crowning moment, in the UK, of a 'long process of juridical and legislative activity' whose result was 'to overthrow bowdlerism and Comstockery, and to enable literature to explore sexuality as readily as any other aspect of social reality' (Dolin 2007: 49). In a similar fashion, David Bradshaw characterizes the trials of 1954 as an 'orgy of banning and burning' (Bradshaw 2013: 138) and suggests that 'the passage of the 1959 Act undoubtedly marks a defining moment in modern British cultural history' (Bradshaw 2013: 156).

Other recent historians have called for greater 'scepticism' towards 'the libertarian suppositions that inform this history when it's told by the lawyers who participated in it' (Glass 2009: 869; cf. specifically Stevas 1956, Rembar 1969, Rolph 1969) and consequently have been hesitant about adopting the 'point of view of a narrative recounting successive steps in a continuing march towards complete freedom of expression' (Ladenson 2007: xvii). Most substantially, Peter D. McDonald (2008) has argued that to understand the Obscene Publications Act (OPA) of 1959 as a landmark event in a narrative of progress and modernization is to ignore its fundamental continuities with the goals, the anxieties and the fundamental assumptions which had already guided the Victorian critics and legislators.

Building *inter alia* on earlier work by Gisèle Sapiro, Kees van Rees, Ralf Grüttemeier, and of course by Pierre Bourdieu (2011), Ralf Grüttemeier and Ted Laros have recently proposed a field-theoretical perspective that might provide a conceptual framework for this question. Calling for a 'comparative approach in reconstructing structural, regional and temporal differences and similarities in the process of the institutional autonomisation of literary fields' (Grüttemeier and Laros 2013: 217), the authors test their hypothesis that '[t]he recognition of the *exceptio artis* in the legal field can be taken to constitute a decisive step in the formation of a relative[ly] autonomous literary field' (Grüttemeier and Laros 2013: 205) in relation to the Dutch literary field, where they find that: 'The moment of the first occurrence of the concept of *exceptio artis* within judicial practice turns [around 1920] out to be a strong and decisive indication of the recognition of the independence of the literary field by the political and juridical elite' (Grüttemeier and Laros 2013: 217).

The following review of the parliamentary process triggered in the UK by the literary obscenity trials of 1954 will not quite bear out the same conclusion. The new OPA indeed indicates the existence of relatively autonomous literary field in the UK, but the final shape in which it becomes law appears in many aspects incidental and contingent rather than 'strong and decisive'. The result is contingent on a power struggle in which the participants cannot adequately be classified under the headings of literary 'autonomists' v. 'heteronomists'. It is contingent to an even greater degree, as I will propose, on the underlying conceptions of power that inform the stances of all participants in the debates (and which I will suggest are best captured by reference to the Foucauldian notions of 'governmentality' and 'biopower'). Even when the larger picture is taken into account – the comparison with previous legislative processes concerning obscenity in the mid-nineteenth century and the early twentieth century, as well as the literary trials of the 1960s – the adoption of *exceptio artis* into the 1959 OPA does not seem 'decisive': it does not bring a decisive alteration to a situation in which the autonomy of the literary field had traditionally been relatively well-established, though the risk of incidental prosecution on the count of obscenity had also existed, and continued to exist, often in a fairly incalculable, if not statistically predominant fashion.

Before I seek to carry this discussion further (in my final section), I propose to offer a brief factual summary of the five literary cases as well as a survey of the main steps in the prolonged parliamentary process that led to the revised legislation, and go on to single out what appear to me to be some of the remarkable features of these debates.

Five trials and five years of parliamentary debate

Starting in May 1954, five literary works in brief succession, and partly overlapping, faced legal charges on the count of obscenity, leading to court cases whose courses and outcomes varied substantially (cf. Sova 2011 as well as Kauffmann 1988 and the coverage in *The Times* newspaper for the information summarized in the following paragraphs). After Stanley Kauffmann's *The Philanderer*, a novel about a married, but compulsively promiscuous young man, published by Secker and Warburg in the spring of 1953 (original US publication 1952), was acquitted in July 1954, the second case ended with a conviction. Vivian Connell's novel *September in Quinze* described erotic entanglements among the international residents of the Côte d'Azur resort Cannes (involving some fierce descriptions of sexual activity featuring, for example, one man 'savag[ing one woman] with his manhood in the forest of her hair' or breasts 'glow[ing] like gourds of love in the moonlight' [quoted after

Sova 2011: 208]). The novel was indicted at Marlborough Street Magistrate Court in May 1954 and even though both the prosecution and the defence asked for a summary trial by the magistrate, Magistrate Milton committed the case to the Central Criminal Court. The trial at the Old Bailey took place in September 1954, and the publisher Hutchinson and Co., the printer Taylor, Garnett, Evans and Co. and Katherine Webb, director of both companies, were fined £500 each. We may note that expert evidence of a kind had been initially allowed. As *The Times* reported, 'September in Quinze ... had been reviewed in conservative and most sober journals. No reviewer had suggested that there was anything in the book to offend against public taste or morals. Mr. MacDermot [the prosecutor] contended that reviews of the book were second-hand opinions and would not necessarily help the jury to form an opinion on it, but the magistrate allowed reviews to be put in as evidence' (*The Times* 1954a). According to Sova (2011: 209), the reviews were however 'disallowed when the case was heard at the Old Bailey'.

The third case attracted attention as a passing embarrassment to the legal system, because it concerned a literary classic. In July 1954, the Swindon Borough Magistrates Court, issued a destruction order for an edition of Giovanni Boccaccio's *The Decamerone* which had been seized along with other materials in a bookshop specializing in obscene publications, but the sentence was overturned by a higher court in September 1954.

In October 1954, the author Walter Baxter, the publishing company William Heinemann and Stewart Frere, one of its directors, were put on trial for obscenity at the Central Criminal Court for publishing *The Image and the Search* (1953), the story of a woman who lost her beloved husband in the war and embarked on an ultimately unsuccessful quest to find another lover like him. After two juries failed to agree, a third trial took place in December 1954, in which the prosecution offered no evidence and the jury returned a verdict of 'not guilty'.

The last novel prosecuted in 1954 was *The Man in Control* by Charles McGraw, the story of a middle-aged widower who marries a young woman and 'then discovers that she is frigid and has lesbian tastes' (Charques 1953: 26), as the *Spectator* reported in its dismissive notice of the book. The publishing company Arthur Barker Ltd., Edinburgh and its director Herbert Van Thal, were found not guilty of 'publishing an obscene libel' by a jury in the Central Criminal Court in December 1954.

A brief review of the trajectory of these trials shows that the first two judges offered highly divergent interpretations of the law and that the juries in each case followed the indications given by the judges. In the trial relating to *The Philanderer*, the judge stated in his summing up of the case that 'the literature of the world … represented … the sum total of thought of the human mind', and stressed that '[a] mass of great literature was wholly unsuitable for reading by the adolescent, but that did not mean the publishers were guilty of a criminal offence for making these works available to the general public' (*The Times* 1954a). In the trial against *September in Quinze*, the defence quoted extensively from these remarks. The presiding judge, however, described the book as 'repugnant to every decent emotion which ever concerned man or woman' and welcomed the verdict by saying: 'It is a very comforting thought that juries from time to time take a very solid stand against this sort of thing, and realise how important it is for the youth of this country to be protected and that the fountain of our national blood should not be polluted at its source' (*The Times* 1954b). The prosecution of Boccaccio's novellas appears to have been seen as passing embarrassment soon put right again, while the final two trials show that no further convictions can be brought about. One might be tempted to conclude that after an intermittent reaction against the liberalism displayed in the first trial, the uncertainty of the situation manifested itself both in the overeagerness of the Swindon magistrates and in the hung juries of the trial against *The Image and the Search* though the year closed, as it had opened, with the acquittal of a literary work from the charge of obscenity.

But while the situation is still unresolved and the last two cases are still pending, in November 1954 voices were raised in the House of Commons to point out the need to reform the law in order to remedy the uncertainty which was manifesting itself. Lieut.-Colonel H.M. Hyde (the MP for Belfast, North) criticized the 'anomalies and inconsistencies' of the present legislation on literary obscenity, where there was one law concerning publishers, printers and authors (and dealing with the criminal offence of publishing an 'obscene libel'), another law enabling the destruction of obscene books and the punishment of the retailers who stock them, a third and fourth law governing the importation of books through the Customs and the circulation of materials through the Post Office (Hansard 1954). At the core of the critique, however, is the perceived arbitrariness of the legal standard that applies in trials of this kind, and the long (and apparently ineffective) tradition which this critique already has: 'The Cockburn test is purely speculative. It regards neither the author's or the publisher's intention, nor the merit of the work. It is solely concerned with its hypothetical effect on a susceptible reader.' A reform of the law, making '[e]xpert literary or scientific evidence... admissible', appeared long overdue. Nearly fifty years earlier, '[a]s long ago as 1908 a Select Committee of both Houses considered the question of indecent literature and recommended that evidence of this kind should be considered in the courts' (Hansard 1954).

A long and laborious process is thus set in motion, carried by the energy and determination of a number of individuals over the period of nearly five years. Roy Jenkins, MP for Labour and one of the key promoters of reform, lists among the main achievements of the new legislation that the work as a whole has to be considered, that likely readership has to be taken into account, and that defendant may plead that the publication was in the interest of the public good, and may have this claim supported by expert evidence (cf. Jenkins 1959). But the details of the 'five-year struggle' summarized by Jenkins bring into view a highly precarious process whose course and outcomes depend on a whole array of contingencies. The following summary highlights only a few of the tactical moves and manoeuvres in this process which one of the promoters 'compared to a game of "snakes and ladders"' and whose fuller version can be found in Jenkins's account.

Since the government does not follow up the discussions of November 1954 with any proposed legislation, Roy Jenkins in March 1955 and the conservative MP Hugh Fraser in November 1955 unsuccessfully introduce private members bills. In November 1956, Viscount Lambton's bill is successful and during the second reading in March 1957 expressions of support are so widespread that the government proposes to second the bill and refer it to a Select Committee instead of the standing committee. This Select Committee, appointed to look comprehensively into all issues relating to obscene publications consists of 'a substantial group of convinced reformers, a number of determined "censors"... and a few neutrals'. It works from May 1957 to March 1958 and produces a compromise in which the 'reformers' had to accept 'the additional powers for which the police had asked' in exchange for securing agreement for 'some of the liberalising provisions' (Jenkins 1959: 65). But late in 1958 there is still no progress. The government shows no readiness to propose legislation on the basis of the published report. None of the twenty MPs who win a place in the ballot on private members bills is prepared to sponsor the bill. Attempts to use the Ten Minute Rule to introduce the bill are blocked twice by objections from conservative back benchers. At this point, Sir Alan Herbert threatens to split the conservative vote at an important by-election and '[w]ithin a week we were offered a debate and with it the promise of an unopposed second reading'

(Jenkins 1959: 65). The government's plan to sabotage the bill in April 1959 by voting out the 'liberalising provisions' in the standing committee while leaving in the 'police provisions' fails, according to Jenkins, on account of the absence of many conservative MPs, which results in an unexpected majority for the reformers. In July 1959, the bill finally passes the House of Lords.

In Roy Jenkins's telling, this is the story of determination and progress prevailing after a long and often frustrating process shaped by a series of contingencies. The progressive principles of a labour backbencher have overcome a conservative government which had been motivated by an outdated fear of moral corruption as much as by a well-founded fear of appearing 'ridiculous to a highly articulate section of the public' (Jarvis 2005: 115), to pay the price of allowing greater autonomy to literature, in order to attain better control of pornography. If we map this opposition on the question of the relative autonomy of the literary field, then we may gloss the term 'reformers' as 'advocates of literary autonomy' and the term 'censors' as 'proponents of heteronomous views of literature'. Jenkins thus carries the political struggle into the literary field, with the labour opposition as the agent of progress and modernization and the conservative government as the agent of regression and heteronomy.

But it is to be questioned, how far Jenkins's account of the successive power struggles, tactical shifts and manoeuvres with highly contingent outcomes really bears out his claim that there is a clear-cut opposition between 'reformers' on the one had, and 'censors' on the other. Clearly neither of the respective party leaderships takes an actively visible role in the process. Moreover, most of the other 'reformers' have unmistakeable Conservative affiliations: Viscount Lambton and Sir Hugh Fraser are conservative MPs, and so is the publisher Nigel Nicolson (though he will not be re-elected later in 1959, after having published Vladimir Nabokov's *Lolita*). Sir Alan P. Herbert, the spokesperson for the Society of Authors in favour of law reform, was an independent MP for Oxford University until 1951 and his 'general political allegiance was firmly Conservative', as quoted above. Norman St. John Stevas, the legal advisor to the Society of Authors, was not an MP at the time though he had stood unsuccessfully for the Conservatives in a safe labour seat in 1951 (and became a conservative MP in 1964, as well as leader of the House of Commons under the government of Margaret Thatcher; on all actors in the process, cf. the respective articles in the *Dictionary of National Biography*).

The 'reformers', then, do not neatly fit the political binary of 'left' and 'right' which Jenkins uses to structure his account; and neither are the representatives of the government willing to accept the label of 'censors': '[Roy Jenkins] has ... on occasion described the supporters of the Bill as liberalisers and its opponents and critics as at heart censors', says the Attorney-General in the final debate on the bill in the House of Commons: 'I do not put myself in the latter category' (Hansard 1959a).

We ought to be aware, therefore, that the process that leads to legislative reform in 1959 can neither easily be mapped onto the confrontations between opposing political camps, nor can it always be adequately described as a contention between proponents of greater or lesser autonomy for literature. The adoption of the factors of 'the work as a whole', of 'likely readership', 'literary merit' and 'expert evidence' into the legislation on obscene publications is – from the perspective of some actors in the process – the final recognition of literary autonomy and thus the completion of a goal they have long aspired to. It may as much be seen as a concession that some are forced to make against their better judgements, or as a by-product of a parliamentary process that involves various agents and divergent stakes. From the government's perspective, I will suggest the issue is one they would have preferred not to legislate on, but on which – once they accept new legislation as inevitable – they see themselves as championing the autonomy of literature – over, for example, the economic interests of publishers.

In the following sections I will review of the positions voiced in parliament in the course of these debates and tell the story not by adopting the perspective of one of the contestants, but by looking in some detail at the conflicting positions voiced in the course of the parliamentary process, before seeking to widen the perspective in my concluding analysis.

A consensus on the need to suppress pornography

If there is one point, on which all participants in the debates on obscene publications appear to be in fundamental agreement, it is that pornography ought to be suppressed. The debates are characterized by 'a general consensus of opinion, as much on the part of those who support the Bill as those who oppose it, that the Bill must be sufficiently armed to deal with mere pornography' (J.E.S. Simon, Joint Under-Secretary of State for the Home Department, Hansard 1957). Whatever we may surmise about the degrees of sincerity on the part of individual MPs, there are no explicit expressions of disagreement from this goal.

The idea that sexual excitement in itself is inoffensive and that consequently materials which are conducive to sexual stimulation are similarly inoffensive as long as they contain nothing else which constitutes an offence (an idea which proved central to the ruling in the US trials against *Fanny Hill* in the 1960s, cf. Ladenson 2007), never remotely enters the horizon in these debates. The chief concern is how pornography can be suppressed effectively, and much casuistry is expended on anticipating potential abuses of well-intentioned revisions and on preventing the inadvertent creation of 'new loopholes' for pornography (cf., e.g., the extensive discussions about the terms 'matter' v. 'an article' during the final reading in the House of Commons, Hansard 1959a; cf. also the revisions of the OPA of 1964, which were designed to close the 'loopholes' left by the Act of 1959, cf. Williams 1965).

As McDonald (2008) has noted, this position is in unmistakeable continuity with the paternalistic concerns of Victorian legislators seeking to suppress pornography in the interest of safeguarding the moral well-being of the population. Nor is this view limited to those whom Jenkins has classified as 'censors'. Even the celebrated summing up in the *Philanderer* case uses this point. Justice Stable warns the jury, that a conviction could provoke a radical reform that might create openings for genuinely pornographic materials: 'If we drive the criminal law too far, in our desire to stamp out the "bawdy muck", isn't there a risk that there will be a revolt, a demand for a change in the law, so that the pendulum may swing too far the other way and allow to creep in things that at the moment we can keep out?' (Stable 1957: 283; cf. also Rolph 1969: 103) Such advocacy makes the *exceptio artis* appear like a concession whose purpose it is to protect the ulterior goal of suppressing pornography.

Recognizing the uncertainty of the legal framework of literature

There is widespread agreement, too, among members of parliament and government representatives participating in the debates that the legal situation as it stands in the mid-1950s creates a substantial degree of uncertainty for individual literary publications. But there is disagreement about how to reformulate the law so that it will provide greater certainty, and whether it will be possible to do so at all.

In introducing the Bill at its second reading in March 1957, Viscount Lambton deplores this lack of consistency. He evokes the contradictory interpretations of the law which had guided the several judgements in the cases of *The Philanderer* and *September in Quinze* and concludes that 'the law [is] uncertain', and 'judgments [are] dependent upon the whim of the judge' (Hansard 1957).

The voices disturbing this consensus do not advocate a heteronomous view of literature. Instead, they point out the difficulty of remedying this uncertainty. In a previous debate, Sir Beverley Baxter (Southgate) had expressed 'sympathy' for the reformers, but had also struck a note of scepticism, warning that 'there are some problems for which there is no solution. It seems to me that this question of censorship and the clarification of the law of obscenity is so complex and confusing that the Bill will only add to the present mess' (Hansard 1955).

In addition, opponents of legal reform question the magnitude of the problem. In the debate on 29 March 1957, only one member (Dudley Williams, Exeter) voices a sceptical attitude. Reviewing the literary obscenity cases of the past decades Williams concludes that the number of questionable prosecutions had been relatively small and that all important works which might have been initially banned or withheld had since become available. In relation to the trials of 1954, his view is 'that no serious harm was done by those five prosecutions' (Hansard 1957), and moreover that the legal system itself has proved capable of correcting its mistakes, as the destruction order issued against the *Decamerone* showed. After all, he argues, 'that decision was put right by the machinery of the law when the case was taken on appeal to the Wiltshire Quarter Sessions', and concludes: 'Surely, if a mistake is made by a bench of magistrates, it does not necessarily prove that there should be an alteration to the law of the whole country' (Hansard 1957).

Even though Jenkins reproaches Williams for his 'complacency' (Hansard 1957), the course of the debates shows that along with the praise for their laudable goals, the proponents of reform have to face the fact that the legal detail of their proposed revisions carries the danger of 'adding to the present mess' rather than solving it.

Proposing and abandoning the criterion of intention

One of the most prominent differences between the initial bill and the one finally enacted consists in the fact that the explicit use of intention in the bill was entirely abandoned. In the original proposal for revised legislation, the question of intention is one of the paramount elements. The promoters see the fact, that intention has not played an explicit role in the legal consideration around obscene publications, as one reason for the difficulties they try to remedy. At its first presentations in 1955 Roy Jenkins describes the Bill as 'a liberalising measure which would give greater security to *works of good intent*' [my italics, AK], and expresses his belief 'that if we act on the basis of intent it will be possible to give a greater security to valuable literary work without in any way opening the gates to a stream of pornographic publications, and I believe that we can put the law on a clearer and more sensible basis' (Hansard 1955). His position received a fair degree of support among MPs in this as well as in subsequent debates. 'I welcome the provision in the Bill which makes the intention of the author or publisher an ingredient of the offence,' declared MP Anthony Kershaw in the debate on 29 March 1957. 'That absence of intention at present is a very serious defect' (Hansard 1957).

The promoters of the bill have to concede, however, 'that it is difficult to prove in law that a publisher or author intends to corrupt by what he publishes' (Viscount Lambton, Hansard 1957). But '[e]ven this Bill could not be said to make impossible the prosecution of reputable publishers and authors for obscene intentions which never entered into their minds', says one of its supporters, Nigel Nicolson (Hansard 1957). In the interest of practicability, the reformers settle for 'guilty knowledge' as a more limited and specific version of intentionality (Hansard 1957). The Report of the Select Committee contains an argument advising against the inclusion of the term 'guilty knowledge' (Select Committee Report 1958b: xi) and the bill as it is finally enacted makes no explicit reference to the aspect of intention.

The (non)existence and the (un)desirability of censorship

Some of the most remarkable exchanges in these debates arise when the topic of censorship is addressed. Roy Jenkins is surely right in pointing out, that the 'five-year struggle' for the new act 'has been illuminating … about British attitudes to censorship' (Jenkins 1959: 63), but this is so not least because the positions of the different participants tend to undermine the binary arrangement into 'censors' on the one hand and 'reformers' on the other, that Jenkins has suggested.

From the beginning, the government is emphatic in its commitment to the freedom of literature. In the first debate, the Home Secretary insists that it is essential to a free country, as 'one aspect of the freedom of speech generally'

(Hansard 1954), and that consequently there is no place for any censorship of literature. At the same time, it is the sense of an incalculable and unofficial censorship hanging over all UK literature without being definitely graspable, that constitutes a central motivation behind the wish to revise the law. As Viscount Lambton points out in presenting the bill in 1957, there is a perception that 'publishers and printers had been so uncertain of the law that they were imposing upon authors a censorship which could be far stricter than any which the law could enforce' (Hansard 1957).

Concrete examples for the effect and the extent of this unofficial censorship are comparatively hard to come by. In the course of the Select Committee meetings, Lord Lambton asks the authors E.M. Forster and T.S. Eliot if they have 'ever been restricted in [their] writing by the present law' (Select Committee 1958b: 17). T.S. Eliot offers an unhesitating 'No' and goes on to discuss the past case of *Ulysses* which is no longer controversial, while E.M. Forster suggests in very general terms that '[s]ome authors – I will not say Mr. Eliot or myself – are inhibited by the harsh and at present uncertain position of the law as regards obscenity' and that 'many of them wish to introduce scenes or phrases and hesitate to do so in case they get into trouble' (Select Committee 1958b: 18).

While the authors who may have feared or suffered censorship do not wish to say so, the representatives of the law themselves do not wish to be considered as censors, even though the current situation makes this position difficult to maintain. Anticipating the Attorney-General's rejection of the label (cf. Hansard 1959a) by a year, Mathew Theobald, the Director of Public Prosecutions had declared in his memorandum to the Select Committee: 'I should strongly deprecate my Department being placed in the position … of being a literary or moral censor' (Select Committee 1958a: 25). Questioned by committee members, he is nevertheless compelled to concede that 'to [a] limited extent the office of the Director of Public Prosecutions is a censorship department'.

The intricacies of the issue of censorship do not stop here, however. Instead of objecting to censorship, the questioner suggests that, in order to be performed properly, censorship requires expertise: 'I think it is alarming that you as a semi-censor, if we can discover a censor anywhere in the whole cosmogony of the legal and police services, can do these things and can pass such a book [as *Ulysses*, AK] merely because, as you have admitted, you found it completely unintelligible' (Select Committee 1958a: 33). In the end, the reluctant censor admits that he would gladly be relieved of this role and its attendant difficulties: 'I should welcome, as Director of Public Prosecutions, obviously, any other form of censorship authority who could deal with these matters before coming to me' (Select Committee 1958a: 40).

While the gist of the questions throughout this exchange is to demonstrate the desirability of establishing a board of literary experts who could arbitrate on literary works prior to their publication (as is the case elsewhere in the British Commonwealth), and while the Director of Public Prosecutions might be glad to leave responsibility to such a board, the authors make it clear in the Select Committee that they unequivocally reject this idea. 'Would you like to see literary men, both authors and publishers, pass judgment before the courts pass judgment, on books which fall on the borderline? In other words, ... would you like to see a board of people, like yourselves perhaps, ... giving advice to the Director of Public Prosecutions?' one questioner suggests. To which E.M. Forster replies: 'I should not like to see it at all' (Select Committee 1958b: 20). Instead, the authors advocate greater tolerance along with a minimum of legal interference in all doubtful cases. T.S. Eliot suggests in his concluding statement 'that really obscene literature is fairly easily identifiable to any person of education, intelligence and some sensibility', so that problems only arise with respect to 'certain border-line cases one way or the other' and that in these cases, decisions 'should be in favour of laxity rather than of strictness' (Select Committee 1958b: 21).

The publishers' representatives, however, find it harder to abandon the idea of consistency through censorship. In the parliamentary debate on the Report, Nigel Nicolson, a conservative MP and member of the select committee, as well as a partner in the widely respected publishing house Weidenfeld and Nicolson, declares that it 'would be quite wrong to imagine that the publishing profession is against a censorship' and mentions two reasons. Firstly, 'it demands a censorship, because it shares with all hon. Members who have spoken in the debate a desire to eradicate pornography'. Secondly, '[i]t wishes to publish works which it considers contribute towards the stock of literature. It does not wish to be deterred from such publications by the fear of a law which in the opinion of every enlightened person is already out of tune with public opinion' (Hansard 1958).

In this situation it falls to the government representative, in this case the Home Secretary R.A. Butler himself, to reiterate the unequivocal rejection of a censorship of literature. Censorship 'has been adopted in one way or another for the theatre and the cinema, but I would most violently rebel at the idea of a censor or board of censors applying his or its activities to literature and art. It would not only be complex, but utterly unacceptable in a free country' (Hansard 1958). The autonomy of literature is then asserted in the strongest terms by the government, and from this commitment arises the task of defining the scope of the *relative autonomy* of literature by casting it in effective legal form – even though the question to what degree it will be possible to reconcile the dual goals of safeguarding the population from moral corruption and safeguarding the progress of literature, remains open. It is the conflict between these two goals that creates the difficulty of 'trying to find a limit for the law' on the one hand, and 'trying to make it ... effective in this very difficult matter' on the other (R.A. Butler, Home Secretary, Hansard 1958).

Even in the final draft of the bill, the promoters of legal reform seek to involve the Director of Public Prosecutions in all prosecutions on the count of obscenity, in order to ensure greater consistency in the legal practice. The government representatives oppose this on the grounds of a principal opposition to literary censorship. In the debate on the bill, the attorney-general, warns that in effect the Director of Public Prosecutions 'will be asked by publishers to operate a kind of censorship' (Hansard 1959a), and in the end, the Clause is dropped.

As a consequence, 'borderline' cases will still be decided by the courts, even if the defences of the public good and of literary merit, on which experts may be called to testify, are now available. To this extent, the institutional autonomy of literature has no doubt been strengthened. But the debates about censorship have shown two additional and significant points: On the one hand, the promoters of legal reform appeared to be ready to make the literary field more heteronomous for the sake of establishing greater consistency. And on the other hand, the absence of an *exceptio artis* clause in obscenity legislation has been quite compatible with a principal recognition of the autonomy of literature.

Conclusion: 'Adding to the present mess'? Protecting public morality and the *exceptio artis* in 1857, 1908 and 1959

Looking back over the process of legal reform, one might be tempted to agree with the MP who warned 'that this question of censorship and the clarification of the law of obscenity is so complex and confusing that the Bill will only add to the present mess' (Hansard 1955). The difficulty of encoding literary autonomy in legal terms is indicated clearly by the abandonment of the criterion of intention along the way, as well as by the fact that the proponents of the bill were prepared to place the Director of Public Prosecutions in the position of a quasi-censor in order to remedy the inconsistencies of the legal situation, while the government opposed this on the grounds of practicability as well as of an emphatic commitment to the autonomy of literature. Clearly the protection of literature from interference by extra-literary institutions was a 'complex' matter.

This point is made late in the final debate on the bill in the House of Commons, which is about to conclude with a series of congratulations extended to Jenkins and the supporters of the Bill when one speaker rises to express his utter incomprehension of the core provisions of literary merit and expert evidence:

> [W]hat has been said to be the main improvement in the Bill is not … understood by anyone … . Mr. Roy Jenkins … was in favour of … experts … sometimes because he thought that their evidence might go to upset what would otherwise be *prima facie* obscene, and sometimes … because even if the article were obscene, if the experts thought that it had sufficient literary value it would not be interfered with. That is the deepest thing in the Bill. I have heard not a word about it today. We have not heard a word about it on the Floor of the House either before today. What was the intention of the Bill … on that point I do not know. What is the intention of hon. Members opposite or the Solicitor-General at the moment, I do not know, and if I knew both those things I should not have the least idea what the effect is going to be. (Hansard 1959a)

No one replies to this speech; instead Hansard drily records the conclusion of proceedings: 'Bill … read the Third time and passed' (Hansard 1959a).

As Peter McDonald (2008) has noted, the OPA of 1959 does not ultimately address this central issue whether something can be obscene and literature at the same time. It places an ultimately unfounded confidence in critical expertise: '[N]o expert witness could ever give an incontrovertible answer' to the questions 'What is obscenity? What is literature?' because literature 'constitutes a labile, even anarchic space', rather than being 'a determinate object nor, indeed, an incontestable "public good"' (McDonald 2008: 301). A similar point had been made by T.S. Eliot in the course of the Committee hearings, and as Roy Jenkins records, 'gave some ammunition to those who were against "expert evidence"' (Jenkins 1959: 65) by doing so. What is at stake here, is the role of literature in modern or modernizing societies, and the question to what extent it is part of this role to challenge existing conditions by transgressing norms – and hence to what extent literature needs to retain the capacity to enter into conflict with existing norms (cf. Levine 2007).

In a larger historical perspective, I suggest that the issues around literature and obscenity are best understood in relation to what Michel Foucault has called 'bio-power' (Foucault 1978: 140; cf. also Hunter, Saunders and Williamson 1993: 135–48). They are effects of a conception of power which links the legitimacy of exercising power to the goal of fostering, promoting, nourishing the lives of citizens. In fact, what emerges from the debates on obscenity, pornography and literature is the existence of conflicting goals which can nevertheless be traced to a common source. Problems of literary obscenity arise, wherever – and as long as – the goal of safeguarding the moral well-being of the population by the suppression of pornography comes into conflict with the – equally biopolitical – goal of protecting literature and creating the best possible conditions for a flourishing national literature. For a long time, politicians have recognized both goals, but placed the legislative focus exclusively on the former goal. The conflict between the two goals is preserved by the OPA of 1959, which retains the general idea that politics must protect the population against materials that have a tendency to deprave and corrupt; it all but disappears when this idea is partly abandoned and partly refocused on other (mainly visual) materials and media. This shift definitely changes the conditions under which literature is practiced, but it occurs in the field of what Foucault has called 'power-knowledge', and it concerns the relationship in which sexuality is thought to stand with the moral well-being of the population. It is as an effect of this shift, that the two bio-political goals – that of creating conditions in which the moral well-being of the population will be ensured and that of creating conditions in which the literature of the nation will prosper – whose conflict produced the political and juridical dilemmas, for example, in the literary trials of 1954, have largely lost their specific potential for conflict.

This proposition also enables a perspective on the conflicts and confrontations in the wider legal history of obscenity in the nineteenth and twentieth centuries. As in the entire course of the process of the 'governmentalisation of the state' (Foucault 1991: 104), not all politicians have readily accepted or contributed to the acceptance of responsibility for more and more areas of social, personal and biological life by the institutions of the state. There was resistance to the suggestion that the production and distribution of obscene publications needed to be policed or prosecuted, just as there was resistance to the idea that a legal provision was required to safeguard literature from such prosecution. And there has been the view that the absence of legal provisions might be the better way of creating conditions in which a particular aspect of human life or creativity might flourish.

In 1857 there is resistance to the idea that there should be a law against obscene publications, and part of this resistance is motivated by the potential damage that might be done to literature by such a law. In 1959, in the House of Lords, this resistance is evoked in the debates on the Obscene Publications Bill:

> In this House the Bill [of 1857] was very strongly opposed, notably by Lord Lyndhurst, who made a speech which is still most interesting to read, and by Lord Brougham, and the objection which they made is one that has been raised almost ever since. They said that the Bill was too severe, in that it would injure the true interests of literature; and they cited the classics, Rochester's poems, plays of Wycherley and Congreve and so on. I mention the point for this reason. Lord Campbell said in this House: 'It is not within my most distant contemplation that works of literature should be affected by this Bill at all. This Bill is aimed exclusively at those who have the single purpose of corrupting the morals of youth or of shocking the conscience of reasonably minded people.' In a word, my Lords, the Bill of 1857 … a Bill aimed at pornography … I do not suppose that anywhere in this House there is a noble Lord who would not be extremely keen that the strongest possible measures should be maintained in our law against pornography of that kind. (Hansard 1959b)

As the conclusion of this quotation shows, the dilemma arising from the potential conflict between two biopolitical goals exists in 1857 in very similar terms as in 1959. It shows as well, that in some form the recognition of literary autonomy was widespread even among Victorian legislators. It shows, finally, that no one saw the need or the possibility to codify this recognition of literary autonomy in legal terms.

The findings of a Select Committee appointed in 1908 in order to look into 'lotteries and indecent advertisements' as well as the obscene literature associated with these in popular print media, present a similar picture. As it is supposed to do, the committee devotes its energies overwhelmingly to questions concerning 'lotteries and indecent advertisements'. The forty-sixth and final recommendation it makes in its report, however, states:

> A provision should also be inserted to exempt from the operation of the Act any book of literary merit or reputation or any genuine work of Art. The Committee consider that it would be almost impossible to devise any definition which would cover this exception. In their opinion the decision in such cases should be left to the discretion of the Magistrate; but they believe that, if a provision such

> as they recommend were inserted into the Act, a Magistrate would be enabled to take into consideration all the circumstances of the case, and would be free from a supposed obligation merely to decide upon the decency or the indecency of the particular literary or artistic work brought to his notice. (Select Committee 1908: ix)

This recommendation was not followed up, but it is brought up early in the parliamentary debates in the 1950s, where the government representative, Sir Hugh Lucas-Tooth, uses it as an argument for the difficulty of devising any legal provision that would effectively make the *exceptio artis* operational. 'As an expression of ideal opinion, that recommendation was admirable and would, I think, be agreed in all parts of the House,' he declares, 'but it is equally clear that the Committee itself was quite satisfied that, beyond expressing the ideal, it was unable to suggest any method by which it could be carried out' (Hansard 1954).

This examination of the moves, issues and positions in the parliamentary debates which have led to adoption of such a 'method' has clearly illustrated the difficulties involved in the legal recognition of literary autonomy. Moreover, it has demonstrated that there were other threats to literary autonomy involved here than the well-known ones posed by the bio-political imperative of governmental responsibility for the moral well-being of citizens, as well as by the inconsistencies of legal practice. Specifically there was the threat of instituting one of several varieties of pre-publication censorship that would reduce the economic risks for publishers while reducing the options that authors had as part of the contingent process of getting a work that might be considered 'borderline' in the parlance of the time published. If the OPA of 1959 brought to literature a limited increase in institutional autonomy, the process of making it can also serve as an illustration of the significant degree of literary autonomy that had existed long before its enactment. While legislators as a body accept the integration of external expertise into the legal discourse when they see that there is no longer any alternative to doing so, they also resist any moves – even on the part of the reformers – that might work to reduce the autonomy of literature.

References

Baxter, W. (1953), *The Image and the Search*, London: Hutchinson.

Bourdieu, P. (2011), *The Rules of Art: Genesis and Structure of the Literary Field*, Cambridge: Polity.

Bradshaw, D. (2013), 'American Beastliness, the Great Purge and Its Aftermath (1946–1959)', in D. Bradshaw and R. Potter (eds), *Prudes on the Prowl: Fiction and Obscenity in England, 1850to the Present Day*, 138–58, Oxford: Oxford University Press.

Charques, R.D. (1953), 'New Novels', *Spectator*, 27 November: 26.

Dolin, K. (2007), *A Critical Introduction to Law and Literature*, New York, NY: Cambridge University Press.

Foucault, M. (1978), 'Right of Death and Power over Life', in *The History of Sexuality: An Introduction*, tr. R. Hurley, 133–59, London: Penguin Books.

Foucault, M. (1991), 'Governmentality', in G. Burchell, C. Gordon and P. Miller (eds), *The Foucault Effect: Studies in Governmentality*, 87–104, London: Harvester Wheatsheaf.

Glass, L. (2009), 'The Ends of Obscenity', *American Literary History* 21(4): 869–76.

Grüttemeier, R. and T. Laros (2013), 'Literature in Law: *Exceptio Artis* and the Emergence of Literary Fields', *Law and Humanities* 7(2): 204–17.

Hansard (1954), 'Obscene Publications', HC Deb 22 November 1954 vol 533 cc1012–20.

Hansard (1955), 'Obscene Publications Bill', HC Deb 25 November 1955 vol 546 cc1883–92.

Hansard (1957), 'Obscene Publications Bill', HC Deb 29 March 1957 vol 567 cc1491–581.

Hansard (1958), 'Obscene Publications', HC Deb 16 December 1958 vol 597 cc992–1051.

Hansard (1959a), 'Obscene Publications Bill', HC Deb 24 April 1959 vol 604 cc803–57.

Hansard (1959b), 'Obscene Publications Bill', HL Deb 02 June 1959 vol 216 cc489–531.

Herbert, Sir A.P. (1956), 'Introduction', in N. St. J. Stevas, *Obscenity and the Law*, xi–xvii, London: Secker and Warburg.

Hunter, I., D. Saunders and D. Williamson (1993), *On Pornography. Literature, Sexuality and Obscenity Law*, London etc.: Macmillan.

Jarvis, M. (2005), 'Obscenity and Pornography', in *Conservative Governments, Morality and Social Change in Affluent Britain*, 113–22, Manchester: Manchester University Press.

Jenkins, R. (1959), 'Obscenity, Censorship, and the Law: The Story of a Bill', *Encounter* 13(4): 62–6.

Kauffmann, S. (1988), 'Album of Obscene Libel', *Grand Street* 8(1): 176–85.

Ladenson, E. (2007), *Dirt for Art's Sake*, Ithaca, NY etc.: Cornell University Press.

Levine, C. (2007), 'Obscenity and the Democratization of Culture', in *Provoking Democracy: Why We Need the Arts*, 103–45, Malden, MA: Blackwell.

McDonald, P.D. (2008), 'Old Phrases and Great Obscenities: The Strange Afterlife of Two Victorian Anxieties', *Journal of Victorian Culture* 13(2): 294–302.

Obscene Publications Act, 1959, 7 & 8 Eliz. 2 CH. 66, London: Her Majesty's Stationery Office.

Rembar, C. (1969), *The End of Obscenity: The Trials of Lady Chatterley, Tropic of Cancer and Fanny Hill*, London: Deutsch.

Rolph, C.H. (1969), *Books in the Dock*, London: Deutsch.

Select Committee on Lotteries and Indecent Advertisements (1908), *Report from the Select Committee on Lotteries and Indecent Advertisements Together with the Proceedings of the Committee, Minutes of Evidence and Appendices*, HC 1908 (275), London: Her Majesty's Stationery Office.

Select Committee on Obscene Publications (1958a), *Minutes of Evidence Taken before the Select Committee on the Obscene Publications Bill, and Appendices, in Session 1956–57*, HC 1957–58 (122), London: Her Majesty's Stationery Office.

Select Committee on Obscene Publications (1958b), *Report from the Select Committee on Obscene Publications, Together with the Proceedings of the Committee, Minutes of Evidence and Appendices*, HC 1957–58 (123), London: Her Majesty's Stationery Office.

Sova, D.B. (2011), *Banned Books: Literature Suppressed on Sexual Grounds*, 3rd ed. New York, NY: Facts On File.

Stable, Mr. Justice (1957), 'The Summing Up by Mr. Justice Stable', in S. Kaufmann (ed.), *The Philanderer*, 273–83, Harmondsworth: Penguin.

Stevas, N. St. J. (1956), *Obscenity and the Law*, London: Secker and Warburg.

The Times (1954a), 'Judge on Role of the Novel', 3 July: 4.

The Times (1954b), 'Obscene Libel in Book', 18 September: 3.

Williams, D.G.T. (1965), 'Obscene Publications Act, 1964', *Modern Law Review* 28(1): 73–6.

3

Law and the Literary Field in South Africa, 1910–2010

Ted Laros

There is a fairly significant body of research available on the administrative regulation – that is, censorship – of both imported and domestically produced literature that was carried out in South Africa in the period between, roughly, 1870 and 1990 (cf. e.g., Coggin 1983; Silver 1984; Ehmeir 1995; de Lange 1997; McDonald 2009). In this body of research, the period 1948–90, the period of apartheid censorship, has long since formed the focus of attention. The period before the rise of Afrikaner nationalism has been underrepresented in scholarly studies on South African censorship of literature. The *judicial* treatment of literature has also been covered only minimally. This essay attempts to partly fill this gap as it presents an overview of the way in which literature has been treated by the South African judiciary in the period 1910–2010. Among other things, it intends to demonstrate that when one seeks to adequately understand apartheid censorship of literature, one cannot ignore the way in which the judiciary dealt with the medium both prior to and during the period 1948–90.

Furthermore, it aims at exploring what the judicial treatment of literature in twentieth-century South Africa might tell us about the autonomization of the nation's literary field. Departing from the premise that literary trials might serve as a barometer registering the presence – or absence – of a relatively autonomous literary field in a country and that by submitting literary trials to an institutional and literary conceptual analysis one might be able to put this barometer function to use (cf. Grüttemeier and Laros 2013), this essay will present the results that such analyses have yielded with regard to the case of South Africa.[1] That is to say that it will attempt to formulate an answer to the question how the institutional and literary conceptual treatment that literature was given by the South African judiciary since 1910 – the year in which the nation became independent – might be described and explained.

In doing so, it will proceed as follows: the next section will treat the trials held in the period 1910–55 that in a direct or more indirect manner pertained to literature. After that, my essay will deal with the trials that were held in the period 1955–75, that is, the 1965 trials of Wilbur Smith's novel *When the Lion Feeds* and Can Themba's short story 'The Fugitives' and the 1974 trial of André Brink's *Kennis van die Aand* (translated by himself as *Looking on Darkness*). Continuing chronologically, I will go into the judicial treatment of literature in the period 1975–80, first and foremost into the 1978 case concerning Etienne Leroux's *Magersfontein, O Magersfontein!* The penultimate section will go into the legal and semi-legal regulation of literature in the period 1980–2010, followed by conclusions that formulate an answer to the essay's main question.

Legal groundwork, 1910–55

Until 1963, when a whole new censorship act was introduced, the regulation of literature produced abroad was an entirely administrative affair in South Africa: customs was responsible for banning offensive works of literature, and appeals against customs' decisions were dealt with by the responsible minister – who until 1934 was the Minister of Finance and as of 1934 the Minister of the Interior (cf. Geldenhuÿs 1977: 24). The regulation of domestically produced literature, on the other hand, was partially an administrative and partially a judicial affair in the period prior to 1963. Taking statutory measures so as to direct the regulation of domestically produced publications was a colonial and, as of 1910, provincial affair up until the 1963 censorship act came into effect, making it a national issue (Marais 1960: 50–1; Kahn 1966: 283, 285; Dean 1973: 78). J.F. Marais, judge of the Transvaal Division of the Supreme Court and a patron of literature and the arts (Kahn 1966: 292), commented that this did not mean that the legislation in this area was inadequate though, as the standard that was being prescribed was essentially uniform, as was the body responsible for prosecution: the Attorney General[2] (Marais 1960: 50–1).

Although apparently little use was made of the statutory provisions to suppress domestically produced books or other publications (Hepple 1960: 35; Marais 1960: 52; Kahn 1966: 286), four cases were taken to court that in a more indirect manner tell us something about the institutional status of literature within the law in the period that South Africa formed a Union (namely *Rex v. Shaw* [1910]; *Rex v. Meinert* [1932]; *Rex v. Webb* [1934]; and *Goeie Hoop*

Uitgewers v. CNA and Another [1953]). Two cases concerning allegedly obscene publications that were heard in the decades immediately preceding the birth of the Union (*Queen v. de Jong* [1894] and *G. W. Hardy v. Rex* [1905]) are of concern too, as they by common law logic would go on to form precedents on which later cases would be built. These six cases form the only cases indicative of the legal status of literature that were treated in court in pre-Union South Africa and in the actual Union since South Africa's first censorship act, the Obscene Publications Act of 1892, entered the statute books.[3]

Although no works were put on trial in this period that would have been characterized by literary experts or the literary socialized public as representing works of literary merit, the judiciary did come to introduce a number of concepts and procedures that would go on to play a crucial role in the legal autonomization of literature within the nation. Firstly, it required for adjudicators to apply a contextual approach when dealing with literature: incriminated passages should be judged in the light of the whole work, not in isolation. Secondly, it ruled that testimonies regarding an incriminated work might be admitted. Thirdly, it required that adjudicators would, as a matter of principle, observe tolerance with respect to changing societal norms regarding certain themes. Indeed, in the 1932 case of *Rex v. Meinert*, the presiding judge, Bok, specifically contended that a certain amount of tolerance had to be observed with regard to evolving norms concerning modern literature. In regard to the question of themes concerning sexuality, he emphatically declared that such themes

> are discussed with ever increasing freedom in the literatures of all civilised peoples and to hold that all such books are obscene within the meaning of the law in this territory, because on the minds of immature, uneducated or uncivilised persons they might have a deleterious affect [sic], would mean to deprive educated people from contact with modern literature and thought in other countries and I cannot think that such could have been the intention of the Legislature. (60)

With this statement, Bok was actually taking a highly remarkable standpoint vis-à-vis the institutional status of literature. The status that Bok was granting literature with his positioning amounted to what might best be described as a colonial *exceptio artis*,[4] a very early form of *exceptio artis* in South Africa – indeed, the first time it seems to have appeared in South African law – which also represented a very specific form of the concept.

Evidently, Bok respected that a certain amount of freedom to depict or write about sexual matters had been conquered by literature and the arts internationally, and what is more is that he also allowed for literature to enjoy this amount of autonomy within South-West African law. Bok quite clearly gave priority to the right to read of literary socialized readers, or 'educated people', at the expense of the right of non-literary socialized readers, or 'immature, uneducated or uncivilised persons', to be protected from potentially harmful material. By granting literary socialized readers this special right, he at once, albeit implicitly, bestowed upon 'modern literature' a (relative) *exceptio artis*. Indeed, he declared that 'the test [of obscenity] cannot be whether there are persons who, incapable of understanding the real spirit of the writing, might suffer morally by being allowed to read it' (*Rex v. Meinert* 1932: 60).

The concepts and procedures which the judiciary thus came to introduce in the first half of the twentieth century effectively prepared the ground for a future recognition of a relative institutional autonomy of the South African literary field by the nation's judiciary – an autonomy which in this period did not seem to be a reality yet. That one could not speak of a relatively autonomous literary field in this period appears to be confirmed by the fact that no trials regarding 'proper' literary works were held in the Union period. Further evidence for this seems to lie in the fact that when Justice Bok in the 1932 case of *Rex v. Meinert* evidenced to be in favour of an *exceptio artis* pertaining to literature, he was exclusively referring to *foreign* literature, that is, modern European literature – not to domestically produced literature at all. Bok's advocacy of what might be termed a colonial *exceptio artis* did not receive the judicial and statutory consolidation that its conceptual relative, the *exceptio scientiae* – a concept that appears to have been introduced in another 1930s case, namely that of *R. v. Webb* of 1934 (cf. Laros 2013: 42ff) – did receive in South Africa at the time. This also seems to underline the hypothesis that the literary field, unlike its academic counterpart, had not yet reached a mature stage in this period.

Hesitant legal recognition, 1955–75

By the time South Africa became a Republic, that is, by the early 1960s, this appeared to have changed. A first indication for this can be found in the fact that the new censorship act introduced at this point, the Publications and Entertainments Act of 1963 (hereafter: PEA), contained sections that provided for literary experts to take up positions within the new censorship bureaucracy. Another indication can be found in the fact that the act introduced the concept of the likely reader, a concept which had been borrowed from the English Obscene Publications Act, 1959. This concept had been introduced in the latter act to adapt the old Hicklin test, a test that had been dominant within the Anglophone world since 1868. The concept of the likely reader effectuated that courts no longer had to estimate what the effect of a publication would be on the *possible* reader but what its effect would be on the *probable* reader. With this concept in hand, one did not necessarily always have to take 'weak' readers (according to prevalent thought, youth, women, uneducated people, native populations, etc. fell under this category) into account when judging a publication: now it was also possible to postulate a readership comprised of 'strong' readers (i.e. adults, [well-] educated citizens, literary socialized people, etc.). The fact that in the 1960s, the first trials concerning works of fiction written by South African literary actors took place – namely the 1965 trials of Wilbur Smith's *When the Lion Feeds* and the 1965 trail concerning Can Themba's 'The Fugitives' – provides even further evidence for the hypothesis that the South African literary field had reached a higher stage of development around that time.

When one examines the trials regarding Smith's novel and Themba's short story that were held in the Cape Provincial Division of the Supreme Court, one can discern that the majority of this court was of the opinion that a certain degree of institutional autonomy should be granted to the literary field. In the Cape trial of Smith's work, both the majority and minority judgements contained critiques of the new act: both lamented that literature had not been given enough protection under the PEA and that the act had not followed to a greater extent the line of the English Obscene Publications Act of 1959. Whereas the latter act had instituted an explicit *exceptio artis* pertaining to literature through its four fundamental instruments of the contextual approach, the likely reader test, the public good test and the admissibility of expert evidence, only one of these instruments had been incorporated into the former act – the concept of the likely reader. This notwithstanding, the majority of the Cape Court appeared to employ a number of means it had at its disposal to guarantee a certain degree of institutional autonomy for literature after all. They found a way to demand that the contextual approach be applied and a publication thus be judged as a whole and not on the basis of isolated passages; they appeared to be applying the concept of freedom of expression as an argument for granting literature some (legal) space; and, finally, for the very same purpose, they applied the likely reader test. The unanimous Cape judgement in the case of Can Themba's 'The

Fugitives' cohered with the judgement concerning Smith's *Lion* in that it secured a considerable amount of legal autonomy for the 'intellectual' reader (cf. *S v. Insight* 1965: 777; Laros 2013: 76).

In the Appellate Division (hereafter: AD) trial concerning Smith's *Lion*, a quite different position was taken, however. To be sure, two minority opinions were filed that followed the same autonomy-oriented line as the majority judgement in the Cape trial of Smith's novel and the judgement in the trial of Themba's 'Fugitives' had mapped out. Yet, the majority came to set a quite different precedent. Among other things, they stipulated that literary expertise could play only a minimal role in judicial proceedings regarding literary works. Furthermore, they restored the isolated-passage criterion, thus making it possible to ban books on the basis of isolated passages. They declared it legally invalid to compare an incriminated work with other books, whether modern or classic. And lastly, they added an extra clause to the likely reader test, thereby effectively rendering it an average reader test, comparable to the one that had been applied before the statutory changes of 1963. For the majority, the PEA was aimed *inter alia* at combating contemporary sexually explicit literature; with their judgement, they provided the judiciary with a number of instruments with which to do this.

Some ten years later, the Cape trial of André Brink's *Kennis van die Aand* reversed much of the heteronomy-oriented line of approach that had been laid down by the AD in the *Lion* case. True, one of the three judges hearing the case, Justice van Wyk, adopted a position that for the largest part cohered with the position of the majority in the case of Smith's *Lion*, yet van Wyk did reveal to be recognizing the value of literary expert evidence. Indeed, he determinedly underpinned his judgements with the literary conceptual analyses of the literary behaviour of Brink that had been delivered by the literary experts testifying on behalf of the Publications Control Board, the party defending the banning of Brink's novel. To be sure, the amount of legal autonomy that van Wyk effectively granted the literary field through the validation and employment of expert evidence was relatively insignificant when viewed in the light of the most fundamental aspect of his position: for him, the sovereignty that the field of power enjoyed over the literary field was namely virtually absolute. Yet, at the same time the very fact of his recognition of literary expertise did appear to reveal that the literary field had already reached a considerable degree of (internal) institutional autonomy.[5]

The supposition that the literary field had already reached a significant degree of institutional autonomy by 1974, the year in which the trial took place, was further underlined by the motivations of the Justices Diemont and Steyn. The opinions of these two judges were much more autonomy-oriented and thereby effectively rendered the position of van Wyk the minority position. Both Diemont and Steyn allowed the literary field a quite significant degree of autonomy vis-à-vis the law. This was brought about first of all because both categorically favoured a freedom-oriented approach to publication regulation. Moreover, it came about because of the way in which the two judges conceptualized the likely reader, both on the more theoretical and on the more practical levels. The recognition of the (judicial) value of literary expertise and the application of arguments advanced by such experts represented a third way in which it was brought about. Lastly, the legal recognition and, indeed, judicial employment of literary conceptual arguments adhered to by contemporary literary actors[6] contributed to the creation of an institutional autonomy of literature vis-à-vis the law. Yet, although both adopted a position that established a considerable degree of artistic freedom for literature, this freedom clearly remained but relative. In the end, both namely declared that Brink's novel was undesirable in terms of the PEA and that the ban on the novel thus had to be upheld, because both found that it had transgressed the boundaries of the permissible by its thematization of religion, that is, Christianity – not with its thematizations of 'political' or 'moral' issues. Apparently, the amount of institutional autonomy that the two were willing to grant literature was smallest when it came to religion.

Despite rollback efforts, ongoing recognition, 1975–80

By the time that the judgement was delivered in the case of Brink's *Kennis*, the Vorster administration had already begun making an apparently determinate effort to reduce the amount of autonomy that literature had acquired vis-à-vis the law at that point. The PEA of 1963 was repealed and replaced with the Publications Act, 1974 (hereafter: PA). With the latter act, the Legislator had chosen to get rid of the only two instruments incorporated into the former statute with which literature could be granted a certain amount of legal autonomy. Firstly, the concept of the likely reader was scrapped from the statute books.

And secondly, it was no longer stipulated that individuals could be appointed members of one of the censorship bodies by virtue of their 'special knowledge of art, language and literature': the provisions of the old act that had enabled literary experts to take such central positions in the censorship bureaucracy had also completely vanished in the new act. Moreover, the right to appeal to the Supreme Court against decisions of the censors was also abolished. A semi-judicial body called the Publications Appeal Board (hereafter: PAB) was set up to deal with such appeals instead, and the only role that the Supreme Court was left to play was to review decisions of this PAB, when it was called upon to do so. Censorship thus became an entirely executive affair – an affair that was indeed firmly in the hands of the Minister of the Interior.

Indeed, the approach towards literature taken in the initial phase of the PAB's existence, that is, the period 1975–8, effectively reduced the amount of autonomy that literature had come to attain over the years considerably. Chaired by former Supreme Court Justice J.H. Snyman, the board substituted the concept of the average man for the concept of the likely reader. As the latter concept had proven to be one of the most important instruments for effectuating a significant amount of legal autonomy for literature in South Africa, the re-implementation of the concept of the average reader effectively cut off one of the foremost paths to an artistic freedom for literature. Two other aspects of the PAB's approach further underlined its rather heteronomist orientation. Snyman's board refused to admit evidence aimed at comparing an incriminated work to other works circulating within the community, as it reasoned that the act had clearly been meant to be interventionist and that it was, therefore, aimed at reducing the rights of literature rather than promoting them. Furthermore, the board appeared not to be following the precedent that had been set by the Supreme Court in the 1972 case of *PCB v. Republican Publications* – this case did not revolve around a work of literature but around a popular magazine – with regard to the question of contextualism, another instrument that had proven to be fundamental to the institutional autonomization of literature in South Africa. Whereas former Chief Justice Ogilvie Thompson had in the latter case explicitly ruled out the isolated-passage criterion and declared that a careful contextual approach be applied when it came to the written word, the board did not adopt such a principled contextual approach. In fact, by adopting the criterion of the average reader and declaring that this reader would not read contextually, the board in effect seemed to be disregarding the precedent that had been established by Ogilvie Thompson. In these three crucial ways, Snyman's board considerably reduced the amount of institutional autonomy that the literary field had reached in the period before the PA had come into force.

The approach of the PAB also revealed that Snyman et al. did realize that the literary field had become a societal fact that could not be ignored, however. The board made sure to carefully stress that literary merit was a factor that had to be taken into account when adjudicating works in terms of the PA and that functionality, that is, the functionality of textual elements within the entire text, was also a factor that had to be taken into consideration. Furthermore, the board admitted evidence by literary experts, and in principle it did indeed leave the establishment of the literary merits of an incriminated work entirely up to them. In practice, this ostensible recognition of a certain amount of autonomy of the literary field did not amount to much, however, as the PAB case of Etienne Leroux's *Magersfontein, O Magersfontein!* clearly demonstrated. For although the literary experts delivering testimony in this case generally held this work to be of outstanding literary value, it still had to succumb to the supposed convictions and feelings of the postulated average man.

The heteronomy-oriented approach of Snyman's PAB was not entirely endorsed by the Supreme Court, however. In fact, in the Transvaal Provincial Division's review of the PAB's decision on *Magersfontein*, the court came to invalidate the most fundamental features of the board's line of approach. First of all, it effectively salvaged the concept of the likely reader, the concept that had been eliminated from the statute books and that, on the basis hereof, was considered to be no longer lawful by the PAB. The court underpinned this decision by referring to the judicial tradition with regard to censorship, that is to say that it referenced opinions that had been handed down in the trials of Smith's *Lion* and Brink's *Kennis* and the judgement delivered by former Chief Justice Ogilvie Thompson in the case of *PCB v. Republican Publications*. As the concept of the likely reader had proven to be of such vital importance for the legal autonomization of literature in South Africa, the court's decision delivered a quite crucial contribution to shoring up the amount of institutional autonomy that the literary field had come to attain in the period before the Vorster Cabinet and Snyman's apparent rollback efforts. The second way in which the court came to check the heteronomist efforts of Snyman's Board lay in its emphasis that the contextual approach was the only valid approach when it came to judging works of literature. The court again underpinned its decision by pointing towards the nation's judicial tradition: it again referred to the AD case of *Lion* and the judgement of Ogilvie Thompson in the *PCB v. Republican Publications* case. As the contextual approach had proven to be about as decisive an instrument in the legal autonomization of literature within the nation as the concept of the likely reader had, the court's position taking in this issue was indeed crucial too. The final way in which the court came to restrengthen literature's position vis-à-vis the law was through its ruling that a strong meaning should be attached to the all-important statutory term of 'offensiveness'. The strategy of attaching a strong meaning to the terms that the statutes pertaining to censorship gave for testing whether or not a work was 'undesirable' had also proven to be a means by which the freedom of literature could be increased. By maintaining this principle, the court thus secured yet another legal instrument with which the literary field could be granted an amount of autonomy vis-à-vis the law.

Yet, although the Transvaal Bench so clearly respected the autonomy-oriented course that the Supreme Court had come to take over the years, it did choose to disregard a very important precedent that had been set by the majority in the case of Brink's *Kennis*, namely the precedent pertaining to the question of the relevance of the concept of the likely reader for the religious provisions of the act. The *Kennis* trial had been the only literary trial in which this question had come up. In this trial, the majority of the judges had declared in so many words that it was relevant, both to the religious and to the political provisions of the law. Both Diemont and Steyn had advanced that it was of vital importance to determine who was going to read a book when one was to adjudge it in terms of the law. Indeed, as Steyn argued, it was absurd to ban a publication because it would offend people who were not going to read it. Diemont and Steyn's position taking effectively expanded the (relative) legal autonomy of literature to also cover the religious and the political stipulations of the law: their position effectuated that the literary reader was the determinate factor not merely when it came to the moral provisions of the law but also when it came to the law's religious and political provisos. The Transvaal Court, however, chose not to follow the precedent set by the majority of the Cape Bench in the *Kennis* case but to adopt the position that van Wyk had taken in the same trial instead. The latter had stated that the likely reader should not be read into the religious and political sections of the act. So, although the judgement of the Transvaal Court effectively shored up the institutional autonomy of literature in three very significant ways, at the same time, it effectuated a crucial setback when it came to the autonomy of the literary field vis-à-vis the religious stipulations of the act. As a consequence of its principled position taking, the court had to uphold the PAB's judgement that Leroux's *Magersfontein* constituted an undesirable work in terms of the PA and should therefore be banned.

The furore accompanying the *Magersfontein* case prompted the new Minister of the Interior, Alwyn Schlebusch, to break with the heteronomy-oriented approach towards literature that had been instigated by his predecessor Mulder through the PA. By amending the act, he enabled the PAB to grant literature a more autonomous position vis-à-vis the law than it had had since the PA had come into force. The Publications Amendment Act of 1978 made it in principle possible to grant literary socialized readers more freedom of choice once again by allowing the board to release books under an age restriction. Moreover, the act arranged for literary experts, who had effectively been written out of the statutory regulations regarding censorship through the PA, to once again play a more prominent role within the system. The response to these statutory amendments of Snyman's Board was quite indifferent, however. Indeed, despite the changed statutory framework and despite the fact that the majority of the cultural, judicial, and political elites apparently felt that the literary field should be granted a relative institutional autonomy vis-à-vis the law, the board chose to continue its restrictive approach. But with both the judiciary and the government being in support of a relative freedom for literature, the board could not keep up its line of approach very long. In fact, the next year, at a point at which Snyman's tenure was coming to an end, the retired judge was not given a second five-year term as Chairman of the PAB. Instead, the 37-year-old J.C.W. van Rooyen, the PAB's Deputy Chairman of the period 1975–80, was appointed Chairman for the next five years.

Decisive legal recognition, 1980–2010

With van Rooyen taking over from Snyman, the board started to consistently continue the approach towards literature that the Supreme Court had taken in the period 1963–78. Van Rooyen's Board came to guarantee a fairly high degree of institutional autonomy for literature through the instruments of the contextual approach, the concept of the likely reader, a fundamental tolerance towards the written word, and a consistent recognition of literary expertise. Moreover, the board increased the degree of freedom that the Supreme Court had granted the literary field through its particular application of the adjudicating factor of literariness – an application that was justified through van Rooyen's interpretation of the Publications Amendment Act of 1978: as he declared, this latter act had expressly been aimed at acknowledging what he termed the 'minority rights' of literature.

The board further expanded literature's institutional autonomy by consolidating the recognition that Justice Steyn had given to pragmatic literature (*sensu* Abrams 1975) in the trial of Brink's *Kennis*. In addition to giving (semi-) legal recognition to the autonomist conception of literature that the contemporary disciples of van Wyk Louw adhered to – a recognition that this poetics had enjoyed ever since the first Publications Control Board had been instigated in 1963 (cf. McDonald 2009) – the board namely chose to also recognize the pragmatic conception of literature that was dominant amongst black literary actors; it did so on the basis of its own concept of protest literature. In effect, van Rooyen's approach, with its crucial explanation of the concept of literariness, amounted to the institution of a quite far-reaching institutional autonomy for literature. The semi-legal freedom that van Rooyen's Board instigated for the medium did have its limits though, certainly when it came to religion. The 1979 and 1984 bans of Anthony Burgess's novel *Man of Nazareth* represented a clear demonstration of this.

In the interim period 1990–4, van Rooyen's successors continued the autonomy-oriented approach of the latter's Board. The relatively precarious position of literature vis-à-vis the religious stipulations of the PA was also reaffirmed when Burgess's *Man of Nazareth* was again brought before the PAB in 1992. For the third time, the board declared the novel to be undesirable, and it did so basically on the same grounds as van Rooyen's Board had done earlier.

The way in which literature has been regulated since 1994, that is, since South Africa became a non-racial constitutional democracy, cannot be regarded as an absolute break with the past. The infrastructure set up for regulating literature and other media through the Films and Publications Act of 1996 (hereafter: FPA) largely resembles the one that was in place under the Publications Act since 1975. The statutory superstructure guiding the regulation of literature did change quite drastically, however. First and foremost, an *exceptio artis* pertaining, *inter alia*, to literature was instituted on the constitutional level. Moreover, on the level of the FPA, some quite significant statutory changes were also effectuated. For the first time in South Africa's legal history, the contextual approach was proscribed statutorily. Furthermore, literature was granted absolute exemption from the Act's stipulations regarding XX and X18 classification.[7] These statutory novelties were not entirely new to the nation's history of literature regulation at large, though. Both of them had been implemented before: the contextual approach by the judiciary, and the literature exemption – albeit in rudimentary form – by van Rooyen's PAB in the 1980s. Indeed, the new statutory superstructure stands firmly in the nation's century-long tradition of literature regulation. This is borne out by other evidence too: The FPA's spirit of promoting freedom of choice for adults, while at the same time protecting children against harm continues a tradition that had begun as early as 1932 with the judgement of Bok in the *Rex v. Meinert* case.[8] Likewise, the insistence of the FPA's draftsmen that in dealing with an alleged literary work, the literary merits of such a work should be assessed 'objectively' by literary experts, on the basis of a text-oriented approach, continues a long tradition in the nation's legal regulation of literature. The new statutory dispensation thus for a large part brought continuity in the regulation of literature within the nation, although the instigation of a constitutional *exceptio artis* and the guaranty of what seemed to be absolute protection to art on the level of the FPA of course both effectuated a proper legal ratification to the merely semi-legal art exemption that van Rooyen's PAB had instigated. Furthermore, the Constitution and FPA's respective ways of protecting literature effectively expanded the art exemption that had been instituted by van Rooyen's Board: Whereas the board had given but a relative protection to works of literary merit on the level of the PA, such works now received a significantly higher degree of protection on the level of the FPA. What is more, is that literature had now been given (relative) protection on the level of the sovereign Constitution.

As it turned out, however, the apparently absolute protection given on the level of the FPA was perhaps not as absolute as it seemed. The 2002 Film and Publication board case of Rushdie's *Satanic Verses* namely demonstrated that the in principle absolute exemption on the level of the act did in effect not prevent the new board from imposing sanctions on Rushdie's work in terms of the act read together with the Constitution. Whereas the FPA explicitly granted literature absolute exemption from the Act's stipulations regarding XX and X18 classification, the board decided to give an X18 classification to the book anyhow, and even added extra restrictions to it. This despite the fact that the FPB, *inter alia*, on the basis of the judgements of literary experts, held the book to represent a work of *bona fide* literature. As a result of the board's decision, a far-reaching ban on distributing Rushdie's novel remains intact in today's South Africa – a ban that is not that different from the one that was initially instigated in 1988. Apart from the fact that the case of *The Satanic Verses* appeared to reveal that literature in practice did not enjoy absolute protection on the level of the

FPA, the case seemed also to be evidencing that the institutional autonomy of literature as it is being recognized through the Constitution and the FPA is still most likely to be restricted when it comes to religious issues.

In recent years, the artistic freedom of literature has been subjected to a certain degree of erosion. The far-reaching protection that was given to literature on the level of the FPA was reduced to a certain extent through the Films and Publications Amendment Act of 2009. When it comes to child pornography, literature is no longer exempted from the act's stipulations. However, considering both the century-long tradition of the legal treatment of literature in South Africa and the way in which the FPB dealt with Rushdie's *Satanic Verses*, it is highly unlikely that the 2009 amendments could in practice have the result of restricting the institutional autonomy of literature vis-à-vis the law to such an extent as to render possible a total ('XX') ban on a work that would 'objectively' – by literary experts, that is – be labelled a work of literature. It is not probable that the administrative or judicial bodies entrusted with the task of regulating literature would go further than to impose certain restrictions on the distribution of a work of literature – as the FPB did in the Rushdie case. Over the past fifty years, the recognition of a relative institutional autonomy of literature has gradually become so firmly rooted in South African law that it is virtually unthinkable that any graver sanctions than a limitation of distributional rights would be imposed on works of literature. Besides, existing research suggests that when an *exceptio artis* is established in a parliamentary democracy, it is far too robust to easily disappear from the legal – let alone constitutional – stage.

Conclusion

Systematic research into the judicial – and semi-judicial – treatment of literature in South Africa in the period 1910–2010 reveals that the 1994 institution of a constitutional *exceptio artis* pertaining, *inter alia*, to literature did not represent an unprecedented novelty in the nation's legal tradition. Rather, it formed the constitutional culmination, and crystallization, of a process that had already been set in motion in the period 1910–55. This legal autonomization of South African literature appears to have unfolded along different lines than it did in former motherland the Netherlands or in other continental European nations such as Germany and France, for instance (cf. Beekman and Grüttemeier 2005;

Grüttemeier 2007; Sapiro 2011). The *exceptio artis* that was established in South African law was for the largest part established through different parameters than it was in the latter nations. This is undoubtedly due to South Africa's orientation towards UK and US law, instead of the continental legal tradition. Yet, as South African law began to go its own way in the 1950s, the particular parameters it came to set with regard to literature regulation cannot entirely be explained by its orientation towards the latter two countries. As the Legislature revealed to be heavily inspired by Australian and Irish law when developing its PEA in the 1960s and its PA in the 1970s (cf. Laros 2013: 57ff.), it might prove to be fruitful to compare the legal treatment of literature in South Africa to the way in which it was regulated in these latter two countries. It appears, indeed, that the commonalities in the legal infra- and superstructures implemented for governing literature regulation in these countries – not to speak of the shared roots of these nations' respective legal systems in UK law – do not provide the only rationale for undertaking such an endeavour. The fact that the institutional autonomy of literature in South Africa has revealed to be rather weak when it comes to religion might provide a further ground for doing so, as religion also seems to play an important role in the censorship histories of Australia and Ireland (cf. Kennedy 1990; Moore 2012). The fact that just like South Africa, these two nations appeared to have been quite restrictive in their legal dealing with literature, compared to other Anglophone nations (cf. Kennedy 1990; Moore 2012), provides yet a further reason for comparing the three countries. Perhaps, indeed, systematic comparative research into the legal treatment of literature in these three countries will reveal that their literary fields underwent a markedly 'postcolonial' process of institutional autonomization – a process that represents a relatively slow progression towards artistic freedom.

Notes

1 This essay presents some of the main findings of my dissertation 'Long Walk to Artistic Freedom: Law and the Literary Field in South Africa, 1910-2010' (Carl von Ossietzky University of Oldenburg 2013). The dissertation was written within the framework of the German Research Foundation funded project 'The Judicial Treatment of Literature in Belgium and South Africa'.

2 With regard to this latter point, Natal formed an exception (Marais 1960: 51).

3 On the basis of systematic research of Supreme Court decisions in cases concerning literature, decisions on literary works and memos of the Publications Appeal Board – the administrative body of appeal that was created through new censorship legislation in 1975 – and all of the major South African law journals and existing studies on South African censorship, I would argue that ten cases have been treated by the South African judiciary from pre-Union times until today that either directly or more indirectly pertained to literature and its status within the law. In addition to the six cases mentioned above, there were four cases between 1963 to today (namely *Publications Control Board v. William Heinemann, Ltd and Others* (1965), i.e. the Smith case; *S v. Insight Publications (Pty) Ltd and Another* (1965), that is, the Themba case; *Buren Uitgewers (Edms) Bpk en 'n Ander v. Raad van Beheer oor Publikasies* (1975), that is, the Brink case; and *Human & Rousseau Uitgewers (Edms) Bpk v. Snyman NO* (1978), that is, the Leroux case). One of these trials, namely the 1932 case of *Rex v. Meinert*, took place in South-West Africa, which at that point fell under South African jurisdiction.

4 The concept of *exceptio artis* implies that utterances that in principle constitute an offence can be judged otherwise when they occur in a literary work (Grüttemeier and Laros 2013: 204).

5 For a lucid discussion of the concept of internal field autonomy, cf. Dorleijn, Grüttemeier and Korthals Altes (2007: xvii).

6 Diemont endorsed the autonomist conception of literature that Brink had defended in court and Steyn quite elaborately came to defend a conception of literature that appeared to be rather coherent with the Louwian poetics that was dominant particularly amongst the older generation of the Afrikaans literary establishment at the time. Moreover, he explicitly referenced Henry James as a literary theoretical authority. (For a more systematic reconstruction of the conceptions of literature employed by the judges in the *Kennis* trial, cf. Laros, forthcoming.)

7 The FPA's classification XX amounts to an absolute ban. X18 limits distribution to persons of eighteen years or older. XX classifications are reserved for publications that contain visual representations of *inter alia* extreme forms of pornography, notably child pornography, and extreme violence. X18 classifications are given to publications that contain 'explicit sexual conduct'.

8 In his judgement in Meinert's case, Bok qualified his position regarding literature exemption somewhat by stating that he should add that he arrived at his conclusion 'with considerable hesitation bearing in mind the large uncivilized class of our population' (63) and that his conclusion 'must not be understood as implying that conditions peculiar to a country like this do not necessitate a stricter view of what is permissible in this respect in the interests of art and culture, than might possibly be accepted in European countries' (63). The prioritization of the right to read of the

'civilized' over the right to protection from harm of the 'large uncivilized class' of the South-West African population was thus not categorical; it did have to be balanced against the latter's right and at some point, it seemed to be implied, the scales would tip in favour of the 'uncivilized class'.

References

Abrams, M.H. (1975), *The Mirror and the Lamp: Romantic Theory and the Critical Tradition*, Oxford: Oxford UP.

Beekman, K. and R. Grüttemeier (2005), *De wet van de letter: Literatuur en rechtspraak*, Amsterdam: Athenaeum – Polak & van Gennep.

Buren Uitgewers (Edms) Bpk en 'n Ander v. Raad van Beheer oor Publikasies (1975), 1975 (1) SA 379 (C), Western Cape Provincial Division of the Supreme Court of South Africa, *The South African Law Reports (1947 to date), Juta Law*, n.d. Accessed 17 February 2011.

Coggin, T., ed. (1983), *Censorship: A Study of Censorship in South Africa by Five Distinguished Authors, Johan van der Vyver, André Brink, Allan Boesak, Ian McDonald and André du Toit. Introduction by Geoff Budlender*, Johannesburg: S.A. Insitute of Race Relations.

Dean, W.H.B. (1973), 'Judging the Obscene: A Critical Analysis of the Criteria Used for Determining What Are Undesirable Sexually Explicit Materials in South Africa', in B. Beinart, W. de Vos and J.D. Thomas (eds), *Acta Juridica 1972*, 61–150, Cape Town: Juta.

De Lange, M. (1997), *The Muzzled Muse: Literature and Censorship in South Africa*, Amsterdam etc.: John Benjamins.

Dorleijn, G.J., R. Grüttemeier and L. Korthals Altes (eds) (2007), *The Autonomy of Literature at the Fins de Siècles (1900 and 2000): A Critical Assessment*, Leuven etc.: Peeters.

Ehmeir, W. (1995), *Literature in Time with History: South African Literature in English and Political Change in the 1960s*, Essen: Die Blaue Eule.

Geldenhuÿs, P.B. (1977), *Pornografie, Sensuur en Reg*, Johannesburg: Lex Patria.

Goeie Hoop Uitgewers (Eiendoms) Bpk v. Central News Agency and Another (1953), 1953 (2) SA 843 (W), Witwatersrand Local Division of the Supreme Court of South Africa, *The South African Law Reports (1947 to date), Juta Law*, n.d. Accessed 27 October 2012.

Grüttemeier, R. (2007), 'Law and the Autonomy of Literature', in G.J. Dorleijn, R. Grüttemeier and L. Korthals Altes (eds), *The Autonomy of Literature at the Fins de Siècles (1900 and 2000): A Critical Assessment*, 175–92, Leuven etc.: Peeters.

Grüttemeier, R. and T. Laros (2013), 'Literature in Law: *Exceptio artis* and the Emergence of Literary Fields', *Law and Humanities* 7(2): 204–17.

G.W. Hardy v. Rex (1905), Supreme Court of Natal, *All South African Law Reports 1828 to 1946, LexisNexis South Africa*, n.d. Accessed 27 October 2012.

Hepple, A. (1960), *Censorship and Press Control in South Africa*, Johannesburg: n.p. Human & Rousseau Uitgewers (Edms) Bpk v Snyman NO (1978), 1978 (3) SA 836 (T), Transvaal Provincial Division of the Supreme Court of South Africa, *The South African Law Reports (1947 to date), Juta Law*, n.d. Accessed 27 October 2012.

Kahn, E. (1966), '*When the Lion Feeds* – and the Censor Pounces: A Disquisition on the Banning of Immoral Publications in South Africa', *The South African Law Journal* 83(3): 278–336.

Kennedy, B.P. (1990), *Dreams and Responsibilities: The State and the Arts in Independent Ireland*, Dublin: The Arts Council.

Laros, T. (2013), 'Long Walk to Artistic Freedom: Law and the Literary Field in South Africa, 1910–2010', diss., Faculty III: Language and Cultural Studies, Carl von Ossietzky University of Oldenburg.

Laros, T. (forthcoming), 'Literary Autonomy on Trial: The 1974 Cape Trial of André Brink's *Kennis van die Aand*', in A. Allo (ed.), *The Courtroom as a Space of Resistance: Reflections on the Legacy of the Rivonia Trial*. Surrey: Ashgate.

Marais, J.F. (1960), 'Regsaspekte van Literêre Sensuur', *Standpunte* 13(6): 49–53.

McDonald, P.D. (2009), *The Literature Police: Apartheid Censorship and Its Cultural Consequences*, Oxford: Oxford UP.

Moore, N. (2012), *The Censor's Library: Uncovering the Lost History of Australia's Banned Books*, St. Lucia: U of Queensland P.

Publications Control Board v. Republican Publications (Pty) Ltd (1972), 1972 (1) SA 288 (A), Appellate Division of the Supreme Court of South Africa, *South African Appellate Division Reports (1910 to date), Juta Law*, n.d. Accessed 1 November 2011.

Publications Control Board v. William Heinemann, Ltd and Others (1965), 1965 (4) SA 137 (A), Appellate Division of the Supreme Court of South Africa, *South African Appellate Division Reports (1910 to date), Juta Law*, n.d. Accessed 17 February 2011.

Queen v. de Jong (1894), 11 S.C.R. 326, Supreme Court of the Colony of the Cape of Good Hope, *All South African Law Reports 1828 to 1946, LexisNexis South Africa*, n.d. Accessed 27 October 2012.

Rex v. Meinert (1932), 'High Court of South-West Africa', in I. Goldblatt and R.E.G. Rosenow (eds), *The South African Law Reports [1927] South-West Africa: Decisions of the High Court of South-West Africa. January to December, 1927*, 56–63. Cape Town etc.: Juta.

Rex v. Shaw (1910), Cape Provincial Division of the Supreme Court of South Africa, *All South African Law Reports 1828 to 1946, LexisNexis South Africa*, n.d. Accessed 27 October 2012.

Rex v. Webb (1934), 1934 AD 493, Appellate Division of the Supreme Court of South Africa, *All South African Law Reports 1828 to 1946, LexisNexis South Africa*, n.d. Accessed 27 October 2012.

Sapiro, G. (2011), *La responsabilité de l'écrivain: Littérature, droit et morale en France (XIXe-XXIe siècle)*, Paris: Seuil.

Silver, L. (1984), *A Guide to Political Censorship in South Africa*, Johannesburg: Centre for Applied Legal Studies, U of the Witwatersrand.

S v. Insight Publications (Pty) Ltd and Another (1965), 1965 (2) SA 775 (C), Western Cape Provincial Division of the Supreme Court of South Africa, *The South African Law Reports (1947 to date), Juta Law*, n.d. Accessed 26 October 2011.

4

De Sade as a Benchmark. Dutch Legal Actions Against Obscenity in Literature, Theatre and Film in the 1960s and 1970s

Klaus Beekman

In the twentieth century in the Netherlands, several literary trials took place. These concerned various types of texts, like novels, essays and letters. The most important ones concerned works which were held in high regard by critics in the literary field. W.F. Hermans, for example, was put on trial for insulting the Catholic community on the basis of the following passage in his novel *Ik heb altijd gelijk* (I'm always right 1951: 31): 'Catholics! That's the most filthy, rotten, retarded, crummy part of our people! Fucking like crazy! Multiplying! Like rabbits, rats, flies, lice. Not emigrating! But staying in Brabant and Limburg with pustules on their cheeks and rotten teeth from wolfing wafers!' The question was whether this passage itself was offensive and if so, whether the author was responsible for this statement of his fictional character in a legal sense. The court was of the opinion that the challenged passage should be considered within the whole of the novel and that the intention of the author had to be derived from the function of the passage within the text (Beekman and Grüttemeier 2005: 100–3). On these grounds, the judge decided not to proceed to a conviction. In subsequent trials too, like the one against Theo van Gogh in the 1980s, judges stated that the incriminated passage had to be considered within its context (*idem*: 106–7). In his essayistic publications he used expressions such as: 'What a smell of Caramel. Today they only burn diabetic Jews', with which he could have insulted the Jewish community. In this case too, the authorial intention was not of significant importance for the judgement. According to the judges, one primarily had to look at the intention as embodied in the text.

However, in some cases authorial intention did play an important role. The so-called 'Donkey trial' is an example. In 1966 Gerard Reve was charged with blasphemy with regard to *Nader tot U* (Nearer to Thee), a collection of letters, and with regard to a letter he had published in a literary magazine, which reads as follows:

> If God again catches Himself in the Living Substance, He will return as Donkey, only able to formulate a few syllables, misunderstood and maligned, and whipped, but I will understand Him and go to bed with Him immediately, but I put bandages around His little hooves, to ensure that I don't get too many scrapes when He flounders in the ejaculation. (*idem*: 80)

In his defence, the author emphasized that he wanted to write literature and that he felt free to propagate his own conception of God, without having the intention to defame the God of the Christians. Especially on the basis of this intentional argument, the author was acquitted (Beekman and Grüttemeier 2005: 82–91).

Until the 1960s, the criminal relationship between literature and law in the Netherlands seems to be marked by great benevolence towards literature. An appeal to the intention of the text and/or to authorial intention could free literature from prosecution. To achieve this, in the 1990s, one also referred to the literary character of a text, which would constitute its own reality. Legal proceedings were instituted against Pieter Waterdrinker, for example, because in his novel *Danslessen* (Dancing Lessons 1998) he could have insulted the Jewish community. In this case, the defence made an appeal to the coherence of the text, as well as to its character. The incriminated passage had to be considered within its context, and the text in its entirety should be seen as free from the reality outside. But this view, which is known as an autonomist conception of literature, was not shared by all courts. Acquittal was chiefly based on the premise that a passage should be viewed and judged on the basis of its place in the whole text (Beekman and Grüttemeier 2005: 169–78).

The juridical basis for the *exceptio artis* in the literary trials mentioned above can be found in the early twentieth century. In 1919 and 1920, a number of trials with regard to *De Hel*, a Dutch translation of Henri Barbusse's *L'Enfer* (The Inferno/Hell 1908), took place. The novel allegedly contained passages which were 'aanstotelijk voor de eerbaarheid' (offensive to public decency). However, the indictment was dismissed by the court, as well as by the Court of Appeal and the Supreme Court, with the view that the incriminated passages should be seen in their context and that one had to prove that the text as a whole is offensive. A work of art always has to be judged in its entirety, the argument goes. By taking this position, the Supreme Court, actually, recognized the special status of art.

The idea of the Supreme Court that a work of art had to be considered as an organism, a living creature, is in line with the so-called idealistic conception of literature, where form and content are considered to be a whole and the successful work of art as an organic unity, which transcends everyday reality, although from this reality elements could be lifted to a higher level (Beekman and Grüttemeier 2005: 63–5, 79; Grüttemeier and Laros 2013).

The point of view formulated by the Supreme Court in the 1920s can also be found in the case of *Bob and Daphne*, a series of novels Han B. Aalberse published in the 1950s and 1960s. With regard to these books, the judge took the view that the passages which were said to be scandalous should be viewed in their context, to trace the intent of the text. The conclusion of the Supreme Court was that the books were more titillating than aesthetic. The novel *Liesbeth en de wereld van Bob en Daphne* (Liesbeth and the World of Bob and Daphne) was considered to be an offence to public decency in its entirety, also because it was not literary enough (Beekman and Grüttemeier 2005: 70–3).

The outlines concerning art sketched by the Supreme Court in the 1920s forced legal experts to clarify when exactly something can be called art. The discrimination trials, however, showed that jurisprudence avoids giving an explicit definition of art and literature. The pornography trials investigated by Ralf Grüttemeier and myself, gave the same impression, for example some trials that were instituted against *Fanny Hill* (*idem*: 60, 75). Research has shown that, although legal experts did not base their statements on explicit definitions, they did have a conception of literature which quite often turned out to have an idealistic character. In this essay the question of the use of literary concepts, in a more systematic way, will be raised again, also with regard to Dutch trials with respect to the sale and distribution of *Fanny Hill* in the Netherlands, in order to get a more specific answer to the question of which line legal experts follow in expressing their conception of literature.

In *Literatuur en moderniteit in Nederland* (Literature and Modernity in the Netherlands), a history of Dutch literature, academics argue that one of the characteristics of the 1960s was the blurring of the boundaries between mainstream and mass culture. According to the literary historians, *Schund* (Trash) was no longer considered to be taboo. As an example of a novel that teeters on the border of high and low literature, they mentioned *Ik Jan Cremer* (I, Jan Cremer) (Ruiter and Smulders 1996: 310–21). Some critics called it a modern form of literature, others labelled it pornography. Publishers too started to put the distinction into perspective, for example the editor of the novel: 'What we publish cannot be pornography, because we only publish literature' (Beekman 2010: 464). In those days one found this perspective quite often in publishing houses. Publishers specializing in pornography suggested that the anonymously edited novels could have been written by famous literary authors. On the other hand, publishers specialized in literature set up pornographic series (Beekman 2007: 226–30; Etty 2012: 176–91). In this light, the purchasing policies of the Dutch Royal Library also are telling. Initially, the policies were based on a dichotomy between high and low literature, but since the 1960s, when the contrast became less sharp, the library collected more and more pornographic texts, including 'pulp series' (Kuipers 2012: 203).

Apparently, starting from the 1960s, in the literary field – to speak in terms of Pierre Bourdieu – representatives of institutions, like the library, publishing houses and literary criticism, considered the distinction between high and low culture as less sharp than before. This raises the question whether in this period also in the legal field prosecutors and others dealt in a more flexible way with lower forms of art and were willing to apply *exceptio artis* to pornography. To what extent are there indications of systematic interrelatedness of changes in the literary field concerning pornography in the 1960s and the view on pornography of legal experts? If legal experts were following the changes in poetics or value ascription in the literary field, this would show the impact literary gatekeepers can have in the field of power. At the same time it would illustrate what Bourdieu calls the 'homology' between both fields, in which legal experts are part of the field of power, which as such is supposed to dominate the literary field (Bourdieu 1996: 367; Grüttemeier and Laros 2013: 204–5). Then, declaring low culture, like pornography, valuable, would also mean a departure from the dominance of the idealist aesthetics, which seems to have been dominant in the Dutch literary field from the Barbusse case up to the Reve trial. Are there any signs for a change in the poetics of the legal experts? Another question concerns authorial intention. Do legal experts use this as an instrument to give pornography more freedom? The last question concerns different forms of pornography: books, performances and films. Is it possible to identify a systematics of degree of *exceptio artis* in the prosecution of pornography?

To answer these questions, the following steps will be taken. First of all the political background will be sketched against which the trials concerning pornography in the 1960s and 1970s played, including the judicial policy from which prosecutors, judges, and others, condemned or defended alleged pornographic texts. Then two cases, in which booksellers stood trial, are analysed. One case concerned *keukenmeidenromannetjes* (pulp novels) and the distribution of writings of de Sade, the other a translation of John Cleland's *Fanny Hill*. In a third step, performances that were considered to be pornographic are at the centre, especially *Oh! Calcutta!* The next part will be dedicated to only one case, *Blue Movie*, which turned out to have consequences for the censorship of other films. In conclusion, my questions posed earlier will be answered.

For my analyses of the literary cases, I used the judicial archives of the *North-Holland Archives* in Haarlem (Netherlands) and for the ones concerning film, the Archive of the Central Commission for Film Censorship (*Filmkeuring*). For the investigation of reactions in the media, I have used the database *Historische Kranten* (Historical Papers) of the Royal Library (available online: *Kranten.delpher.nl* – all quotes from dailies and weeklies are from this site). For my sociological approach, I am indebted to Pierre Bourdieu and his theory of relational research between various fields and institutions, as well as to his terminology.

Judicial policy concerning pornography

In the 1960s and 1970s, several Ministers of Justice were very active when it came to pornography, whether they represented a Christian party, like A.C.W. Beerman (1959–63), Y. Scholten (1963–5), A.A.M. Struycken (1966–7) and A.A.M. van Agt (1971–7), or a Socialist one, like I. Samkalden (1965–6). Also under C.H.F. Polak, who was a minister on behalf of the Liberal Party from 1967 until 1971, a large number of pornography cases came to court, among others the trial of bookseller Gerrit Naujoks, which will be analysed later in detail. As a rule, the ministers defended their actions by saying that they were just following the law, which prohibits writings or images that are *aanstotelijk voor de eerbaarheid* (Hazeu 1972: 5).

Prosecutors who implemented judicial policy argued in the same way, but emphasized that an exception should be made for pornography with a literary quality. W.H. Overbeek, Chief Prosecutor of the District of Utrecht from 1955 to 1978, expounded his ideas on this in *Pornografie voor het gerecht* (Pornography in Court 1966). The purpose of this book was to clear up the misunderstanding that Justice tried to keep literary authors within the generally accepted morality. The relevant articles of the law only had to prevent the distribution of 'artistically worthless *schund*' (trash), so Overbeek (1966: 71). Justice would only be allowed to take action against publications known as *pikante romannetjes* (spicy novels), which are characterized by gross descriptions of all kinds of sexual situations without any artistic value, publications that only want to titillate consciously (*idem*: 102–4, 108–9). So, according to Overbeek, it was possible to make a dichotomy between high and low art. The first is valuable, the second worthless and could be recognized by gross sexual descriptions and by the authorial intention to titillate and make money.

Later, Overbeek would lead a group of six prosecutors whose task was to achieve a clear judicial policy on pornography. The committee drew up guidelines for pictures and texts in specific publication media, such as 'stories, letters, etc. in sex magazines, which are characterized by an accumulation of highly sexually charged situations' (*De Telegraaf*, 15 October 1970). The report of the committee was sent to the district courts in October 1970. In a hearing, Overbeek again emphasized that the committee wanted to make an exception for art and literature. With regard to narrative categories he remarked: 'In judging letters and stories we had to be careful not to touch art forms. Everything that has some literary value falls outside the standards, but short stories with a strong sexually loaded situation and the intention to create sexual excitement, of course, are punishable' (*De Telegraaf*, 15 October 1970). When Overbeek was asked how to determine when indecent assault was at stake, he replied: 'That you shiver for a moment. No, I never do that, I can't afford it. If it were so, I have to put it off me, because it's not a matter of what I think about it myself' (*Leeuwarder courant*, 15 July 1971; *Limburgs Dagblad*, 16 July 1971). In other words, a legal expert had to work with a definition of art, without appealing to his personal idea of it.

Book publications and pornography

Prosecutors were particularly concerned with the distribution of 'artistically worthless trash', as Overbeek called it, and tried to make a distinction between spicy novels and eroticism in real art. At the same time, prosecutors tried to take into account that the view on pornography in society was changing. So, they had to deal with two unclear factors – the view on the phenomenon of pornography and the one on literature. The following cases will show how they tried to solve these problems.

In 1966, C. van Emde Boas, psychiatrist and sexologist, concluded that after the Second World War, liberalization of censorship in the United States, England

and Germany was increasing. At the same time he found that in the 1960s a crusade against obscene literature took place in these countries, for example against John Cleland's *Fanny Hill* (Van Emde Boas 1966: 49). After the first edition, in 1748–9, this novel had frequently been translated. Many translations, however, turned out to be adaptations. Passages were often omitted or changed. That in the 1960s many legal proceedings were instituted, especially in the United States and England, had to do with the fact that precisely in that period this novel was published as a cheap pocketbook and thus could more easily fall into the hands of young people (Riess 1967: 228–38; Ashbee 1969: 267–78; Englisch 1977: 628–33; Kearney 1982: 66–9; Fuld 2012: 70).

In the Netherlands, in 1964, different editions of *Fanny Hill* were on the market: three in English, one in Dutch, printed in Antwerp, and an expurgated version, also in Dutch. Mr J.F. Hartsuiker, a prosecutor, demanded that the publishers stop the distribution of the English editions, as well as the Dutch one printed in Belgium. Otherwise, he would take 'other measures' (*De Tijd*, 29 May 1964; *Nieuwsblad van het Noorden*, 29 May 1964; Hazeu 1972: 18). After this threat, the publisher, NV Keurboekerij, stopped the import of the Dutch translation of *Fanny Hill* (*Het Vrije Volk*, 30 May 1964). The threat of the prosecutor also immediately led to a fierce reaction in the press. Critics could not reconcile the threat with a trend which was determined by Eberhard Kronhausen and Phyllis Kronhausen, namely the assimilation of two categories, which Justice tried to keep apart: pornography and art, or 'obscene books' and 'erotic realism', as the psychologists called them in *Pornography and the Law* (1959): 'For the assimilation of the differences between porn and art, like those which have been determined in recent years by Mr and Mrs Kronhausen and others, a lot of time will be required again in the Netherlands' (*De Groene Amsterdammer*; *Friese Koerier*, 11 June 1964). The analysis of the next case will show how *Fanny Hill* fared in the second half of the 1960s in the Netherlands.

On 14 September 1967 the Amsterdam publisher Gerrit Naujoks was summoned to appear in court. He was charged with having in stock 149 copies of a Dutch translation of *Fanny Hill*, which he was going to distribute, 'knowing the content of the book, which was offensive against public decency'. On the sitting of 5 October the prosecutor, Mr H.E. van Renesse, explained his point of view: 'The text describes, for the most part, adventures in the sexual field of a young girl and mainly consists of detailed and penetrating descriptions of sexual acts, excesses and perversities.' According to him, the separate scenes, as well as the complete text, and the intent of the text, made a case against the Dutch version of *Fanny Hill*: 'The text is in and by its parts together, in view of their interrelationship and intent, offensive against public decency'. On the basis of this argument, he demanded a suspended sentence of six weeks with three years' prison and a fine of 750 Dutch guilders.

When the accused was told that Mr Hartsuiker already in 1964 asked not to import the book from Antwerp, he answered to have interpreted this as a request only, and he said not to have known that the court in Breda and the one in Den Bosch, earlier, had considered this publication as pornography (Beekman and Grüttemeier 2005: 75). To the question what he thought about the 'detailed and penetrating descriptions of sexual acts, excesses and perversities', he answered by appealing to 'the literary and historical value of the work', and referred to de Sade, apparently assuming that by this comparison, he could provide evidence for its literary quality and that since the publications of de Sade were free for sale, this should also apply for *Fanny Hill*.

Whereas the publisher defended himself by appealing to 'the literary and historical value of the work', the prosecutor had his doubts about exactly these qualities. 'For fifty years, since the introduction of the obscenity laws of Regout, this is a joke', so Mr H.E. van Renesse, who further said: 'The literary value is zero: I have never read such lousy Dutch. If one would replace the words "horse and carriage" and "candles" by "car" and "lamp", nothing remains of the historical value either' (*Het Vrije Volk*, 6 October 1967).

At the sitting of 5 October, the president of the court adjourned the case against Naujoks for more detailed research, to get an answer to two questions concerning the translation by G.B. Revis: (1) 'did the sexual adventures of the main character in this translation get a stronger accent and are they described more extensively and in more detail?'; (2) 'Are reprints of the original edition at this moment in English speaking countries (especially England and the USA) free for sale or are they considered to be "pornography" by Justice, and/or is the distribution forbidden, or has it been prevented in any way?' (*Arrondissementsrechtbank* 1960–9). The answers to these questions played an important role in the deliberations of Mr Van der Waerden, the president of the court, to clear the accused of the charge on 19 October. Research had shown that the Dutch translation 'corresponds to a great extent with the content of the original text, which had been edited in 1947 in London and then had been left undisturbed by Justice, and that the sexual adventures of the main character did not get a stronger accent and were not described in a more extensive and detailed way'. Furthermore, the president concluded, 'that the Dutch morals concerning what had to be considered offensive against public decency were strongly changing in the last few years'.

To determine the literary value of *Fanny Hill*, the judge compared the novel with modern literature and plays in which, according to him, increasingly, sexual passages did appear, but which were allowed to be published and performed, because of their overall 'literary value'. For the president this was a reason to proceed to acquittal. At the end of his verdict, he once again emphasized that it is impossible to insist that the novel is offensive against public decency, if one were to look at the text in its entirety and keep the potential reader in mind: 'One cannot say that this edition of *Fanny Hill*, which has not been illustrated and even does not have a titillating cover, considered as a whole, is offensive for people with a normal developed sense of decency.'

Not only with regard to *Fanny Hill*, but also in other cases an appeal was made to De Sade in order to free a publication from prosecution. Janna G. Hageman, for example, who translated *The Pearl*, which in 1969 was confiscated by order of Mr Hartsuiker because the Dutch translation contained offensive passages, also referred to de Sade for her defence: 'I omitted the sadistic passages, plus all those passages in which daughters have sex with their fathers. *Justine* by de Sade is full of sadistic passages and that is freely available now for years in our country' (*Het Vrije Volk*, 28 June 1969; cf. Beekman 2011: 140).

For prosecutors and judges de Sade had become a benchmark too, as the trial against G.W.R., a trader in second-hand books, shows. According to the prosecutor, Mr W.D. Meeter, the bookseller was guilty of distributing pornographic reading material. In an interview the prosecutor said he was aware of the fact that the boundaries of 'pornography' were shifting. But, as no one exactly knew to what extent such reading material was 'really harmful' especially for young people, he thought it would be wise to proceed carefully. He did rate the memoires of de Sade, which were also sold by the bookseller, as possibly harmful reading material. He further remarked about de Sade that 'personally' he thought the memoires 'were just annoying and even tedious'. However, he saw a difference between the work of de Sade and the two publications by others that were found in the possession of the bookseller. These he qualified as semi-literature and described them in pejorative terms as 'slechte keukenmeidenromannetjes' (bad kitsch novels). These novels did contain some erotic passages, although without a clear pornographic character. The material found caused the prosecutor, anyhow, to demand a fine of 400 Dutch guilders or a month detention and the confiscation of the writings of de Sade (*Het Vrije Volk*, 20 March 1968).

The Rotterdam judge, however, did not follow the demands of the prosecutor. In his sentence of 2 April 1968 he only demanded a fine of 75 Dutch guilders or seven days' detention for the distribution of pornographic literature. For his sentence, the judge also used a literary value judgement. In contrast to the so-called bad kitsch novels, the judge considered the memoirs of de Sade not as pornography, 'because of their literary value and the changed social norms regarding the concept of *aanstotelijk voor de eerbaarheid*' (*Het Vrije Volk*, 2 April 1968).

In the Netherlands, the work of de Sade had not been freely available for a long time. Abroad, justice also had problems with his publications: in the 1950s Dutch papers still extensively wrote about the confiscation of his oeuvre in France (*De Tijd*, 12 January 1957). Even having a look at it in the Royal Library was no sinecure (Kuipers 2012: 192–4). This would not change until the beginning of the 1960s. Then, also the image of de Sade as a pornographer was changing. After Walter Soethoudt, a Flemish publisher, had placed a translation of his work on the market which could only be sold under the counter, Bert Bakker, a Dutch literary editor, published his complete works in the 1960s without serious problems (Leemans n.d.). The Dutch editor engaged famous translators, like Gemma Pappot, who took responsibility for *Justine* and who also published a book about him: *De markies De Sade* (The Marquis de Sade) (1967). At that time renowned literary authors and journalists dedicated articles and books to the Frenchman, like W.F. Hermans – the above mentioned author of *Ik heb altijd gelijk* – who wrote a famous essay about him under the title *Het Sadistische Universum* (The Sadistic Universe 1964). But also Rudi Kousbroek, Alfred Kossmann and, in Belgium, René Gysen drew attention to de Sade already at an early stage: *De slecht befaamde Markies De Sade* (The notorious Marquis de Sade 1961). In their essays, they argued that, on the basis of the sexual descriptions, de Sade's oeuvre can be classified as pornography. On the basis of a deeper level, however, it could be seen as philosophical literature. For his work would have been based on an idealist concept of literature and society. It was not de Sade's intention to titillate, the argument goes, but to show that in every human being a sadist lurks (see also Otterspeer 2012: 147–58). It is uncertain whether legal experts have been influenced in a direct way by these changed views on de Sade in the literary field. But considering the number of times they emphasized wanting to take into account the changed view on pornography in society in general, considering also the critical notes of sexologists, psychologists and literary authors concerning actions of the police against pornography they had received, and finally the fact that they began to use De Sade as a benchmark and put pornography into perspective by comparing it to modern literature and plays in the second half of the 1960s: considering all these arguments one only can conclude that legal experts must have been aware of the changed view on de Sade in the literary field.

Performances and pornography

An appeal to de Sade could provide acquittal, at least with regard to book publications. With regard to performances this was more complicated. The legal action against *Oh! Calcutta!*, which at the end of 1970 was staged in the Netherlands, will show this. *Oh! Calcutta!*, which contained many nude scenes, was labelled as 'pornography' after the performance in New York. Mr Hartsuiker, the Amsterdam prosecutor, first ordered the acting head of the Vice Squad to make a report on the performance and later decided to have a look himself. There was one scene he wanted to have cut: 'Bang, bang, bang, I (almost) shot you!' (*pief, paf, poef, ik schiet je [bijna] dood!*). This scene was about group sex of older married couples, who all had physical defects. According to Mr Hartsuiker this scene was 'so coarse and would affect human dignity so deeply', that he wanted it to be removed.

The prosecutor, 'for the time being', did not take further action against *Oh! Calcutta!*, although the show, actually, should have been prosecuted for *openbare onfatsoenlijkheid* (public indecency), according to Article 239 of the Penal Code. That he did not take steps had to do with the fact that in a similar case – *Erotisch Panorama* (Erotic Panorama) – the Supreme Court (*Hoge Raad*) had passed no final judgement. Meanwhile, he wanted to have people know what he thought about the show himself. Probably he was aware of the intention of Kenneth Tynan, the maker of the show, who said he had used 'short parodies' of Edward Albee and Samuel Beckett. Perhaps he also was familiar with the reviews, in which *Oh! Calcutta!* was characterized as 'an ordinary persiflage on the system of swingers, key clubs and all kinds of underhandedness that goes with it' (*Het Vrije Volk*, 29 December 1970; 24 June 1971; *De Waarheid*, 24 June 1971). For he said he had seen that the show had 'partly a satirical and partly an ironic character'. But, apparently, the authorial intention for the prosecutor was less important than the form of presentation, the level and the used language. In any case, he had no high impression of *Oh! Calcutta!*: 'I consider the artistic value low. The performances are rude, just like the language used.' To avoid the impression he would use his personal conception of art for a legal judgement, he at once added that here violation of Article 239 of the Penal Code was at stake.

When the show went into the country, problems arose again. The Mayor and Aldermen of Geleen, a small Catholic town, decided to prohibit the performance on the basis of the conception of art of the cultural committee of Geleen, which thought that the show 'is obscene and has low, if any, artistic quality' (*Limburgs Dagblad*, 16 November 1971; Hazeu 1972: 108, 112). The Dutch book edition of *Oh! Calcutta!* (Pleiter 1969), published in 1969, which included the incriminated scene, was not mentioned in the debates. It shows that Justice especially had problems with performances. This seems to be confirmed by the fuss about *Het buitensporige seksuele genie van Markies De Sade* (The Excessive Sexual Genius of the Marquis de Sade), a documentary theatre performance. The city council of Amsterdam and Breda forbade the performance (*Het Parool*, 31 January 1970). The Alderman for Culture in Breda gave a short comment on his decision. He had no objection if one were to read aloud from de Sade's work, he said. His objection concerned 'a performance based on quotations from de Sade' (*de Volkskrant*, 13 February 1970; *Het Vrije Volk*, 20 February 1970; Hazeu 1972: 84).

However, in the 1970s the views on visual presentations of pornography also changed gradually (Sorgdrager 2003: 90). The Mayor of Utrecht, for example, after consulting the prosecutor, decided not to prosecute. He had two arguments for his decision. First, he pointed out that the works of de Sade were freely available in the bookstore. His second argument concerned the intention of the text, as well as the authorial intention: the performance would not be 'intentionally' blasphemous and did not have 'the intention' to hurt religious feelings: 'The performance is meant to be a realistic representation of the peculiar views of de Sade' (*De Tijd*, 7 March 1970).

Film and pornography

In 1964 Hella Haasse, a famous Dutch literary author, was nominated to become a member of the *Centrale Commissie voor de Filmkeuring* (CCFK, Central Committee for Film Censorship). The invitation came from J.C. Schuller, who from 1963 to 1977 was chairman of this committee. He knew Haasse from other advisory bodies. Haasse groped in the dark as to why exactly she was approached. She supposed Schuller asked her because she was someone 'without a political or religious background', because she was an author and, probably, because she was a woman (Du Mée and Boost 1971: 78).

The Committee for Film Censorship consisted of at least sixty members, who were appointed by the Minister of the Interior on the advice of the executive committee of the CCFK. Members had to reflect the main ideologies of the Netherlands, such as clergymen (Roman Catholic or Protestant), members of the judiciary (judges), teachers, doctors and people who were involved in youth problems (*Filmkeuring*: 9). The chairman and secretary were appointed by the Crown. The censorship of individual films was carried out by subcommittees of five members. The films had to be approved in advance, on the criterion of 'admissibility'. Age limits were used to decide on admissibility. In addition to this, the CCFK could decide that films could be shown only after certain cuts had been made. In fact, it was the CCFK's job to determine whether a film was contrary to public order or decency.

Thanks to Hella Haasse, we know which criteria were used in the subcommittees, namely 'the motives', or authorial intention of the filmmaker, 'the effects on ourselves and on other potential viewers', and, not least, the quality of the film. Haasse herself especially had eyes for 'the composition', the structural coherence of a film, which she explained from her profession as a literary author. Reasons for her to ban a film or to have it cut were sadism and masochism. But she wanted to make an exception for those sexual actions which were presented 'on the level of de Sade', she said. In other words, if a pornographic film had been brought to a higher level and the erotic passages had attained a function within the whole, according to her, it had to be approved (*idem*: 78–9). From this point of view, Haasse also looked at the Dutch film *Blue Movie* by Wim Verstappen and Pim de la Parra, which should have had its premiere in 1971. On 24 May, however, the Board of Film Censorship concluded that the movie, which tells the story of a young man who, after leaving prison, ends up in a society in which sexual freedom reigned, was not permitted for public display, 'because depiction of certain scenes and the showing of parts of pornographic films and scenes in this movie are in defiance of decency' (Verstappen 1971: 4). So censorship took place on the basis of certain components with which the film had been constructed. In the USA, by the way, the movie was confiscated, as well as in Belgium, in Surinam it was banned after two inspections, and in Germany, where it was shown under the title *Das Pornohaus in Amsterdam*

(The House of Porn in Amsterdam), the so-called *Freiwillige Selbstkontrolle* (Voluntary Self-Control) saw to it that some small cuts were made.

In a comprehensive report, in which he asked for re-examination, Verstappen argued why his film had to be approved. His main argument was that the movie, falsely, was labelled 'pornography' because it only had the intention to titillate. According to Verstappen (1971: 5) the intention of the movie was 'to comment on specific contemporary developments'. This external intention of the filmmaker fully corresponded with the internal intention of the movie, which gave 'clear and evident arguments' for this view. To clarify what the intention exactly was, Verstappen used a sociological essay of Simon Vestdijk, a famous Dutch literary author: *De toekomst der religie* (The Future of Religion). According to Vestdijk, in the Netherlands a new religion (read: ideology), with a new sexual morality, had come into being. In the 1960s, one was finished with the morality of marriage, based on Christian ethics. But the newly acquired sexual freedom led to new sexual difficulties, because the brake of the morality of marriage was missing. So, in making *Blue Movie*, Verstappen would have used a mimetic-ethic conception of art. 'From the movie speaks a very strong moral and social preoccupation', so Verstappen (1971: 8).

Another important argument Verstappen put forward was the coherence of the movie. He used a structural criterion to argue that removal of the 'documentary moments', or pornographic fragments, from *Blue Movie*, would mean that the society to which it referred could not be recognized. By removing these fragments, the film would lose its function as 'social comment' (*idem*: 12). In fact, he criticized the idea of the board to reject the film on the basis of some fragments. He argued that this is also legally reprehensible, because Dutch jurisprudence with regard to pornography says that 'one should never pay attention to the character of fragments extracted from a work of art, but only to the character of the work as a whole' (*idem*: 15). On the basis of his authorial intentions and the coherence of the movie, Verstappen concluded: 'This movie, on an artistically considerably high level, deals with some problems with regard to liberalization of sexual morals in the Netherlands, which can be seen in daily life' (*idem*: 15).

The plea Verstappen made had the desired effect. On 28 July, the Board of Film Censorship approved the movie at second stage and decided it was permitted for persons of eighteen years and older. One of the members of the board was the above-mentioned Hella Haasse. The report of re-examination shows that the board largely accepted Verstappen's intentional and structural criteria. The board accepted his argument that flashes of 'pornographic' material had been incorporated 'in a functional way', that the movie 'as a whole defends an intelligent and thoughtful, i.e. *not* obscene and only physical approach to sexuality', as well as the argument that 'cutting would weaken the intention of the makers, i.e. showing that so-called sexual freedom contains a lot of danger' (*idem*: 17). The board of re-examination not only used a structural and intentional, but also a pragmatic argument, to borrow a term of M.H. Abrams (1974): in *Blue Movie* ideas on morality with regard to sexuality were brought up for further discussion. Actually, the board, using an idealistic conception of art, accepted the artistic concept of the filmmaker.

Although some critics believed that Verstappen's intentional arguments were only used in a strategic way, namely to get approval, most of them reacted positively to the re-examination (Dronkers 1971: 38–9). Especially because, as Peter van Bueren, a well-known film critic in those days, wrote, 'the Board of Film Censors pays less attention to what has been shown, than to the intentions of the filmmaker'. They also welcomed the decision of the Board of Film Censors to no longer use 'the criterion of centimetre', i.e. measuring the quantity of nudity, but was willing to examine a fragment within the entire movie (*De Tijd*, 30 July 1971). According to the film critics, but also according to the board of re-examination, the approval of *Blue Movie* made it possible that *Flesh* by Andy Warhol, after having been rejected six times, was finally also released in the Netherlands (*De Telegraaf*, 22 September 1971; *De Tijd*, 15 October 1971).

Conclusion

In the Netherlands, under the rule of Christian, as well as socialist and liberal Ministers of Justice, prosecutors frequently took action against pornography in the 1960s and 70s. The prosecutors seemed to have more problems with performances and films than with book publications. This had to do with the premise that performing sexuality was more harmful than an appeal to the imagination of the reader. The policy concerning pornography was based on a theoretical distinction between high and low art. In practice, however, this dichotomy caused difficulties. The prosecutors did not want to rely on their own conception of art, but they did not have a well-described definition either. The dichotomy ran up against still another problem. Views on morality in society were changing. Sexologists, psychologists and writers talked about this to politicians as well as to lawyers. Meanwhile, in the literary field a lot was changing too. Literary novels were published and plays performed, with scenes one only knew from pornographic works. At the same time literary essayists defended de Sade, who had previously been put aside as a pornographer, on the basis of the deeper layers in his work, i.e. as a philosophical literary author. Legal experts also began to consider him as a literary author and even used him as a benchmark. So, the distinction between high and low art actually was removed.

It is hard to prove that legal experts took their view on de Sade directly from the changed view in the literary field. But it seems quite likely. Legal experts began to consider de Sade's works as a higher form of pornography in the same period, and they had themselves been guided by the social acceptance of erotically charged modern literary novels and plays. So, in the second half of the 1960s, there were changes on the level of theories of literature in the legal field, which seem to have been triggered by the rise of corresponding poetics becoming dominant among experts in the fields of literature and the arts. That pornographic texts and films were considered to be valuable by literary experts and members of film censorship committees does not mean that the time of idealist aesthetics was over. Just like writers and critics in the literary field, literary experts attached value to the unity of a work. In both fields, novels and films were judged on the basis of their organic coherence. Structural coherence was by far the most important standard concerning texts. With respect to performances, but especially to film, authorial intention also mattered greatly. From the end of the 1960s, a work which had previously been put aside as pornography, whether it was a book or a movie, was increasingly acquitted after prosecution, often via de Sade, on the basis of the artistic criterion that it was layered and did not transcend everyday reality, but rather said something about society.

References

Abrams, M.H. (1974), *The Mirror and the Lamp: Romantic Theory and the Critical Tradition*, Oxford: University Press.

Arrondissementsrechtbank Amsterdam 1960–1969, Inv. 46; Rolnr. 676566; Naam: Naujoks, G., Rechter: Vijfde Kamer; Zitt. Datum: 7-3-1968; Vonnis: 2504-144-1-67-R. In: *Noord-Hollands Archief.*

Ashbee, H.S. (Pisanus Fraxi) (1969), *Index of Forbidden Books*, London: Sphere Books.

Beekman, K. (2007), 'Mystificaties en intenties', in L. Kuitert, C. Dauven and J. Koopmans (eds), *Wie is de auteur? Dertien opstellen over schrijverschap, toeschrijvingen, pseudoniemen en anonimiteit*, 219–33, Amsterdam: University Press.

Beekman, K. (2010), 'Jan Cremer en de literaire kritiek', in H. Dütting (ed.), *Jan Cremer. Portret van een legende*, 459–82, Soesterberg: Aspect.

Beekman, K. (2011), 'Overheidscensuur en zelfcensuur in de twintigste en eenentwintigste eeuw in Nederland en Vlaanderen', in M. Mathijsen (ed.), *Boeken onder druk. Censuur en pers-onvrijheid in Nederland sinds de boekdrukkunst*, 137–51, 172–5, Amsterdam: University Press.

Beekman, K. and R. Grüttemeier (2005), *De wet van de letter. Literatuur en rechtspraak*, Amsterdam: Athenaeum – Polak & Van Gennep.

Bourdieu, P. (1996), *The Rules of Art: Genesis and Structure of the Literary Field*, trans. S. Emanuel, Stanford: University Press.

Dronkers, A. (1971), 'Vestdijk, de sociale religie en Verstappen', *Skoop* 8(2): 38–9.

Du Mée, R. and Ch. Boost (1971), 'Hella Haasse. Interview', *Skoop* 7(1–3): 78–83.

Englisch, P. (1977), *Geschichte der erotischen Literatur*, second ed., Wiesbaden: Fourier.

Etty, E. (2012), 'Duistere driften in deftige dorpen. Naoorlogse Nederlandse pornografische lectuur', in J. van Driel and R. Honings (eds), *Pornografie in de Nederlandse literatuur*, 176–91, Amsterdam: Nijgh & Van Ditmar.

Filmkeuring, *Inventaris van het archief van de Centrale Commissie voor de Filmkeuring, (1926) 1928–1977*, pdf available online: http://www.gahetna.nl/collectie/archief/ead/index/eadid/2.04.60 (accessed 15 October 2014).

Fuld, W. (2012), *Das Buch der verbotenen Bücher. Univeralgeschichte des Verfolgten und Verfemten von der Antike bis heute*, Berlin: Galiani.

Grüttemeier, R. and T. Laros (2013), 'Literature in Law: *Exceptio Artis* and the Emergence of Literary Fields', *Law and Humanities* 7(2): 204–17.

Hazeu, W. (1972), *Wat niet mocht… Een overzicht van censuur, ernstige en minder ernstige gevallen van vrijheidsbeknotting in Nederland (1962–1971) of de stem van de 'zwijgende' meerderheid of nog een jeugdsentiment van de jaren Zestig*, Amsterdam: De Harmonie.

Hermans, W.F. (1951), *Ik heb altijd gelijk*, Amsterdam: Van Oorschot.

Hermans, W.F. (1964), *Het Sadistische universum*, Amsterdam: De Bezige Bij.

Kearney, P.J. (1982), *A History of Erotic Literature*, London: MacMillan.

Kranten.delpher.nl, available online: http://kranten.delpher.nl (accessed 15 October 2014).

Kronhausen, E. and Kronhausen, Ph. (1959), *Ponography and the Law. The Psychology of Erotic Realism and Pornography*, New York: Ballantine Books.

Kuipers, A. (2012), 'De signatuur van de Hel. Erotica, pornografie en pulp in de Koninklijke Bibliotheek', in J. van Driel and R. Honings (eds), *Pornografie in de Nederlandse literatuur*, 192–207, Amsterdam: Nijgh & Van Ditmar.

Otterspeer, W. (2012), 'Slaan en geslagen worden. Willem Frederik Hermans en de pornografie', in J. van Driel and R. Honings (eds), *Pornografie in de Nederlandse literatuur*, 147–58. Amsterdam: Nijgh & Van Ditmar.

Overbeek, W.H. (1966), *Pornografie voor het gerecht*, The Hague: NVSH.

Pleiter, A. (n.d.), *Oh! Calcutta!* Dutch version, photos C. de Vogel, Utrecht: Aquarius Groenekan.

Riess, C. (1967), *Erotica! Erotica! Das Buch der verbotenen Bücher*, Hamburg: Hoffmann und Campe.

Ruiter, F. and W. Smulders (1996), *Literatuur en moderniteit in Nederland 1840–1990*, Amsterdam: De Arbeiderspers.

Sorgdrager, W. (2003), *Zonde, zeden en strafrecht*, Breda: De Geus.

Verstappen, W. (1971), '*Blue Movie* en hoe (Verstappen er voor zorgde dat) de film toch door de keuring kwam', *Skoop* 7(6): 2–18.

Van Emde Boas, C. (1966), *Inleiding tot de studie van de pornografie*, The Hague: NVSH.

Waterdrinker, P. (1998), *Danslessen*, Amsterdam: De Arbeiderspers.

5

Freedom of Satire? Oskar Panizza's Play *Das Liebeskonzil* in a Series of Trials in Germany and Austria

Claudia Lieb

When in 1895 Oskar Panizza was sentenced in Munich to prison because of his satirical play *Das Liebeskonzil* (The Love Council), he triggered a debate: did the play violate the right to protection of religious sentiments as the court had ruled? Or should the play be protected by the freedom of expression? This debate continued well into the 1990s, because, on the grounds of blasphemy, in 1985 a filmed version of the play was seized and banned by a regional court in Austria. In the second instance, the 1985 trial was taken to the European Court of Human Rights (ECHR) in Strasbourg. Although in the contemporary worlds of art, the play and the film were not seen as extraordinarily provocative, both trials ended up with harsh and strongly disputed judgements: while Panizza was sentenced to a severe punishment of one year in prison, the ECHR ruled that the banning of the film was justified. The rulings form a sharp contrast to western society's liberal circles where people are usually regarded as witty and intellectual when they mock the church.

It is true that from a religious perspective, blasphemy is regarded as a sin, as a culpable action. However, this must not be true from other perspectives such as art and jurisprudence. The secular state has problems when it comes to protecting religious sentiments. The evaluation of blasphemy is ambivalent, for the right to protection of religious sentiments is typically contrasted with the rights to freedom of expression and freedom of the press (cf. Keller and Cirigliano 2010). This conflict between fundamental rights hints at the fact that blasphemy itself is ambiguous. But it is also entertaining, which is why blasphemy is not at all seldom in western literary fiction. Throughout the history of literary fiction, discourses of blasphemy have been all the rage: examples range from Greek and

Roman myths to contemporary authors such as Elfriede Jelinek; they include Madonna's music videos and concerts, Terrence McNally's drama *Corpus Christi* (1997) and the animation series *Popetown* (2003), to name but a few.

For artists and writers, blasphemy is a way to attract a great deal of attention, all the more so if it is legally proven. The juristic condemnation of Panizza's play had a strong impact on the audience's response to the play as also to the film. The legal context even influenced the play's initial printing. Right from the start, Panizza was smart enough to work with a foreign publisher who had already published one of his earlier works: the first editions of *Das Liebeskonzil* were launched by Jakob Schabelitz' *Verlags-Magazin*, a Swiss printing and publishing house based in Zurich. Dated 1895, the first edition actually came out in 1894. Right after the trial, Schabelitz prepared the second edition which came out in 1896 and only one year later, he published the third. Nobody took offence in Switzerland, but in Munich the authorities did. This is all the more remarkable as Panizza's play is rooted in a turn-of-the-century movement known as 'Münchner Moderne'.

Munich-based authors like Panizza, Thomas Mann, Alfred Kubin, Alexander Moritz Frey and Gustav Meyrink created an imaginary fiction that refers to paradigms such as eroticism, crime and the grotesque. They depicted literary worlds of unbridled fantasies, of exoticism and of perversion. As they did so by citing medical and psychological disciplines, we can loosely describe their fiction as science fiction. Panizza, who gave up his early career as a psychiatrist to be a writer, fused medical discourses and criticism of the Catholic Church and of papacy in his play. In his literary works, Panizza repeatedly voices criticism of the Pope, for example, in his satirical pamphlets *Die unbefleckte Empfängnis der Päpste* (The Immaculate Conception of the Popes, 1893) and in *Der deutsche Michel und der römische Papst* (The German Michel and the Roman Pope, 1894). Although these texts were confiscated and banned shortly after publication (cf. Bauer 1984: 139), they did not provoke a trial as *Das Liebeskonzil* did: 'No author within the realm of emperor Wilhelm II was approximately as severely punished as Oskar Panizza for his publication' (Bauer 1984: 185).[1] As the play fulfils a common literary standard, it is strange that it prompted the greatest literary scandal of its time (cf. Bauer 1984: 16). The reason is possibly that Panizza appeared to be a repeat offender; *Das Liebeskonzil* was perhaps regarded as a calculated offence.

Panizza used the scandal to promote himself and his play. In 1895, he published a pamphlet commenting his own case: *Meine Verteidigung in Sachen*

'Das Liebeskonzil'. Nebst dem Sachverständigen-Gutachten des Herrn Dr. M. G. Conrad und dem Urteil des k. Landgerichts München I (My Defence in the Matter of 'Das Liebeskonzil', including the expert report by Dr. M. G. Conrad and the Judgement of the regional Court of Munich I). In the play's second edition, Panizza added a lengthy introductory part that alludes to his case and condemns censorship, while the third edition contains an extra preface about the trial. As it stresses the freedom of literary art, poor Panizza appears as a victim of the law. Right from the beginning, the story was reported in the press, too; the 1896/7 editions of the play actually quote a wide range of articles covering Panizza's case.

In 1930, it was Walter Benjamin who said that Panizza was remembered for his trial (Benjamin 1989: 645), and ever since, it has raised scholarly attention (Breuer 1982; Bauer 1984; Boeser 1989; Brown 2001, 2010; Mitterbauer 2007). In contrast to the trial itself, the surrounding legal history has not yet been appraised. To explore the importance of legal history for Panizza's case, I will compare several cases, taking into account the contemporary legislation. In the deluge of legal actions against turn-of-the-century writers, literary trials resulting in sentences seemed to occur less frequently than censorship cases – which is why Panizza's imprisonment was met with harsh protest. This might also explain why scholarly research cared about the history of censorship in Germany (cf. Houben 1965; Breuer 1982) but paid little attention to that of courtroom trials (cf. Seiler 1983: 233–59). With regard to France, historical studies on literary trials have been made (cf. Sapiro 2011), but the German history of literary trials has yet to be written.

A few examples may illustrate how literature was at the focus of criminal prosecutions before and after Panizza's case. Plays on stage, rather than books, were seen to pose a special threat to the authorities and to the audience. Hence writers and theatre directors had to take far-reaching legal action to gain official permission for stage performances. In this context, Gerhard Hauptmann's play *Die Weber* (The Weavers, 1892) paved the way for one of the most prominent trials in Wilhelmine Germany. In 1892 and 1893, the Berlin-based *Deutsches Theater* (German Theatre) asked for the permission to perform *Die Weber*. The police, however, prohibited this because it feared riots caused by the play. At the *Berliner Bezirksausschuss* (Berlin Administrative Court), Hauptmann appealed against the ban, but he failed as the court confirmed the police's decision. It was the *Oberverwaltungsgericht* (Higher Administrative Court) where Hauptmann appealed next. In the meantime, *Die Weber* premiered in February 1893 when the *Freie Bühne* (Free Stage) organized a private performance. It was only in

October 1893 that the Higher Administrative Court lifted the ban and gave permission for performance. In its judgement, the court held that *Die Weber* did not pose an imminent danger for public order and security, as people who could afford to visit the German Theatre did not tend to be violent. After the play had been presented to the public in September 1894, it was Emperor Wilhelm himself who counteracted it: because of the play's demoralizing effect, he terminated his own royal box at the German Theatre, the president of the Higher Administrative Court was rebuked while the police were praised for having banned the play. As a consequence, *Die Weber* scored a smashing success on the stage – since the play was in all the newspapers and magazines, everybody wanted to see it. However, this did not stop major German cities such as Hamburg, Munich, Frankfurt and Hannover from banning Hauptmann's socio-critical play (cf. Breuer 1982: 192).

As far as religious and biblical subjects were concerned, prohibitions seemed completely arbitrary. This goes especially for Prussia, where biblical topics were forbidden on the stage (Houben 1965 vol. I: 430–1). Nonetheless, in Berlin-based theatres such as the *Königliches Schauspielhaus* (Royal Theatre) and *Hofoper* (Royal Opera), biblical plays were all the rage: Franz Grillparzer's *Esther*, Friedrich Hebbel's *Judith* and Paul Heyses *Die Weisheit Salomos* (The Wisdom of Salomon) were celebrated works (Houben 1965 vol. I: 590). Other plays such as Hermann Sudermann's *Johannes* were banned. A forbidden drama that became famous was Heyse's *Maria von Magdala* (1899) which was prohibited in 1901. The Ministry of the Interior (*Ministerium des Inneren*) declared: 'The content of the play appears liable to injure the religious sentiments of the Christian population in several ways because the method of presenting the personality and the Passion of Christ cause offence' (Houben 1965 vol. I: 432). *Maria von Magdala* was then revised to get the ban lifted, but, in 1902, the police renewed it. Heyse appealed against this prohibition at the Berlin Administrative Court, and in October 1902, the court did in fact revoke the ban. It ruled that Heyse's drama posed no danger for the public order; what is more, the play glorified the Passion of Christ, it said. While the court took a favourable view of the play, the police did not accept it. Hence, the police appealed against the judgement, and the case was taken to the Higher Administrative Court which viewed the play as an 'attack on the Christian religion'. In the meantime, the play was performed in the United States, while the trial was being discussed in the press. When in 1903 *Maria von Magdala* was finally released for performance in Berlin by nobody less than Theobald von Bethmann-Hollweg, the prime minister of the Federal State of Brandenburg, the play turned out to be a clear flop. The media coverage had raised false expectations (cf. Houben 1965 vol. I: 437–52). This leads back to Panizza who used the media coverage of his own trial to promote *Das Liebeskonzil*.

Artistic liberties, artistic prosecutions: Panizza's drama and Schroeter's film

Das Liebeskonzil is based on a myth saying syphilis was God's punishing gift for mankind's sinfulness and fornication. It was the humanist Ulrich von Hutten who addressed this myth in his work *Von der wunderbarlichen arztney des holtz Guaiacum genant, und wie man die Frantzosen oder blatteren heilen sol* (On the wonderful medicine called wood Guaiacum, and how to cure the French disease) dating from 1519. Panizza's play is dedicated to Hutten and his work is cited at the beginning of the play. Set in heaven and in Pope Alexander VI's Renaissance court of 1495, the play displays a fictional version of the myth. While the Borgia Pope plays sinful erotic games with the members of his court, we learn that a heavenly council – God the Father, Virgin Mary, Jesus Christ, the Holy Spirit, and others – plans to punish sexual intercourse. Mary charges the devil with inventing something that counteracts sex: she needs 'a thing, an influence, a force, a person, a poison, a something... which would stem the bestiality of men and women in those relations and apparently necessary contacts and comminglings intended exclusively for the purpose of procreation' (Brown 2010: 47; cf. Panizza 2005: 41). Reluctantly, the devil starts to work for Mary. In a lurid and hallucinatory scene, he revives a number of mythological sinners. With Salome, the worst sinner of all, he procreates a beautiful and seductive daughter who at last transmits syphilis – after having infected the Pope, she also infects bishops, cardinals, ministers and the rest of mankind ('das übrige Menschenpack', Panizza 2005: 78), too. One, and only one girl is enough to erase mankind, and the Virgin Mary commanded it – Panizza's narration of heavenly blessed evil is, of course, ironic.

The play's first edition stresses the power of female eroticism by displaying a representation of syphilis on the front page: it shows a female figure, large and naked. Her abdomen is embraced by a black beast whose mouth is wide open and points at the figure's bare breast. Looking over her shoulder, the figure sees a group of clergymen and lords. She holds a pan flute in her hand, thus hinting at the mythological god Pan who is well known for his lasciviousness:

Figure 5.1 Max Hagen: Cover illustration (n.d.), cf. Panizza (2005). N. pag.

In addition to the threats of eroticism and a fatal disease, the play raises matters such as madness, conditions of fear and suffering, cruelty, violence, crime and murder. The first scene in heaven displays a dead young girl who has turned into an angel. The girl died on earth because her mother made her work as a prostitute and she was fatally raped by a punter. Using the effects of the grotesque, Panizza had no inhibitions about talking about all sorts of horrors on the stage, but he did so in a satirical and comic way. Take, for instance, the devil's description of a man suffering from syphilis:

> [H]is hair falls out, his eye-lashes fall out, his teeth fall out; ... after three months, his entire skin is perforated like a sieve ...; despair not only constricts his heart but also drips out of his stinking nose; ... after one year, his nose drops into his soup bowl, and he goes out to try and buy a rubber one; ... after two, three years, his liver and other large organs are like rocks in his body, and his mind turns to lighter foods; then an eye begins acting up, in another three months it's closed shut; after five, six years, convulsions shoot through his body like fireworks; ... one day, after about eight years, he picks up a bone from his own edifice, sniffs it, and tosses it aside in horror ... (Brown 2010: 60, cf. Panizza 2005: 70–1)

As the play also gives force to the traditional storyline of the grotesque, it aims at desecrating sacred doctrines and characters. Unsurprisingly, the Pope and his court are depicted as immoral, corrupt, criminal and, of course, horny. The heavenly characters are funnier: God the Father acts as a pitiful senile and sick old man, Jesus is a tubercular and rather stupid fellow who hates to be eaten by Christians ('Mich essen sie', Panizza 2005: 22). As a power-seeking conspirator who wants to rule heaven and earth, the Virgin Mary enters a pact with the devil, while the devil himself is an artist or a writer: His procreation, syphilis, is a work of art ('Kunstwerk', Panizza 2005: 53), and he sees himself as a genius.

The play proved to hold a fascination. Early in the twentieth century, when Panizza was still alive, the *Gesellschaft der Münchner Bibliophilen* (Society of Munich-based Book Lovers) published a new collector's edition of the play which was illustrated by Alfred Kubin. Only fifty copies of this 1913 edition were printed in the Netherlands. To prevent censorship, 'each copy had the name of its future owner printed on the title page' (Brown 2001: 534). In the 1930s, Benjamin regretted that there was no current edition of Panizza's works. This is the case, he says, because Panizza's texts would still attract the public prosecutor, 'just as it happened thirty-five years ago' (Benjamin 1989: 645).

Legal action, as well as liberalization, continued at a later date. After a German edition of the play published by Peter Jes Petersen had been confiscated in 1962 (cf. Brown 2001), Hans Prescher's 1964 edition came out without problems. Since then, the play has been available on the book market. In 1967, *Das Liebeskonzil* was finally performed: it premiered in Vienna (1 June 1967, *Kellertheater Experiment*). The play's first performance in France (2 July 1969, *Théâtre de*

Paris) was met with international attention, and ever since, *Das Liebeskonzil* has been staged more than seventy times. The play's stage performances were perceived as anything but shocking (cf. Mitterbauer 2007).

In 1981, Antonio Salines directed a performance at Rome's small theatre *Theatro Belli*. Supported by the film distribution company Atlas, the Roman performance was filmed under the direction of Werner Schroeter; later on, the producer Peter Berling transformed the stage version into a movie called *Liebeskonzil*. The film differs from the play because it lacks several scenes that take place in the Vatican court. What is more, in his film, Schroeter added a biographical frame: set in court, the first and the last scenes of the film depict Panizza's 1895 Munich trial. Thus, the framing scenes host characters such as a public prosecutor, a lawyer, a judge, a witness and Panizza himself. He is charged, of course, with the crime of blasphemy: 'Swearing religion will be punished, … I listed 93 acts of swearing in the book "The Love Council". The performance itself is even more incredible!' (Panizza, Schroeter and Salines 1982: 26)[2] Establishing an analogy between the courtroom and the stage, the movie is suffused with self-referential imagery of art. The courtroom's theatrical status is joined by allusions

Figure 5.2 *Liebeskonzil* (1982), [film] Dir. Werner Schroeter, Germany: Saskia-Film. Cf. Panizza, Schroeter and Salines (1982: 67).

to performances of the devil on the stage, as all heavenly characters appear in the traditional mask of the devil in Goethe's Faust: Their faces are covered in white make-up and their eyes have black frames. Heaven, it seems, is hell.

The movie premiered in 1982 at the Berlin Film Festival and was shown in cinemas throughout Germany and Austria. Contemporary reviews say the film was boring and as harmless as a puppet show: 'Today, the intended blasphemy appears to be a students' joke and a naughty puppet show' (Geleng 1982). Nonetheless, it served as a starting point for 'one of the most important, yet little publicized, censorship cases in postwar Europe' (Brown 2001: 536) – just as Panizza's case involved one of the heaviest punishments for a piece of literature imposed on a turn-of-the-century author in Germany (cf. Bauer 1984: 15–28, 151–8; Boeser 1989; Mitterbauer 2007).

The trials: Surprises and contradictions

Although *Das Liebeskonzil* had been printed and published outside Germany in Switzerland, on 4 January 1895, the Munich prosecutor accused the Munich-based Panizza of blasphemy. Only four days later, investigations started. It was decided to seize all available copies of the play, but the Munich police did not find more than two (cf. Bauer 1984: 151). The trial took place in Munich on 30 April 1895. Panizza was convicted to one year in prison, he had to pay for the criminal proceedings and the enforcement of the punishment, and it was decided to destroy all copies of the 'publication'. Strangely, the court ruled that all printing plates had to be destroyed, too. In the judgement, Panizza's play is referred to as a 'product of the press', a *Druckschrift* (publication), whereas words such as 'literature', 'drama' or 'work of art' are not used at all. The judgement reads:

> In the name of His Majesty the King of Bavaria, the Jury Court of the Royal State Court Munich I, in the case against the author Dr. Oskar Panizza of Kissingen, charged with an offense against religion committed in print, judges as follows: 1. For an offense against religion committed in print, Dr. Oskar Panizza of Kissingen is sentenced to a prison term of one year, as well as bearing the costs of the trial and the sentence. 2. The remaining copies of the publication The Love Council by Oskar Panizza, as well as the plates and molds for its production, are to be rendered unusable. 3. An arrest warrant for the accused is issued. (Brown 2010: 130; cf. Boeser 1989: 73–4)

Although the judge issued an arrest warrant, Panizza was released on an 80,000 Mark bail until the beginning of his imprisonment on 8 August 1895.

Legally, Panizza's case is rooted in German criminal law. When Bavaria became part of the Deutsche Reich in 1872 the German Penal Code (*Strafgesetzbuch für das Deutsche Reich*) became effective. Article 166 forms the basis for Panizza's trial:

> Whoever through insulting utterances publicly blasphemes God, gives offense, or who publicly insults one of the Christian churches or another corporate religious society in the country or their institutions or customs, also whoever commits insulting mischief inside a church or in another place dedicated to religious assemblies, shall be punished with imprisonment of up to three years. (Brown 2010: 126; cf. *Strafgesetzbuch* 1871: Art. 166)

The court ruled that *Das Liebeskonzil* was a blasphemous product of the press by which Panizza hurt the religious sentiments of his readers. This was, of course, a great trivialization of the play, and the penalty for it was extraordinarily high. As Panizza was convicted on the basis of Article 166, his punishment was more severe than that of other authors who were typically convicted on the basis of Article 184. This latter paragraph was in use to punish *unzüchtige Schriften* (lascivious writings), providing a maximum penalty of six months in prison (cf. Hütt 1990). As a consequence, the judgement and the long sentence in Panizza's trial were met with sharp protest from writers and artists. In the courtroom, it was Michael Georg Conrad's expert report on *Das Liebeskonzil* which protested against the criminal prosecution of Panizza and of poets in general. Hinting at the autonomy of literature, Conrad wrote:

> In the author's vision, the traditional heaven and what goes on there assumes a form that is thus actually beyond any discussion. The author envisioned it as he had to see it, from the artistic necessity of his creative imagination, period. You can accept or reject his vision, but you cannot legally transform it, you cannot punish it. The sole forum to which writers and artists have to answer is aesthetic criticism. (Brown 2010: 164; cf. Panizza 2005: 31)

This concept of *exceptio artis* can be found in numerous articles of the press, too (cf. Houben 1965: *passim*), but in contemporary German law, it is not relevant. In Panizza's case, the court rejected such a concept, and hence, it branded literature as a mere 'product of the press'. Even if notions of artistic freedom were mentioned in an earlier case (cf. Knies 1967: 148; Grüttemeier 2007: 183), this did not affect Panizza's trial, for Germany was – and is – not part of the common law tradition of arguing through precedent. For German judges and lawyers, legal reasoning means applying the abstract norms of a codified law to the particular case at hand.

As far as the film *Liebeskonzil* is concerned, the case is more complicated. In 1985, a non-profit-making organization called *Otto-Preminger-Institut für audiovisuelle Mediengestaltung* in Austria's Innsbruck announced a series of six evening showings of Schroeter's *Liebeskonzil* in its own cinema. Beginning on 13 May, the showings were scheduled at 10.00 pm. The announcement was made in a newsletter of the *Otto-Preminger-Institut*, and the film was introduced as follows:

> Oskar Panizza's satirical tragedy set in Heaven was filmed by Schroeter from a performance by the Teatro Belli in Rome and set in the context of a reconstruction of the writer's trial and conviction in 1895 for blasphemy. Panizza starts from the assumption that syphilis was God's punishment for man's fornication and sinfulness at the time of the Renaissance, especially at the court of the Borgia Pope Alexander VI. In Schroeter's film, God's representatives on Earth carrying the insignia of worldly power closely resemble the heavenly protagonists. Trivial imagery and absurdities of the Christian creed are targeted in a caricatural mode and the relationship between religious beliefs and worldly mechanisms of oppression is investigated. (ECHR 1994: 5; cf. Grabenwarter 1995: 131)

The film was to be shown late at night to a paying audience in an art cinema which addressed a small number of viewers sensitive to experimental films. By means of the newsletter, this audience was warned beforehand about the satirical nature of the film. What is more, the film was forbidden for persons under the age of seventeen. Nonetheless, the Innsbruck diocese of the Roman Catholic Church requested criminal proceedings.

As a consequence, on 10 May 1985, the prosecutor started action and instituted criminal proceedings against *Otto-Preminger-Institut*'s manager Dietmar Zingl. The charge was 'disparaging religious precepts' (*Herabwürdigung religiöser Lehren*), which was prohibited by Article 188 of the Austrian Penal Code. After the film had been shown at a private session in the presence of a duty judge (*Journalrichter*), the public prosecutor applied to seize the film on 12 May. This application was granted by Innsbruck's regional court (*Landesgericht*), and hence, the planned public showings of the film could not take place.

At the Innsbruck Court of Appeal (*Oberlandesgericht*), Zingl appealed against the seizure order, but his appeal was dismissed on 20 July 1985. The court said 'that artistic freedom was necessarily limited by the rights of others to freedom of religion and by the duty of the State to safeguard a society based on order and tolerance.... The wholesale derision of religious feelings outweighed any interest the general public might have in information or the financial interests of persons wishing to show the film' (cf. ECHR 1994: 6).

On 24 October 1985, the trial took place before the Innsbruck regional court (*Landesgericht*). The court ordered the banning of the film as the film was criminally blasphemous; the public projection of it fulfils 'the definition of the criminal offence of disparaging religious precepts as laid down in section 188 of the Penal Code', it said (cf. ECHR 1994: 7). It is true that the court's reasoning considered Article 17a of the Austrian constitution (*Staatsgrundgesetz*) which guarantees the freedom of artistic creation and the publication and teaching of art. However, because of the 'particular gravity in the instant case', the court held that 'the basic right of artistic freedom will in the instant case have to come second' (cf. ECHR 1994: 9). The case's 'gravity' derives from the film's absurd portrayal of Christian icons. In its judgement, the regional court had characterized the film as follows: 'God the Father is presented both in image and in text as a senile, impotent idiot, Christ as a cretin and Mary Mother of God as a wanton lady with a corresponding manner of expression.' What is more, 'the Eucharist is ridiculed' (cf. ECHR 1994: 7).

Zingl appealed against the judgement of the regional court, submitting a declaration signed by some 350 persons who protested they had been denied free access to a work of art by the court's ban of the film. In his appeal, Zingl of course claimed that the freedom of art enforced in Article 17a should be superior to disparaging religious precepts as laid down in Article 188. However, on 25 March 1987, the Court of Appeal declared the appeal inadmissible – since Zingl was not the owner of the film's copyright, he had no standing, it ruled.

On 6 October 1987, the *Otto-Preminger-Institut* applied to the European Commission on Human Rights in Strasbourg, claiming that Austria had violated Article 10 of the European Convention on Human Rights. Article 10 provides the right to freedom of expression. In January 1993, the Commission reported that there had indeed been a violation of Article 10, as regards the seizure and the forfeiture of the film (cf. ECHR 1994: 15). When, in April 1993, the Commission referred the case to the ECHR for a final ruling, this ruling caused great surprise: in contrast to the Commission's report, six of nine judges of the ECHR found 'that there has been no violation of Article 10 … of the Convention as regards either the seizure or the forfeiture of the film' (ECHR 1994: 28). Instead, it was 'the respect for the religious feelings of believers as guaranteed in Article 9' that 'can legitimately be thought to have been violated by provocative portrayals of objects of religious veneration' (ECHR 1994: 22).

In a nutshell, the ECHR based its ruling on the idea that a state must 'protect the right of citizens not to be insulted in their religious feelings by the public expression of views of other persons' (ECHR 1994: 22). The majority of the judges of the ECHR decided that this right was more important than the right to freedom of expression. However, in their dissenting opinion, three judges contradicted this judgement. They argued: 'The Convention does not, in terms, guarantee a right to protection of religious feelings. More particularly, such a right cannot be derived from the right to freedom of religion, which in effect includes a right to express views critical of the religious opinion of others' (ECHR 1994: 30). Although they agreed with the majority that there must be certain limitations to the public expression of such views, they found that the 'repressive action' of seizing and banning the film was not proportionate to the legitimate aim pursued (ECHR 1994: 31).

Concluding remarks

In its defence before the ECHR, the *Otto-Preminger-Institut* argued that 'a work of art dealing in a satirical way with persons or objects of religious veneration' could not be regarded as disparaging or insulting (ECHR 1994: 20). This argument seems to be based on the assumption that *exceptio artis* should be applied to satire: blasphemy might be an offence, but when it occurs in literary satire, it should be judged otherwise. The ECHR did not agree. It confirmed a line of thought that stems from its 1988 case of *Müller v. Switzerland*: the ECHR grants national courts and judges a certain 'Margin of Appreciation' when it comes to moral standards and religious beliefs, because an international institution such as the ECHR should respect cultural and social differences in Europe (cf. Keller and Cirigliano 2010: 419–20).

Historically, the ECHR's 1993 judgement is in line with the 1895 judgement: both argue that when a work of art hurts the religious feelings of its readers or its viewers, it must therefore be forbidden. But there is a contradiction between the ECHR's ruling in this case and the ECHR's earlier ruling, according to which the right to freedom of expression applies to information and ideas regardless of their content. In the famous case of *Handyside vs. United Kingdom*, the ECHR ruled as early as 1976 that freedom of expression does in fact apply to information and ideas which shock or offend a group in society or the state itself. In the case of *Otto-Preminger-Institut* vs. *Austria*, the ECHR came to a radically different judgement. This is why in jurisprudence this judgement was recognized as false. The German jurist Andreas von Arnauld says that seizing and banning the film violates Article 10 of the European Convention on Human Rights (von Arnauld 2012: 280–1). What is more, Arnauld argues that a state cannot possibly protect the feelings of its citizens. It is true that a constitutional law such as Article 10 of the European Convention on Human Rights can protect the freedom to do or not to do something, he says: it can protect inner faith, it can protect the profession of faith and it can also protect the exercise of faith. None of these actions, however, are restricted by a blasphemous film or book (cf. von Arnauld de la Perrière 2007: 75). In addition to this, the ECHR's idea of a right to respect religious feelings cannot be handled in practice, he says:

> A right to respect religious sentiments as such, however, as the ECHR appears to take for granted for the above-mentioned jurisdiction, exceeds the standard message of the right of freedom, and it leads, as an immediate point of contact of legal regulations, in addition to practical difficulties. If one intends to consistently realize the protection of feeling, one has to take the subjective feeling seriously because this is radically a subjective assessment. The 'felt justice', however, is no calculable line of reference which might be the basis of a social network. (von Arnauld de la Perrière 2007: 76)

From a literary critic's point of view, I can only confirm Arnauld's argumentation. It also holds true when applied to the reception of satire or works of art in general: feelings must not be the basis for the evaluation of art or texts. In the end, a taboo-oriented culture of law could lead to a radical loss of freedom, as UK historian Timothy Garton Ash argued: 'in our increasingly mixed-up, multicultural world, there are so many groups that care so strongly about so many different things, from fruitarians to anti-abortionists and from Jehovah's Witnesses to Kurdish nationalists. Aggregate all their taboos and you have a vast herd of sacred cows. Let the frightened nanny state enshrine all those taboos in new laws or bureaucratic prohibitions, and you have a drastic loss of freedom' (Ash 2006).

Notes

1 All translations from German are mine, unless indicated otherwise.

2 As the film has disappeared, I quote the book based on the film (Panizza, Schroeter and Salines 1982).

References

Ash, T. Garton (2006), 'We Must Stand Up to the Creeping Tyranny of the Group Veto', *Guardian*, 2 March, available online: http://www.guardian.co.uk./comment /story/01721390,00html (accessed in September 2006).

Bauer, M. (1984), *Oskar Panizza. Ein literarisches Portrait*, Munich etc.: Carl Hanser.

Benjamin, W. (1989), 'E. T. A. Hoffmann und Oskar Panizza', in R. Tiedemann and H. Schweppenhäuser (eds), *Gesammelte Schriften*, vol. II. 2: 641–8, Frankfurt/M.: Suhrkamp.

Boeser, K., ed. (1989), *Der Fall Oskar Panizza. Ein deutscher Dichter im Gefängnis. Eine Dokumentation*, Berlin: Edition Hentrich.

Breuer, D. (1982), *Geschichte der literarischen Zensur in Deutschland*, Heidelberg: Quelle & Meyer.

Brown, P.D.G. (2001), 'The Continuing Trials of Oskar Panizza: A Century of Artistic Censorship in Germany, Austria, and Beyond', *German Studies Review* 24: 533–56.

Brown, P.D.G. (2010), *Oskar Panizza and The Love Council. A History of the Scandalous Play on Stage and in Court, with the Complete Text in English and a Biography of the Author*, North Carolina etc.: McFarland Company.

ECHR (1994), Otto-Preminger-Institut v. Austria, ECHR judgement dating from 20.09.1994, 13470/87, available online: http://www.worldlii.org/eu/cases/ECHR/1994/26.html (accessed 11 March 2013).

Geleng, I. (1982), 'Der Skorpion im Messkelch', *Badisches Tagblatt*, 23 February, quoted in Brown (2001): 537.

Grabenwarter, C. (1995), 'Filmkunst im Spannungsfeld zwischen Freiheit der Meinungsäußerung und Religionsfreiheit', *Zeitschrift für ausländisches öffentliches Recht und Völkerrecht* 55: 128–65.

Grüttemeier, R. (2007), 'Law and the Autonomy of Literature', in G.J. Dorleijn, R. Grüttemeier and L. Korthals Altes (eds), *The Autonomy of Literature at the fins de siècles (1900 and 2000), A Critical Assessment*, 175–92, Leuven etc.: Peeters.

Houben, H.H. (1965), *Verbotene Literatur von der Klassischen Zeit bis zur Gegenwart, Ein kritisch-historisches Lexikon über verbotene Bücher, Zeitschriften und Theaterstücke, Schriftsteller und Verleger*, 2 vol., Hildesheim: Georg Olms.

Hütt, W. ed. (1990), *Hintergrund. Mit dem Unzüchtigkeits- und Gotteslästerungsparagraphen des Strafgesetzbuchs gegen Kunst und Künstler 1900–1933*, Berlin: Henschel.

Keller, H. and L. Cirigliano (2010), 'Die Krux mit der Blasphemie – Analyse zweier richterlicher Lösungsansätze', *Zeitschrift für ausländisches öffentliches Recht und Völkerrecht* 70: 403–31.

Knies, W. (1967), *Schranken der Kunstfreiheit als verfassungsrechtliches Problem*, Munich: Beck.

Mitterbauer, H. (2007), '"Ihr Herrn, mir scheint, der Streit geht schon zu weit". Performative Konstruktion von Blasphemie am Beispiel von Oskar Panizzas "Liebeskonzil"', in S. Neuhaus and J. Holzner (eds), *Literatur als Skandal. Fälle – Funktionen – Folgen*, 247–56, Göttingen: Vandenhoeck & Ruprecht.

Panizza, O. (2005), *Das Liebeskonzil. Eine Himmels-Tragödie in fünf Aufzügen. Faksimile-Ausgabe der Handschrift, eine Transkription derselben, des Weiteren die Erstausgabe des 'Liebeskonzils' als Faksimile sowie 'Meine Verteidigung in Sachen "Das Liebeskonzil"' und Materialien aus der zweiten und dritten Ausgabe*, ed. P.D.G. Brown, Munich: belleville.

Panizza, O., W. Schroeter and A. Salines (1982), *Liebeskonzil Filmbuch*, ed. P. Berling, Munich: Schirmer/Mosel.

Sapiro, G. (2011), *La Responsabilité de l'écrivain. Littérature, droit et morale en France (XIXe–XXIe siècle)*, Paris: Seuil.

Seiler, B.W. (1983), *Die leidigen Tatsachen, Von den Grenzen der Wahrscheinlichkeit in der deutschen Literatur seit dem 18. Jahrhundert*, Stuttgart: Klett-Cotta.

Strafgesetzbuch für das Deutsche Reich vom 15. Mai 1871, § 166 [version valid from January 1, 1872 to October 1, 1953], available online: http://lexetius.com/StGB/166 (accessed 24 April 2013).

von Arnauld, A. (2012), *Völkerrecht*, Heidelberg etc.: C. F. Müller.

von Arnauld de la Perrière, A. (2007), 'Grundrechtsfreiheit zur Gotteslästerung?', in A. Angenendt, M. Pawlik and A. von Arnauld de la Perrière, *Religionsbeschimpfung. Der rechtliche Schutz des Heiligen*, ed. J. Isensee, 63–104, Berlin: Duncker & Humblot.

6

'Words Are No Deeds'. Trials Against Literature in the Soviet Union

Sylvia Sasse

In September 1965, the two writers Andrei Sinyavsky and Yuli Daniel, the first being also a critic and the second a translator, were arrested for having published 'anti-Soviet literature' in foreign editorials under pseudonyms. In Soviet legislation, both were accused under Article 1, paragraph 70 of the Criminal Code of the RSFSR: 'Agitation and propaganda with the purpose of undermining or weakening of the Soviet power or with the purpose of committing or inciting the committing of particularly grave crimes against the Soviet state, the spreading with the same purposes of slanderous fabrications that target the Soviet political and social system, the production, dissemination or storage, for the same purposes, of literature with anti-Soviet content are punishable by six months to seven years of imprisonment, with possible subsequent internal exile from two to five years.' One year later, Sinyavsky was sentenced by a court in a show trial to seven years of strict-regime labour camp, Daniel to five years. Even though – or perhaps because – it was apparent that both would be convicted, an unusually controversial debate about literature was held in court. Since both of the accused admitted right from the beginning to having spread the writings abroad (publication under a pseudonym), the discussions in court were limited to the question of whether those writings were of an anti-Soviet nature, that is, if they defamed or humiliated the Soviet people. The charge was thus phrased as followed in the newspaper: 'In 1956, Sinyavsky wrote the novella "Sud idet" (The Trial Begins), which is infused with hatred against everything Soviet. It contains malicious attacks against the theoretical maxims of Marxism-Leninism, against the history of the Soviet state, against the culture and moral of the Soviet people' (Ginzburg 1967: 213). One of Sinyavsky's novellas that were tried in court is in itself also a story about the court. At the end of 'The Trial Begins', the narrator, a writer himself, is denounced, tried and sentenced to forced labour camp at the end because he is telling the story in hand. As Sinyavsky had already analysed the connection between denunciation, indictment, court and verdict within the Soviet Union in 'The Trial Begins', it can be read as an involuntary subtext of the trial against Sinyavsky. His fictional writer is also accused of 'defamation' – specifically, of the defamation of juridical processes in the Soviet Union. In the novella, the writer refers to the role of the word in everyday juridical and literary life in the Soviet Union.

The word, so he writes, is fundamentally dangerous – on the one hand, it needs to be surveilled and controlled, on the other hand, it is itself an agent, an agent of denunciation, indictment and verdict. That which is spoken has consequences and leads to arrests and convictions. In some cases, the word is deadly. Sinyavsky's narrator repeatedly compares religious and totalitarian notions of the power of words. While in the Bible the world was created by means of the word, the word thus creatively becoming deed, it now creates deeds by other means – it creates them in court (Terc and Sinyavsky 1992: 278). In his last words in court in 1965, Andrei Sinyavsky refers to these observations made by his narrator in 'The Trial Begins':

> I only want to recall a few arguments essential for literature. Learning them is the beginning of studying literature: a word does not involve a deed, it is a word. A designed image is not real. The writer is not identical with the fictional character. That is the ABC and we tried to talk about it. But the prosecution persistently rejects it as an invention, a deception, a lie.... As a matter of fact I can even understand the attorney. His tasks are far-reaching and he is not obliged to consider literary properties, like what an author, a hero, etc. is. If, however, two members of the Union of Soviet Writers, one being a professional author and one a certified critic, allege such things and consider direct speech of negative fictional characters as the author's opinion, then one really no longer knows what to say. (Ginzburg 1967: 302)

In this statement, Sinyavsky addresses various points that are regularly negotiated when literature is on trial – the differentiation between the speech of narrator, author and character as well as the differentiation between fact and fiction. By mentioning the equation of word and deed, however, he touches upon the neuralgic point which has become the precondition for the condemnation, not only of literary works but also of other 'utterances' in the Soviet Union. Up until this point, nobody before him had addressed the problem this explicitly, and nobody had so clearly spoken out against the notion of literature that Maxim Gorky used in the 1930s with the formula 'words are deeds' in order to establish

Social Realism in literature: 'For the word is equivalent to the deed – essentially, it is also a deed and therefore it is crucial to show how it effects and influences men' (Gorky 1935: 113).

Sinyavsky's defence forwards a theory of literature according to which the literary word is metaphoric, polysemic and can never be understood fully. Thus there can hardly be decisive proof of the political purposefulness of a literary text. This theory, of course, is not accepted by the court. Its acceptance would render the prosecution futile. According to Grüttemeier and Laros (2013), a recognition at trial of literature as a special discourse (*exceptio artis*) can serve as evidence for the recognition of the (relative) autonomy of the literary field by the field of power, and this, in turn, can itself be understood as a major achievement in the struggle of the literary field for its autonomy.[1] Obviously, the debates in the trial of Sinyavsky touch upon this problem of *exceptio artis*. Although matters in the Soviet Union lay very differently from western-style liberal democracies, I would like to offer some preliminary thoughts on this subject.

Firstly, the exact definition of *exceptio artis* seems crucial in our context: '*Exceptio artis* means that utterances that in principle constitute an offence can be judged otherwise when they occur in a literary work' (Grüttemeier and Laros 2013: 204). I think this definition can apply in a stronger and in a weaker sense. The stronger one would apply if a literary work *does* in fact present certain features which it can be indicted for, *but* the literary work is *redeemed* by its 'social value' as a work of art. An instance of such a liberal jurisdiction has for example been established in US legal rulings concerning pornography since the late 1950s. However, it seems that *exceptio artis* in this strong sense is more likely to play a role in trials when literature is charged with pornography (also blasphemy), because here a difficult balance has to be achieved between the protection of the 'vulnerable reader' and the freedom and enjoyment of the sophisticated reader. If a piece of literature is indeed found guilty of libel against a particular person or of inciting hatred against a minority, there is no balancing between types of readers. In such cases, it seems less likely that a court will judge that the literary text can nevertheless be redeemed by its literary worth and the high esteem it is held in within the literary community. Similarly, in the case of Sinyavsky, discourse *presupposed* that a literary work which in fact was 'anti-Soviet' could not be redeemed by its artistic worth.

A less stronger variation of *exceptio artis* seems to apply when the court, upon coming to a decision, recognizes the special knowledge concentrated in the literary field and reformulates concepts of literature found there (cf. Grüttemeier and Laros 2013: 205). This, of course, is the kind of recognition Sinyavsky is pleading for, but the court not only rejects the writer's theories about poetics, it, moreover, breaches the most elementary conventions of how to read a literary text (spontaneous identification of narrator/hero and author).

Trials against literature in the Soviet Union

If one wants to understand the equation of word and deed in Soviet literature and legal rulings, it is necessary to first look at the history of the trials against literature, beginning from the establishment of the Soviet Union. In the early 1920s, the first years after the revolution, the state did not prosecute any authors or their literary works. Rather, a Soviet jurisdiction and a Soviet law first had to become established. One way through which this happened was the arts themselves. The theatre becomes an arena for trying out, and also practising, jurisdiction and law. In the 1920s, for instance, so-called agit-courts (*Agitsudy*) are performed all across the Soviet Union. These theatrical lay courts stage moral misconduct in front of ordinary citizens and have the purpose of demonstrating the practices of confessing, testifying and judging. From the very beginning, it is noticeable that throughout these agit-courts, words are strongly attributed with the ability to form reality: a repentant confession usually enabled the delinquents to change their ways and return into the community. The American writer and sociologist René Fülöp-Miller, who visited the Soviet Union before 1926, writes that all debates, even the debates in the field of arts, were staged as court hearings: 'If, for instance, a well-known director presents a new production to the public, soon after a "trial" will take place in which the new work is discussed. One person from the theater personnel performs the prosecutor, another one the defender; the judge, too, is performed by a director or by an actor. The unfortunate one who is to be blamed for the new production is in the dock and has to face the charges' (Fülöp-Miller 1926: 191). Unsurprisingly, this propagandistic genre was immediately parodied by artists. In post-revolutionary Russia, for example, the 'Trial against the Imaginists' (*Sud nad Imazhinistami*) was held in 1920. The literary group of Imaginists (among others, Sergei Esenin, Vadim Shershenevich and Anatoli Mariengof) was accused of violating contemporary, post-revolutionary poetry. For this, twelve judges were chosen from the audience, the Russian symbolist Valerij Brjusov appeared as literary prosecutor, and Ivan Aksenov was the plaintiff. During the trial, Brjusov cited

Imaginist poems by heart, and Esenin similarly used a poem – 'Confession of a Hooligan' ('Ispoved Chuligana'), a parody of the violent power of words – for his defence. In answer to this 'trial', the Imaginists staged a contra-trial, the 'Trial of the Imaginists against Russian literature' (*Sud imazhinistov nad literaturoj*).

Apart from these parodistic and propagandistic theatrical trials, lay courts with the purpose of dealing with smaller offences are introduced in the mid-1920s. The introduction of lay courts can on the one hand be ascribed to a serious lack of legally trained personnel, but on the other hand, it is also programmatic: the people themselves should be the judges, since codified law (partially pre-revolutionary) was still considered a model in transition in the 1920s. Once the masses gain a socialist consciousness, it would become downright redundant (Solomon 1996: 36). Although the creation of such informally called *tovarishcheskie sudy* (comrade trials) in order to lighten the workload of the courts was initially accepted by the People's Commissar in March 1928 as a temporary experiment, by 1930, lay courts had become firmly anchored in Soviet law (Solomon 1996: 67). This carried consequences for literary or artistic production as well – it was thus possible to try offences against the Soviet conception of art and literature and later, in the years after 1934, against the official doctrine of the Socialist Regime, in front of lay courts, especially the courts of the Union of Writers. One of the first, very early lay courts known to me is the 'Trial against Pornography' in 1925. In this case, it was more of a discussion organized by the local committee of writers on a text written by Alexander Volzhskij 'Druz'ja po Volge' (Friends along the Volga). The court was called in on the request of the writer himself, because he had the impression that his text was being defamed in the *Pravda* (the press). The discussion was mainly concerned with the question of whether the use of profanity in new proletarian literature was allowed or not. Volzhsky defended himself by arguing that the use of vulgarity occurs in character speech and is vital for the characterization of a figure belonging to the Tsarist army, that is, the old order. The vulgar speech had a realist function. The verdict came to the conclusion that 'all charges against comrade Volzhsky are dropped' (*Sud nad pornografiej* 1926: 46), although he received a warning. In the future, the use of such words in literature should not be allowed if they are deemed redundant from an artistic or harmful from an educational point of view.

At about the same time, beginning in 1927, an extensive campaign of self-criticism and criticism spread across the Soviet Union, with devastating consequences for writers and artists. This campaign also prepared the persecution, arrest and murder of artists in the 1930s. With the introduction of this campaign, it is possible to speak of a juridification of society by means of compulsory and public self-criticism and the denunciation of those who transgress Soviet doctrine. In this campaign, Stalin erroneously refers to the Marxist concept of criticism in order to use it for the persecution of so-called deviants – that is, everybody who does not comply with his policies (Marx and Engels 1948: 215). Thus, beginning in the late 1920s, there are numerous instances of self-criticism by writers and artists, at times even prophylactic, in which they apologize for former 'errors' in order to avoid a ban on publication, among other things. Viktor Shklovsky wrote an example of forced self-criticism as early as 1930, which was published under the title 'Pamjatnik nauchnoj oshibke' (Monument to a Scientific Error), published in the *Literaturnaja gazeta*. In the article, he uses the exact same vocabulary for self-defence that was used against him and the Formalists at the time. He has to defend the fact that he – naively – saw literature as a sum of processes, but he now realized that single pieces cannot be summarized into literature but can only work together in a state of interdependence (Shklovskij 1930: 1). Shklovsky's self-criticism occurred parallel to a polemic against 'Formalism' in literature and other arts. As early as 1933, 'Formalism' was considered as an antithesis to 'Realism', though it then became a charge, if not even an offence, in trials against a variety of artists in a broadly conceived campaign. Meetings were organized all over the place in order to verify suspected Formalism, such as in the House of Film in February, and in March, the Union of Writers conducted a session that lasted several days in which Boris Pasternak, Yuri Olesha, Boris Pilniak and Isaak Babel had to justify themselves because of Formalism. Sergei Eisenstein had to publicly justify his errors in 1937 as well, mainly because of 'Formalism' in his film *Bezhin lug* (Bezhin Meadow). The Union of Filmmakers even held a three-day-long colloquium on self-criticism for Eisenstein in 1937, following Eisenstein's article from April 1937, published in *Sovetskoe Kino*, with the title 'Oshibki Bezhina luga' (The Error in Bezhin Meadow). The text has the same title as the article published by one of his critics, Boris Shumyatsky, that was previously published in *Pravda* (Shumyatsky 1937).

Parallel to these instances of self-criticism and lay courts in the unions, the state holds a series of secret trials against numerous writers. Among others, writers such as Daniel Charms, Alexander Vvedensky, Osip Mandelstam, Isaak Babel, Sergei Tretyakov and Vsevolod Meyerhold are brought in front of a court and sentenced to labour camps or even shot immediately. All of these secret trials, with the exception of one, were mock trials. By mock trials, I mean those trials that were held on account of a single charge with the purpose of covering up the actual reason for the indictment. This means that writers were not prosecuted because of their writings but because of counterrevolutionary actions (Article 58 of the Criminal Code of the RSFSR), which covers espionage as well as propaganda or agitation that aimed at overthrowing, undermining or weakening the power of Soviet rule or at the committal of single counterrevolutionary crimes. Sergei Tretyakov, for example, was brought in front of a court for espionage. One exception is the trial against Osip Mandelstam. Mandelstam was arrested in 1934 because of a poem directed against Stalin. He '[h]as written a counterrevolutionary pamphlet about comrade Stalin and distributed it among acquaintances at lectures' (Shentalinsky 1995: 228). The examining magistrate was only provided with a transcript of an informer who claimed to have heard the poem at a reading by Mandelstam. At the interrogation, Mandelstam was forced by the examining magistrate to write down the poem in his own hand and countersign it (Shentalinsky 1995: 229). This transcript, together with a copy of it written down by the investigators, is the only remaining document of two and was hidden in Mandelstam's files until the early 1990s, all the while different versions of the text were circulated orally thousandfold. At the hearing, Mandelstam was threatened to have endangered not only himself but also every other person who had heard the poem. Mandelstam had to name every member of the audience, and all of those were now in danger of indictment as well, due to having heard the poem. Mandelstam's trial showcases how two aspects were combined, something which Sinyavsky had also drawn attention to in 'The Trial Begins' – the connection of a religious and of a totalitarian understanding of the word. The notion of sin that is contagious by hearing recalls an idea practiced in Christianity, according to which the hearing of a curse and failure to report it leads to the listener also becoming infected by the evil as if by illness, and, as a carrier of it, thus becoming infectious to others as well. Within the logic of the Stalinist trials of the 1930s, the sinful, contagious word is the word of the defamatory deed.[2]

Performativity and hermeneutics

The equation of words and deeds will have considerable consequences for conceptions of literature in the official discourse as well as for juridical practices. Gorky reacts in his statement on word and deed to one aspect of a conception of literature from the nineteenth century and further accentuates it. In *What is Art?*, a text he worked on during the 1880s and 1890s, Lev Tolstoy summarizes that art is only art if it infects immediately. Tolstoy reduced the role of art to its medial character and thus highlighted the danger of art being contagious. He moreover drew inferences from the author's condition while writing, as readers are supposedly infected with the very feeling the author had during the writing process. Such a conception of literature legitimized censorship, which explains why the representatives of Socialist Realism were interested in Tolstoy in the 1930s. If art can cause immediate deeds, as, for example, the music of Tolstoy's *Kreutzer Sonata* causing a murder, it is also legitimate to surveil its effects. Tolstoy's conception additionally makes it possible to draw inferences about the author as a person – it literally makes him responsible for the effects of his art – while assuming that a universal reader existed. In the proletarian conception of art in the 1920s, there is a revival of Tolstoy's conception: Anatoly Lunacharsky, for example, takes up Tolstoy's theory of infection, in order to elaborate his concept of agitation and propaganda. Already at the beginning of the 1920s, he clarifies the role of infectious art as 'organizing ideas and emotions' (Lunacharsky 1967: 440).

Whereas Tolstoy primarily focuses on a transference of affects, Gorky takes a step forward in the quote above. For him, spoken and written words are not only effective in organizing the recipients' emotions but are also immediately effective. Here, one could come back to the two aspects of performativity Judith Butler distinguishes in her book *Excitable Speech*, following Austin. She differentiates between illocutionary and perlocutionary speech acts. Illocutionary ones perform what they say in terms of content (promising, inviting, requesting, judging, guaranteeing or baptizing) by saying it. As Butler puts it: in the situations at stake, the word does 'not only name, but in some sense … perform[s] and, in particular … perform[s] what it names' (Butler 1997: 43). In this context, the word is instrumental to the accomplishment of a deed, as well as being the action in itself. Perlocutionary speech acts, however, cause effects which do not necessarily have to realize the content of what is said immediately. They lead to certain effects and realities which result from the speech act but which do not realize its content. Austin categorized both types of speech acts as performative utterances whereby illocutionary speech acts are already performative themselves by the act and process of naming.

In totalitarian cultures' understanding of words and deeds, both speech acts concur. In court, this becomes especially obvious. It is hard to mention an example for a trial against literature here since we have no material about the secret trials. Instead I would like to focus on the famous show trial of 1938, in which Nikolai Bukharin was tried and sentenced to death. In the interrogation of Nikolai Bukharin, one can clearly discern the performative status that words had in court during the 1930s. The fact that they were officially provided with this performative status is linked with a change in the juridical practices before show trials were introduced and with the cultural agreement that words are already deeds. In this context, a performative understanding of words comparable to perlocutionary speech acts was at stake. The attorney Vyshinsky elevated the confession, that is, the word, to the status of being the sole means of evidence. From then on, it was no longer necessary to bring forward any other means of evidence in order to reach a verdict. A confession thus outweighed any evidence. Bukharin, on the one hand, tried to reveal what happens if words are granted such power; on the other hand, he wanted to take advantage of it. So what did Bukharin do? He primarily had two strategies: on the one hand, he engages with the performativity prescribed when it seems useful to him; on the other hand, he tries to thwart the principle of a word's immediate effectiveness by setting interpretation and hermeneutics against performativity. Thus, he was affirmative and subversive at the same time. For example, he always affirmed the attorney's concept – he affirmed that what is said is effective. Bukharin for instance said: 'and because Rykov affirmatively talks about them (the facts), I do not have a reason to deny them' (*Sudebny otchet* 1938: 191). He dealt similarly with testimonies: he did not confirm the witnesses' testimonies because of their content but rather confirmed the effect of the speech genre in court: a testimony as well as a confession are performative due to their genre; what has been said is effective. Conversely, Bukharin continually questions particular terms and dwells on the meaning of certain words. In contrast to Vyshinsky, who understandably was not interested in questions of interpretation, Bukharin had a hermeneutic interest. Vyshinsky demanded not to discuss formulations or terms; he even accuses Bukharin of quibbling and regards it as evidence for his conspirative activity. The attorney makes it clear that exegesis and interpretation do not only defy his principle of performativity but are downright criminal.

One can find various analogies to the equation of words and deeds in the totalitarian culture of the 1930s discussed here in Russia's legal history. The legally legitimized analogy of word and deed was already founded in the 1649 *Sobornoye Ulozheniye* (Legal Code).[3] In the *Ulozheniye* of 1845, it is still stated that 'disclosing one's disposition by oral or written articulation of thoughts (alone) is equal to the accomplished act' (Urysohn 1906: 54). Referring to the *Ulozheniye*, Dostoevsky created the probably most well-known document of the indistinguishability of words and deeds in legal history in his novel *The Brothers Karamazov*, which he finished in 1880. The case, described as a juridical error by Dostoevsky and always understood as such, is no error from the perspective of the valid law at the time. It rather takes up the ambivalence of Russian legal rulings, according to which whoever thought and said the deed was already considered a potential culprit. In *The Brothers Karamazov*, the one who thought of the crime and formulated the intention to do it is convicted, while the actual offender, Smerdyakov, who 'only' became this word's minion and the thought's executor, is called into question by the novel as offender.

Against the background of these examples, I do not want to establish a historical context but rather suggest that specific historical agreements in dealing with public speech and the difference between words and deeds have always been in effect and were re-actualized in the 1930s. However, I briefly want to summarize how I understand the relation between words and deeds in the totalitarian culture of the 1930s. We are concerned with a culture embracing the staged performativity of words. The performativity of words was not only claimed but also artistically represented and staged. In almost every novel written in the context of Socialist Realism, one can find reception scenes showing the danger of words and leaving behind shocked or delighted intradiegetic readers. My point is thus not to ask whether there are performative utterances, but to show how a specific historical context was produced in which words were given this status in the first place.

Effect-witnesses

Effect-witness is a term Sandra Frimmel uses in her book on trials against curators and artists in contemporary Russia (Frimmel 2015). It refers to the witnesses summoned in order to testify to art's negative effects, either by drawing on their own experience, or by witnessing effects of art on other people. For the prosecution, the witnesses act as evidence for the word's or image's/painting's performativity. The practice of relying on effect-witnesses also started in the trials of the 1960s in the Soviet Union. It can then also be encountered in other trials of the former Eastern Bloc and is especially prominent in the cases against the organizers of the exhibition *Ostorozhno religiya* ('Caution, Religion' 2005) and *Zapretnoe iskusstvo* ('Forbidden Art' 2010) as well as the case against Pussy Riot in 2012.

In order to illustrate the practice of effect-witnesses, I want to go back to the 1960s. Based on the material of the case against Iosif Brodsky, it can be demonstrated how witnessing an effect by others works. Each witness of the prosecution starts his or her testimony in the trial as follows: 'I do not know Brodsky personally, but ...', or 'I do not really feel comfortable being a witness in this case, as I only got to know Brodsky here, in court' (Varshavsky 1998: 282). These statements refer to Brodsky as a person as well as to his texts. Such ritualized formulations were not new, they were already known from the denunciative statements of the public campaign against Boris Pasternak. Thus, the witnesses do not present themselves as eye- or ear-witnesses of the text from the outset, they have not read it but are witnesses to its effect on others. However, one cannot call them only witnesses by hearsay, because what they testify, the effect of a text, is indeed seen with their own eyes: 'Prosecution witness Nikolaev, retired: "I do not know Brodsky personally, but I have heard of him for the last three years .... I know him for the harmful influence he has on young people. I saw a big book at my son's place – in it, there were several poems. I did not read them, but I can imagine what is written there"' (Varshavsky 1998: 278).

The legal basis for the case against Brodsky was Article 209 of the Criminal Code of the RSFSR (*tuneyadstvo* – parasitism) as well as the enactment 'on strengthening the struggle against persons who avoid socially useful work and lead an antisocial parasitic way of life' by the Presidium of the Supreme Soviet of the RSFSR on 4 May 1961. The conviction to be expected entailed five years of exile and penal servitude in the Arkhangelsk district. So even though parasitism was negotiated in court, witnesses who were supposed to testify to the harmful effect of his poems on young people were summoned. Consequently, evidence that was supposed to condemn his harmful and illegal way of life alone did not suffice, and the accusation was extended to show how this way of life had its effects on the poems and how the poems had the same effects on young people.

In 1976, the prosecution proceeded similarly in the case against the band Plastic People of the Universe in Prague. Sixteen band members were arrested and convicted of 'organized disturbance of the peace' according to Article 202/1, 2 of the criminal code of Czechoslovakia. In the end, six band members were sentenced to imprisonment of between six months and three years. The indictment includes the following: 'Vulgar expressions were the core of the program. The texts had extremely vulgar contents, containing antisocialist and antisocial elements. Most texts praised nihilism, decadence and clericalism' (Amnesty International 1977: 2). Because of only roughly nine vulgar expressions, from sixty-five compositions on behalf of which the defendants were on trial, the prosecution summoned witnesses who were expected to testify to the texts' shocking effects. Among them were very different people, for example adolescents or workers who had visited one of the illegal concerts or had heard about the concerts from others. In the pre-investigation, all of these witnesses confirmed the lyrics' shocking effects. During the trial, the success of precisely this strategy was at risk, threatening the entire lawsuit. Suddenly, most of the witnesses refrained from introducing themselves as 'effect-witnesses'. Thus, a 15-year-old girl reports that she indeed heard an indecent word but that she was not shocked by it. Likewise, a TV employee changed the testimony he had given during pre-investigation: he claims that he was not shocked but only surprised and that he knew other artworks in which vulgar expressions are used. Also, Plastic People's defence attorney used an argumentative strategy that opposed a simple reasoning of effects. He situates the vulgar expressions in the context of carnivalesque popular culture, that is, he argues with Mikhail Bakhtin's book on Rabelais that was translated into Czech shortly before. For his part, Bakhtin argues that vulgar expressions in popular culture do not have destructive, offensive effects but rather have to be considered as part of a culture of laughter determined by playful language. This culture of laughter is said to be self-referential and is thus precisely not directed against others.

The image as deed

According to my observation, the trials of the 1960s in the Soviet Union (but also in other countries of the Eastern Bloc) as well as the lawsuits against artists in contemporary Russia are not only designed to scare by making an example but moreover become the stage to create a valid understanding of literature, in which the belief in a word's performativity is paramount.

In the post-Soviet cases of the 2000s, one can observe that the notion of art's immediate effect pertaining to Socialist Realism is resumed, although no longer as a conception of words but as a conception of images. Thereby, two things are introduced: a return to the understanding of images in Socialist Realism that is at the same time both religious and iconic. Iconic implies that 'each reproduction is a likeness of the original image of equal value; also digital copies are not considered inferior, but their contents are regarded as being of the same value' (Frimmel 2015: 214). According to Lotman, the iconic notion of the image is based on an iconic understanding of signs in which the expression appears as an image of the content, so to speak. Both share a relation of analogy and the expression is only a materialization of the content. If the expression or the representation were alienated, this would also imply an alienation of the content and in this sense would not only be considered a deviation, but also a heresy (Lotman 1981: 151–71).

During the time of the Soviet Union, it was primarily writers who were put on trial. In the 2000s, it is primarily artists and curators working with religious symbols or exhibiting such artworks. All the trials of the last ten years in which artworks were brought before court referred to Article 282 of the Criminal Code of the Russian Federation according to which 'actions aimed at the incitement of national, racial, or religious enmity' are punishable. All cases presuppose the consent that art can be immediately effective – that images can insult, humiliate, incite hatred and that images can cause shocks or even traumata. All trials were designed to prove the immediate effectiveness of images and to demonstrate this effectiveness through the trials themselves performatively.

The first lawsuit against the artist Avdej Ter'Oganjan in 1998 was carried out because of religious hatred, the latest one against the activists of Pussy Riot because of hooliganism. According to Frimmel (2015), a new or old notion of art should once more be established via the court.

In the 2000s, however, the use of effect-witnesses becomes a real business. While we are concerned with resentful and shocked visitors of the exhibition in the first large case against the curators of 'Caution, Religion', the witnesses in the case against the exhibition 'Forbidden Art' are actually recruited and casted in a media campaign. After initiating an investigative procedure against the curators Andrei Erofeev und Yuri Samodurov, which came about because of prefabricated/pre-formulated letters of complaint written by religious citizens, the organization 'Defence of the People', which had triggered the whole thing, called upon all *neravnodushnye* (sympathizers) a second time to volunteer as witnesses in the case 'Forbidden Art':

> The investigations in the case of the exhibition 'Forbidden Art 2006' have now begun ... We request all sympathisers to participate as witnesses. The investigations are conducted by Evgeny Evgenevich Korobkov, who expects

> everyone willing to testify at the address of the district attorney of Tagan... Not only those who visited the exhibitions, but also those who are indignant at the works shown can appear as witnesses. (*Sledstvie po delu vystavki* 2007)

In the trials, these recruited people in fact appeared as witnesses. Their answers are schematic and constantly seek to stress that the art works had a shocking, in some cases even traumatic, effect. Two examples may suffice. In the case against the curators of the exhibition 'Forbidden Art', the witness Smakhtin, an advisor of a small insurance agency, testified the following: 'I cannot remember, I was so shaken and shocked by what I saw that I cannot remember' (*Dopros Smakhtina* 2004: 4). The witness Garbuzov, an employee of a construction company, stressed: 'The exhibition itself and all that followed took a lot of strength and caused great moral harm to me. Huge damage, I would even say, damage which cannot be made up for. I can say that an ulcer (a cancer) burst open and then damage was inflicted on me, great, significant damage ...' (Dopros Smakhtina 2004: 8) The witnesses suffered emotional, moral and health damage, and they gave evidence of the harmful effects of the images/paintings by means of their own condition. The art's possible effects were confirmed by 'psychological juridical opinions'. Here is an excerpt from a psychological juridical opinion given in the 'Caution, Religion' trial (2005):

> The authors of the exhibits create an image (a likeness) of Christ and thereby try to distort the image of religion and Christianity in public. This is an attempt to change the observer's worldview by means of shocking and provoking representations and to force him to doubt the religious and moral foundations of society's order, the family, his character and the integrity of his mental values. The process... increasingly and clearly reinforces its negative psychological effect and stimulates cultural and moral or psychological shock reactions.... The visitors of the exhibition were exposed to the strongest and most extreme impacts on their psyche while observing the exhibits mentioned. These impacts constitute a direct threat to their personality as a whole and threaten to destroy their worldview, which resulted in an experience traumatic for their psychological constitution. They also represent a strong stress factor causing insurmountable moral anguish and stress, as well as feelings of humiliation and indignity. (Slobodchikov 2008: 14)

The last quote reveals that the iconic notion of the image does not need to be created, it is already postulated as existing. The expert even presupposes the iconic idea of the images. Consequently, the judicial proceedings do not discuss the limits of art by using religious material. The experts of the prosecution and the prosecutor do not mention the interpretability of the images. The use of the effect-witnesses prevents the discussion about art.

Yet the trials not only have the purpose to re-establish a religious idea of art but also to modify and to tighten the law. In 2013, the Russian Duma passed a new law that generally forbids any use of religious symbols. The blasphemy law allows for prison sentences of up to three years for those who offend Russian citizens' religious feelings.

Notes

1 We have to bear in mind that this trial only seemed necessary because writers like Sinyavsky were pushing for freedom of expression by *tamizdat* (publishing abroad) or by *samizdat* (self-publishing) and that the state overall was losing its institutional and ideological grip on the cultural fields. There arose a polarity between a state-sponsored subfield with its material and symbolical gratification of political loyalty on the one hand and a defiant subfield based on artistic merit and political disloyalty on the other. (I'd like to thank Matthias Meindl for the discussion on this point.)

2 In 1938, Mandelstam is convicted a second time, this time because of counterrevolutionary actions, in a secret mock trial. The verdict was five years of hard labour (Kolyma), and on 27 December 1938 he dies in a hospital barrack of a transition camp and is buried in a mass grave.

3 The *Sobornoye Ulozheniye* was a legal code promulgated in 1649 by the Zemsky Sobor under Alexis of Russia. The code was used up to 1849, when its articles were revised.

References

Amnesty International (1977), *ČSSR 1976. Junge Kunst unter Anklage*, Bonn: Amnesty International Publications.

Butler, J. (1997), *Excitable Speech. A Politics of the Performative*, New York: Routledge.

Dopros svidetelya obvineniya Nikolaia Smakhtina (2004), Moscow 15 November (unpublished typescript).

Eisenstein, S. (1937), 'Oshibki *Bezhina luga*', *Sovetskoe Kino*, 17 April.

Frimmel, S. (2015), *Kunsturteile. Gerichtsprozesse gegen Kunst in Russland nach der Perestroika*, Wien etc.: Böhlau.

Fülöp-Miller, R. (1926), *Geist und Gesicht des Bolschewismus*, Zürich etc.: Amalthea.
Ginzburg, A. (1967), *Belaya kniga po delu A. Sinyavskogo i Ju. Danielya*, Frankfurt/ Main: Possev.
Gorky, M. (1935), 'Pis'mo k M. Slonimskomu', Literaturny *sovremennik*, 6: 113.
Grüttemeier, R. and T. Laros (2013), 'Literature in Law: *Exceptio Artis* and the Emergence of Literary Fields', *Law and Humanities* 7(2): 204–17.
Lotman, Y. (1981), 'Zeichen und Zeichensystem in Bezug auf die Typologie der russischen Kultur', in Y. Lotman, *Kunst als Sprache*, 151–73, Leipzig: Reclam.
Lunacharsky, A. (1967), 'Osnovy chudožestvennogo obrazovaniya', in A. Lunacharsky, *Sobraniye sochinenij v vosmi tomach*, vol. 7, 438–74, Moscow: Khudozhestvennaya literatura.
Marx, K. and F. Engels (1948), *Ausgewählte Schriften in zwei Bänden*, vol. I, Moscow: Verlag für fremdsprachige Literatur.
Shentalinsky, V. (1995), *Raby svobody. V literaturnykh arkhivakh KGB. Babel, Bulgakov*, a. dr., Moscow: Parus.
Shklovsky, V. (1930), 'Pamjatnik nauchnoj oshibke', *Literaturnaya gazeta* 4(41), 27 January: 1.
Shumyatsky, B. (1937), 'Ošibki *Bežina luga*', *Pravda*, 17 March.
Sledstviye po delu vystavki 'Zapretnoe iskusstvo – 2006', Moscow 20.11.2007, available online: http://maponz.info/index.php?option=com_content&task=view&id=1010&Itemid=9 (accessed 8 April 2013).
Slobodchikov, V. (2008), *Psichologicheskaya ekspertiza po ugolovnomu delu № 402588*, Moscow, 5 May (unpublished typescript).
Solomon, P.H. Jr. (1996), *Soviet Criminal Justice under Stalin*, Cambridge etc.: Cambridge University Press.
Sud nad pornografiej v literature: Diskussiya ustr. mestkomom pisat. 17 noyabrya 1925 g. v Dome Pechati nad proizved. A. Volzhskogo 'Druzya po Volge' (1926), Moscow.
Sudebny otchet po delu antisovetskogo 'Pravotrotskistkogo bloka' (1938), Moscow.
Terc, A. and A. Sinyavsky (1992), 'Sud idet', in A. Terc and A. Sinyavsky, *Sobranie sochinenij v dvuch tomach*, vol. 1, 251–312, Moscow: Start.
Urysohn, I. (1906), *Das Verbrechen des Hochverrats im russischen Strafrecht*, Breslau: Schletter.
Varshavsky, J. (1998), 'Protokol vyezdnogo zasedaniya Dzerzhinskogo naradnogo suda po delu I. A. Brodskogo, obviniennogo v tuneyadstve', in J. Brodskij, *Tvorchestvo, lichnost, sudba*, 274–82, Sankt Petersburg: Zhurnal Zvezda.

Part Two

Change of Rules? The Challenges of Defamation and Religion

7

Literature Losing Legal Ground in Germany? The Case of Maxim Biller's *Esra* (2003–2009)

Ralf Grüttemeier

In 2007 the highest German court, the *Bundesverfassungsgericht* (*BVerfG*), had to decide on upholding the ban on the novel *Esra* by the established German writer Maxim Biller. Biller had published his debut *Wenn ich einmal reich und tot bin* (Someday, When I am Rich and Dead), a collection of short stories, in 1990, at the age of thirty, and *Esra* was his second novel (Weidermann 2006: 283–8). For the 4,000 readers who bought the first edition in 2003 in the days before it was banned, paratextually the book must have seemed Biller as usual. *Esra* was brought onto the market by Biller's regular literary publisher, Kiepenheuer & Witsch, the subtitle was 'novel' and on the back of the cover a single sentence could be read: 'Is love the last Utopia?' The book was indeed the story of an unhappy love affair between a young writer, Adam, and a woman with a Turkish migrant background, Esra, who had a daughter, Ayla, from a broken marriage. This relationship is described in the novel with all quarrels, sex and conversations in detail:

> When she took my dick into her hand, I touched her between her legs. We stayed like this for a while, but then moved quickly to the large room and undressed. I undressed completely, she kept on her shirt, and we kneeled – facing each other – on the bed and kept on caressing each other. Never before, let alone in the last months, when she was so distant because of Ayla's illness, had we been so close. We were closer than when we would have been sleeping together, the hand on the genitals of the other was like an instantly fulfilled promise, like a connection that can never be broken. It went on like this for a long, a very long time, but not in the way it sometimes is when one wants to force an orgasm. When we came – we came nearly at the same time – Esra sighed very loudly and beautifully. (Biller 2003: 70; my translation)

The only paratextual signal that might have caused second thoughts was a short sentence at the end of the book: 'All characters and actions in this novel are fictional. Any resemblance to persons living or dead is entirely coincidental and not intended.' Biller's former girlfriend and her mother did not agree. Their most obvious argument was that the book talked about the 'alternative Nobel Prize' – the Right Livelihood Award – which Esra's mother received (Biller 2003: 9), while in the novel Esra herself had won a German film award, the 'Bundesfilmpreis', as a 17-year old for her role in a movie (Biller 2003: 50) – which was true for both plaintiffs in real life. The same also went for the serious illness of the daughter mentioned in the quote above – an illness that Esra and her mother had tried to hide from Ayla and which the daughter of Biller's former girlfriend had heard about only after the novel had been published.

The plaintiffs saw in this novel a violation of their personal reputation, as did the courts, resulting in a ban on the book. Finally, the verdict was confirmed by the *BVerfG* in 2007, with five to three votes. There was strong criticism from different sides surrounding the final judgement. In the most substantial book on the trial by a literary critic, Uwe Wittstock came to the conclusion that the constitutional court had restricted the rights of literature in an unacceptable way and warned that already *trying* to prosecute literature had a devastating public effect to the disadvantage of literary freedom (Wittstock 2012: 7, 65). Wittstock's view is typical for the majority of criticizing voices from the literary field. Similar ideas were articulated by literary scholars who had intervened during the trial with reports on behalf of Biller and the publisher, such as Astrid Ohmer and Michael Ansel (cf. Bunia 2007: 162; Wittstock 2012: 73, 81). Shortly before the verdict the literary scholar York-Gothart Mix and the lawyer Christian Eichner had sent a substantial report – on their own initiative – to the president of the *BVerfG*. They held that the ban on the book by the *Landgericht München*, the *OLG München* and the *Bundesgerichtshof* (*BGH*):

> in the end runs contrary to any critique of contemporary society and continues the tradition of a restrictive interpretation of the law that is not compatible with the ideal of an open society. It puts into question the civilized and constitutional basic values that have been written down in positive law with the *Grundgesetz* from 1949 against the background of historical experience. (Eichner and Mix 2007: 9)

For them, the banning of *Esra* obviously constituted a serious rollback of the freedom of literature, implying even a possible opening of the door that the German constitution had tried to close in 1949. This presentation must be seen, too, against the background of similar cases in Germany at the beginning of the twenty-first century when lower courts had banned Birgit Kempker's *Als ich das erste Mal mit einem Jungen im Bett lag* (When I was in Bed with a Boy for the First Time) in 2000 and *Meere* (Seas) by the established author Alban Nicolai Herbst in 2004, because former partners had opposed what they saw as a too intimate presentation of themselves in the novels. Even if not all literary warnings were as dramatically staged as the one by Eichner and Mix, it can be held that a majority of voices from or close to the literary field saw the banning of *Esra* as reducing the freedom of literature in Germany.

This view was not limited to *literary* professionals, as the involvement of Eichner already indicated. Also two of the dissenting judges at the *BVerfG* – Hohmann-Dennhardt and Gaier – claimed in their minority report that by the majority verdict 'the freedom of art was restricted in an intolerable way' (*BVerfG* 2007: 110). They agreed with the reports by Ohmer, Ansel and Eichner/Mix explicitly (*BVerfG* 2007: 110–124; cf. Wittstock 2012: 99). A similar general claim was made by the third dissenting judge, Hoffmann-Riem, who held: 'Anything that has the claim of being fiction, cannot affect the personal rights of others.' (*BVerfG* 2007: 147) This view was also defended in some juridical dissertations (Riedel 2011; 132; Bülow 2013: 163, 131). There were also other juridical concerns brought into the debate, both before and after the verdict of the *BVerfG* (cf. Ladeur and Gostomzyk 2004: 434; Lenski 2008: 282). An indirect confirmation for these concerns is the growing number of dissertations trying to concretize the guidelines of the *BVerfG* with detailed schemes of risk-weighing (cf. Neumeyer 2010; Borutta 2013).

In my paper, I will argue quite the opposite of what the literary criticism summarized above has claimed. First I will put the 2007 verdict into a broader historical and institutional frame,[1] followed by a comparison with the *BVerfG* judgement on literature from the 1971 trial confirming the ban on Klaus Mann's novel *Mephisto* (1936) from the perspective of *exceptio artis* and theories of literature. In conclusion, I will try to give some explanation for the criticism on the verdict and discuss briefly where the judicial dealings with literature might go in the future.

The *exceptio artis* in German law and jurisdiction

The constitutional frame for judicial dealings with literature in Germany today is Article 5, paragraph 3 of the constitution from 1949, the *Grundgesetz*: 'Art and science, research and teaching are free.' The freedom of art is granted by the constitution in an unconditional way, which is different from other basic rights. The constitution explicitly states (cf. Art. 5, para. 2) the limits to freedom of speech as being where it clashes with existing laws – a restriction absent from the paragraph on the freedom of art. But how can the courts nevertheless ban a book that was seen by everyone as literary art?

When looking into the drafting of Art. 5, para. 3 after the Second World War, one cannot find much information. There are hardly any indications of what the legislator, the *Parlamentarische Rat*, had in mind when giving art such a special status within the constitution. No remarks are made concerning a possible absolute freedom of art in the documents, neither in the preparation nor in the parliamentary debates (Oettinger 1981: 182). This could be an indication that the legislator did not intend much revolutionary change while writing Art. 5, para. 3. Indeed, in the Weimar constitution of the German Republic from 1919 a similar law can be found, stating in Art. 142: 'Art, science and its teaching are free. The state protects them and takes part in their development.' As far as I can see, this was internationally the first time that the protection and freedom of art was made part of a constitution, and also in this case there were no explicit legal restrictions made in the law. But again, the discussions around the framing of the constitution do not indicate that something special and new was aimed at.

In fact, there was broad consensus within the Weimar Republic that this freedom did not mean that individual artworks were immune to juridical restrictions; it was primarily the institutional freedom from state interference that was guaranteed by the constitution (Anschütz 1960: 658 *passim*). This is confirmed by the fact that basically not much change can be seen when comparing the rulings on artworks before and after 1919. Trials against writers or artists, also against established ones, were held on the basis of the laws of pornography or blasphemy, and the artist did definitely not win in all cases (cf. Lieb, *infra*), even though the Weimar Republic is deemed to be relatively tolerant towards the arts compared to neighbouring countries (Petersen 1995: 285). The benevolent tradition concerning the arts seems to have already gotten its jurisprudential shape in the nineteenth century (Hütt 1990: 13), when for instance an 1893 verdict of the highest German court, the *Reichsgericht*, acknowledged a special status to art (cf. Knies 1967: 148 *passim*). From the second half of the nineteenth century onwards the German judiciary took into consideration the possibility that art can transform violating utterances in such a way that the charges may be judged differently compared with the same utterances in non-artistic discourses. This legal convention can be conceptualized as *exceptio artis* – that is, art exemption that can guarantee an extra degree of freedom and protection for art and literature compared with referential speech acts. However, this autonomy is only a relative one and definitely not an unconditional situating of art outside the domain of possible legal restrictions (cf. Beekman and Grüttemeier 2005, 63ff.; Grüttemeier 2007).

It is within this context of a relative autonomy of art and literature that the 2007 verdict of the *BVerfG* must be situated, too. The freedom of art is not unlimited in Germany. It finds its restrictions in other fundamental constitutional laws. When two or more of these rights collide, the *BVerfG* has to find a balance. In the *Esra* case the freedom of art (of the writer and publisher) clashed with the general personal rights (Art. 2, para. 1 and Art. 1, para. 1 of the constitution) of the two women who recognized themselves in the novel: 'A solution can only be found in weighing the one against the other, in order to do justice to both basic constitutional rights' (*BVerfG* 2007: 85). Whatever one may think about the intersubjectivity of jurisprudential weighing, the quote gives no signal whatsoever that the court tried to undermine what can be conceptualized as the more than 100-year-old legal tradition of *exceptio artis* in Germany giving to arts and literature an especially protected status.

Taking an overview over juridical dealings with literature since the nineteenth century, it seems that the special protection of art and literature in Germany is relatively stable and has not undergone dramatic changes, at least if one leaves the period 1933–45 out of consideration.[2] More particularly, much of the criticism quoted above seems to mistake specific judgements on specific literary texts for institutional foundations, that is to say: taking accidentals for structures. To put the same argument in the words of Bernd W. Seiler (1983: 247): 'Not the individual verdict is decisive for the restriction that personal rights lay upon the freedom of art; decisive are the leading principles that have founded the verdict.' Even if there were any changes triggered by the 2007 verdict, they are most likely slight ones, given the high specific weight of the established juridical tradition of the *exceptio artis* in democratic Germany over the last century. So, were there any relevant changes? In order to answer this question, I will compare the two last benchmark cases of the *BVerfG* regarding literature, the 1971 *Mephisto* case and the 2007 *Esra* case, providing the guidelines for the judicial dealings with literature in Germany since the Second World War.

Mephisto vs. *Esra* – increasing or decreasing the institutional autonomy of literature?

Klaus Mann's novel *Mephisto*, published in exile in the Netherlands in 1936, narrates the career of an opportunistic careerist in Nazi Germany, Hendrik Höfgen. Höfgen's character in the novel was inspired – to say the least, most see it as a *roman à clef* – by the actor and theatre director Gustaf Gründgens. Gründgens had been a friend of Klaus Mann but had stayed in Germany and in fact made a career in the world of theatre under the Nazi regime – and in Germany after the war. When, after the death of Gründgens in 1963, the novel was about to be published in West Germany for the first time, Gründgens' heir successfully tried to prevent this by claiming that the novel would damage Gründgens' reputation and violate his human dignity guaranteed in Art. 1 of the constitution. The appeal court (*OLG*) in Hamburg banned the novel in 1966, and the *BVerfG* in effect confirmed the ban with a 3:3 draw on 24 February 1971.

In its judgement, the *BVerfG* left no doubt that *Mephisto* fell under what the constitution tried to protect in Art. 5, para. 3. However, 'such a piece of art does not only have an aesthetic reality, but additionally an existence among real objects. These connections to reality are artistically transformed, but they do not lose their effects upon social reality' (*BVerfG* 1971: 1646f.). These social effects are conceptualized by the court 'next' to (*neben*) the domain of art (cf. *BVerfG* 1971: 1647). Therefore, when dealing with art, the judiciary must neither exclusively look at the social effects nor only at the aesthetic domain: both sides have to be weighed against each other. The *BVerfG* acknowledged that the courts had taken both sides into account and could not find sufficient reasons to contradict in the end the judgement that Klaus Mann had given 'a negative misleading portrait' of Gründgens (cf. *BVerfG* 1971: 1648).

This verdict was accompanied by two dissenting votes, of which in our context the one by Erwin Stein is especially interesting. Though the *BVerfG* did acknowledge that *Mephisto* was literature and therefore treated the text in a way that was meant to be adequate for literature, Stein maintained it had not sufficiently done so. The crucial point for him was not that he denied art an existence *in* and an effect *on* reality. But he insisted that also the artwork's ties to reality should be conceived primarily from an aesthetic point of view: 'The artistic presentation therefore cannot be measured against the world of reality, but only against criteria that are specific for art and aesthetics' (*BVerfG* 1971: 1649). In other words: what Stein did not plea for was an absolute autonomy in which being art meant per definition the impossibility of having a judicially relevant effect in reality. This was for him a question of degree and of domination, as it had been for the majority. What he did oppose, however, was the 'one-sided' view of the majority focusing on the 'real' resemblances and differences between Höfgen and Gründgens as if these could be seen and weighed as isolated findings. The majority conception of art and literature was one in which the reality dimension of art was seen as being 'next' to the aesthetic one – while for Stein they were not 'next' to each other but transformed into an 'inseparable union' (*BVerfG* 1971: 1649) – and therefore could not be treated in 'realistic isolation'. This is not the same as saying that novels could not have a – legally relevant – effect on reality. Judging the novel from this viewpoint, however, Stein could not see that the personal rights of Gustaf Gründgens were violated by publishing *Mephisto*.

The 1971 majority vote on *Mephisto* has been the leading case for German judicial dealings with literature for quite some decades, including the one on *Esra* of the *Bundesgerichtshof* (*BGH*) in 2005. When the *Esra* case came before the *BVerfG*, however, the judges not only took a very principled, programmatic stand on arts and literature. They also turned away from some of the views of their predecessors. One of the most striking differences was that the judges in 2007 explicitly and consentingly referred to the dissenting judge from 1971, Stein, with his quote given above: 'The artistic presentation therefore cannot be measured against the world of reality, but only against criteria that are specific for art and aesthetics (cf. dissenting vote Stein)' (*BVerfG* 2007: 83). As we have seen, on a scale between treating literature as factual discourse on one pole and treating literature as not related to judicial reality at all on the other, Stein had shifted what he regarded an adequate treatment of literature more in the direction of the latter. By taking over Stein's view, the *BVerfG* made the same move. Furthermore, this move is not an isolated event at the top of jurisdiction, but obviously had been prepared by jurisprudential discussion in which, in the meantime, the dissenting vote by Stein was now regarded as the 'right, maybe even nowadays ruling opinion', as Bernard von Becker (2006: 78) claimed in an essay on the *Esra* case one year before the verdict of the *BVerfG*. From our perspective, this is a strong indication for what seems to be a growth of the relative autonomy ascribed to literature by judicial rulings since the 1970s in Germany, consecrated by the *BVerfG* in 2007. And there are others, pointing in the same direction.

The most obvious one is the second of the four guidelines (*Leitsätze*) that the *BVerfG* placed at the top of its verdict. In it, the necessity of looking at a novel in a way *adequate for art* – we might add: *sensu* Stein – was translated into the guideline that the starting point when reading must be that the literary text is fictional (*eine Vermutung für die Fiktionalität eines literarischen Textes, BVerfG* 2007: Leitsatz 2). This implies that the court had in mind an educated, mature (*mündig*) reader who can distinguish between a report on what really happened and fiction (*fiktive Erzählung*). Such a competent reader of fiction starts with the presumption that the text in question does not claim to present facts (*keinen Faktizitätsanspruch erhebt*) (*BVerfG* 2007: 84), as the court later explains more explicitly in its verdict. The effect of this presumption and guideline is significant: in fact, it comes down to a shift on whose shoulders the relevant argumentation is burdened. When the starting premise while reading fiction is 'this is not about truth claims', then it must be convincingly argued whether and why this specific fictional text destroys that premise, if a collision with other constitutional rights seems to be at stake. *In dubio pro ficto*, one might summarize.

The effect of the judicially new fiction premise regarding novels can be demonstrated regarding the plaintiff who had recognized herself in the character of Lale, the mother of Esra in the book. All previous rulings on *Esra*, including the one of the *BGH* in 2005, had concluded that the novel violates the personal rights of this plaintiff, too. The reasons were that the mother in the novel, Lale, is clearly recognizable in reality ('alternative Nobel Prize'), and that Lale is presented in a very negative way – among others, as a selfish, greedy alcoholic and dictator cheating on insurance and allying with the mafia. However, recognizability together with a negative presentation in the novel does not already outweigh the freedom of art given by the constitution, the *BVerfG* states. What would be needed against the background of the fiction premise was the proof that the text tried to convince the reader that parts of what was described were facts, and, in addition, exactly those parts had to seem factual which were protected by the personal rights guarantee of the constitution (*BVerfG* 2007: 99), as for example the disclosure of intimate sexual preferences. For the *BVerfG*, this was not the case concerning Lale in the novel, mainly because the judges saw her character as part of a complex literary presentation of the motive of 'guilt' (for Esra's and I/Adam's breaking up) (cf. *BVerfG* 2007: 96). Another reason given by the court for its judgement was that the information on Lale in the novel was mostly not first-hand observation of the narrator (I/Adam) but narrative recycling of other sources in the novel, telling the reader something about Lale (cf. *BVerfG* 2007: 97).

The introduction of the fiction premise is a strong indication that the protection of literature is increased by the 2007 verdict of the *BVerfG*, making it even harder for courts to find that literature violates other constitutional rights. This tendency is strengthened by the court's third guideline stating that artists have the right to take any person from reality as a source of artistic transformation (*BVerfG* 2007: Leitsatz 3). So it seems that the institutional autonomy of literature within the law has reached an even higher degree in 2007, compared with the *Mephisto* case from 1971.

Evidence pointing in the same direction, though more circumstantial from the perspective of this article, comes from the civil trial in which Biller was sued to pay damages to his former girlfriend for violating her personal rights, after the banning of the novel had been confirmed by the *BVerfG*. The *BGH* judged principally and finally on 24 November 2009: 'Therefore, in general, a violation of personal rights that has already caused a banning directed against the artist, weighed against the right of artistic freedom, will not lead to damage fees to be paid by the artist in addition' (cit. Wittstock 2012: 119).

However, such a gradual change must be not be confused with claims that come close to absolute autonomy for (real) art. There is a clear difference between the 2007 verdict and the views of some legal and literary experts who want to exempt art from any 'weighing' against other constitutional values or from the reach of the judiciary in general (cf. von Becker 2006: 10; Eichner and Mix 2007: 31; Wittstock 2012: 127), seeing any prosecution of art as a conceptual fault of the legal system (von Becker 2006: 54). The 2007 verdict strengthened relative autonomy of literature, not absolute autonomy.[3]

Institutional autonomy and poetical fallacy

A possible explanation why many legal and literary scholars obviously do not agree on the line drawn above might be found to some extent in a lack of a broader historical perspective on the matter. The fact that literature 'lost' the *Esra* case (or any singular case) does not say much about the degree of institutional autonomy. This degree can only be assessed over a longer time span and from a systematic perspective comparing the historically specific shape of legal parameters – in the first place the *exceptio artis*. As far as the protesting literary critics and scholars are concerned, their reaction makes sense when looked at from a field theoretical perspective. The protest can be explained not only as defending their own professional specialization (cf. Seiler 1983: 308) but also as a reaction to the fragility of the autonomy of the literary field between the state and the market (cf. Sapiro 2003). Accordingly, the protests against actions of the field of power concerning literature can be taken as an indicator for the degree of relative autonomy of the literary field (cf. Bourdieu 2011: 220) – but these protests should not be mistaken for an analytic description of the relationship between the judiciary and literature.

A similar conceptual warning might be useful when looking at another parameter that has played an important role in the trials and the related debates, although it is rarely addressed explicitly: theories of literature. When dealing with the arts, the courts generally do not see it as their task to define what art is and what art is not, let alone to define what good and what poor art is. But since they have to deal with art, they cannot avoid taking a stand on it, however implicitly and reluctantly they might do so. Concerning literature, a representative and telling poetical position was taken for example in the *Mephisto* trial:

> In this situation it must be taken into account, whether and in how far the 'image' ('Abbild') – compared to the 'original' ('Urbild') – through the artistic transformation ('künstlerische Gestaltung') of its material and its integration and subordination into the whole organism of the work of art ('Gesamtorganismus des Kunstwerks') has become a thing of itself in such a way that the individual, the personal and intimate has been transcended objectively towards the general, semiotic dimension of the 'character'. (*BVerfG* 1971: 1647)

With this conception of art and literature, the *BVerfG* places itself in the tradition of a poetics in which the concept of transformation ('Gestaltung') plays a central role: the function of this artistic principle is a metamorphosis of the empirical, accidental reality of the everyday into something more general – a deeper, higher or more real reality – within the organic unity of the work of art or literature. With this conception of art and literature, the *BVerfG* places itself in a tradition of what can be called idealistic aesthetics (cf. Bürger 1983), playing an important role in western art theory reaching from Plato via Immanuel Kant's *Kritik der Urteilskraft* and George Lukács' *Theory of the Novel* (1971) to Hans-Georg Gadamer's *Wahrheit und Methode* (1960) and further. In the juridical context, the idealistic transformation aesthetics has been dominant in German jurisprudence throughout the nineteenth and twentieth centuries (cf. Knies 1967: 148ff.). A clear indication for the latter claim is that the quote above from 1971 based on 'transcending' can be found literally in the verdicts on *Esra* of the *BGH* and of the *BVerfG* (2007: 83).

However, it is important to add that this transformation is conceptualized as a question of degree by the courts. The *BVerfG* leaves no doubt about this when speaking in the last of its guiding principles ('Leitsatz 4') of the degree (*dem Maß*) to which the author creates an aesthetic reality that is set free from everyday reality. Working out this gradual concept of aesthetic transformation, the *BVerfG* continues: 'The more image and original coincide, the more judicially relevant is a violation of the personal rights. The more the artistic presentation touches upon the especially protected domains of the personal rights, the stronger must be the fictionalization in order to prevent a violation of the personal rights' (*BVerfG* 2007: Leitsatz 4; cf. 2007: 85, 90).

The concept of literature underlying these reflections is one in which literature has a certain poetic autonomy but only a gradual one in which the court has to distinguish between degrees of fictionalization and reference to reality. And it is exactly this gradual concept that many critics of the 2007 verdict were opposed to. The judges Hohmann-Dennhardt and Gaier for example claim in their dissenting vote that fact and fiction cannot be distinguished in a work of art at all: 'their relationship cannot be measured in degrees' because art is not a special way of looking at reality, but makes 'own worlds' from reality (*BVerfG* 2007: 113). This view is corroborated by explicitly referring to the German philosopher of critical theory, Theodor W. Adorno: 'For everything concerning form and material, spirit and content that is in the works of art has migrated from reality into them and in them has left reality completely behind' (*BVerfG* 2007: 124). From this point of view, the poetic autonomy given to art and literature is an absolute one, leading to something that is 'purely aesthetic' (cf. Lenski 2008: 28) and has no intersection with everyday reality at all since it is a world of its own. Art is from this point of view the 'Other' and 'parallel' to reality (*ein aliud*) and therefore cannot violate personal rights, as Eichner and Mix (2007, 33; cf. von Becker 2006: 10, 67) phrase it in the report they offered to the *BVerfG*. They themselves here use – without explicit reference – the same terminology as the dissenting vote by Rupp-von Brünneck from 1971 (cf. *BVerfG* 1971: 1654). Eichner and Mix (2007: 30) underline their view with the Adorno quote which the judges Hohmann-Dennhardt and Gaier have taken over literally in their dissenting vote. To look at art and literature this way probably would have found the consent of writers such as Oscar Wilde or Samuel Beckett – but it is probably not how 'engaged' writers from Multatuli or Emile Zola via Bertolt Brecht or Jean-Paul Sartre up to Heinrich Böll, Günter Grass or Dave Eggers would describe their novels. How influential – at least in Germany – the absolute autonomistic views of Adorno and the *Frankfurter Schule* may have been from the 1960s onwards, in the end they are no more (and no less) than a possible answer to the question 'what is literature?'.

In other words: the judges Hohmann-Dennhardt and Gaier quote a particular theory of literature containing normative ideas on the nature, the function and the qualities of literature. They defend a specific poetics. In the end, this is a normative and arbitrary choice, even if it is legitimized through a renowned German aesthetical theorist. From a historical and systematic perspective on poetics, one could describe Adorno's and others' plea for absolute autonomy of literature as being part of the objective tradition *sensu* Abrams (1971), while the transformation view of the idealist tradition in jurisprudence as quoted above gives room to mimetic, pragmatic, expressive and also objective traditions of literature, as long as they do not try to completely cut the ties that bind them to the judiciary. So there clearly is a poetic conflict at stake in and around the courts.

The conflict however is not only a question of different tastes and different poetic preferences. What is especially striking is that the difference worked out above was nowhere explicitly conceptualized in terms of theories of literature or as a normative poetic battle between different positions in the literary field and in the field of literary scholarship. The introduction of the problem by Eichner and Mix in their report is telling: they do not deny that there is a passionate debate in literary scholarship about what literature is. Nevertheless they claim that there is something like a 'minimum consensus' (Eichner and Mix 2007: 4) in the scholarly debate. It comes as no surprise that this consensus equals their poetics. But what is surprising is that they present their views as 'ontological and epistemological' scholarly fact: it is from this point of view that they criticize the *BVerfG* majority for making 'structural mistakes' and ignoring what they see as the 'standard of general knowledge of art theory' since the 1960s (Eichner and Mix 2007: 30). In other words: they present their poetics as generally shared scholarly knowledge – dismissing differing poetics as not up to date; ignoring differing scholarly views on the matter (Nickel-Bacon, Groeben and Schreier 2000, cf. Bünnigmann 2013: 166–8); and disguising poetics as consensual expertise.

If these twists in the argument of the literary experts had a strategic dimension, it was to a certain extent successful. For Hohmann-Dennhardt and Gaier, judging a novel such as *Esra* from a juridical perspective needs the expertise of literary scholars. They themselves do so by explicitly taking over parts of the two reports the publishing house delivered (by Ohmer and Ansel) and parts of the report by Eichner and Mix, including the Adorno quote, and present them as scholarly consensus (*einhellige Meinung*, cf. *BVerfG* 2007: 122–3). This way, they fall into the same poetical fallacy as Eichner and Mix. They mix up poetics with scholarly consensus[4] and that confusion seems to me another important explanation for the criticism of the *Esra* verdict quoted above. It could account for the fierceness of the opposition as well as for the impossibility to solve questions that are in the end normative questions, for which there is no intersubjective scholarly solution – in these matters, there is only choice, based on taste and poetic preferences regarded as legitimate by specific experts at a specific point in history.

Let me add one last aspect that makes the situation even more complex. Part of the poetical fallacy of the dissenting judgement in this judicial context is, as we have seen, the linking of two different kinds of autonomy, that is, poetical and institutional, by concluding that since the world of the artwork is poetically absolutely autonomous, whatever is written in such an artwork therefore cannot be referential and therefore cannot be held liable for any violation of laws. This fusion is legitimized with reference to scholarly literary expertise, suggesting, as we have seen too, that the majority of judges in the *Esra* judgement does *not* rely on literary expertise (cf. Hohmann-Dennhardt and Gaier in *BVerfG* 2007: 122; Hoffmann-Riem in *BVerfG* 2007: 149, 150; Wittstock 2012: 91, 97). But is that so?

Surely it can be agreed that the majority did not make explicit use of the three reports offered to the court nor did it make use of any explicit reference to literary scholars at all. However, there are at least some indications of a conceptual homology between the judges responsible for the majority verdicts of the highest German courts on the one hand and parts of the literary academic elite on the other. Firstly, this homology can be seen in the field of poetics in which the idealist aesthetics offers common ground for experts on both sides, as we have seen above. When Peter Bürger (1983) still deemed it worthwhile to write a principled critique of the idealistic aesthetics in the 1980s, one can state at least that this conception of literature and art is, also among literary scholars, still taken seriously, since it is worthwhile fighting against for some scholars.

There is more interference on the part of the legal and the literary elites, since the *BVerfG's* analytical tools for the interpretation of literature seem to have quite some affinity with structuralist criticism. On its way of approaching literary texts in a manner even more adequate for art as articulated in the 2007 majority verdict, the *BVerfG* had already mentioned in 1987 the necessity to look at the 'specific characteristics and structural properties' (*BVerfG* 1987: 2661) of works of art. In tune with these structuralist signals are the arguments we already summarized above. In the *Esra* case, the *BVerfG* (cf. 2007: 96, 97) came close to structural criticism for example by analysing the literary motive of 'guilt' and by delivering a sophisticated differentiation between narration (who speaks) and focalization (who sees, cf. Bal 1994: 100–14), both with regard to the literary structural function of the character Lale within the novel as a whole. It is difficult to imagine that this judicial judgement was not informed at all by literary scholarship.

However, due to the lack of explicit references in parts of the judgements, it would take a complex network analysis in order to find out whether and how exactly the homology between the elites of the legal and the literary field were shaped in the last decennia. It seems not unlikely that this analysis might reveal a complex constellation of alliances of parts of the respective elites in both fields, with legal scholars using specific literary expertise to legitimize the position they take in the legal debate. Compared to the first half of the twentieth century, the present homology however turns out to be a more segregated and contested one, given the prominence of dissenting scholarly views.

Conclusion

One can conclude that from a field theoretical perspective, the protest against the *BVerfG* verdict on *Esra* has little descriptive and analytical value. First of all, it seems to ignore the level and the relative stability of institutional autonomy granted to literature by the field of power through law and jurisprudence at the beginning of the twenty-first century in Germany. The introduction of the *exceptio artis* into the German jurisprudence in the second half of the nineteenth century can be seen as the consecration of the view of the political and legal elites that art was something that deserved special freedom and care in order to develop its specific potential for the general good of the state (cf. Grüttemeier 2007: 180–4). The relative stability of that view in the field of power can be inferred from the German constitutions of 1919 and 1949, in which the freedom of art was explicitly guaranteed.

Furthermore, there are indications of a growth of institutional autonomy, at least in the last decades. This relative growth, though neither linear nor teleological, has led to a constellation in Germany where the level of protection of literature in defamation trials in Germany seems to be higher than it was in the 1970s. These developments go along with an increasing presence of absolute autonomy claims for literature, also among legal experts in the last decades. I would not know of any examples for the acceptance of this claim before 1945 by legal experts, but already three of the eight judges in the *Esra* case seem to be willing to give complete freedom in legal terms to literature with regard to personality rights (cf. *BVerfG* 2007: 123, 147) – at least as long as the text is not just falsely pretending to be literature.

The debates around the banning of *Esra* also have a poetic dimension, which is closely connected to institutional autonomy. It turned out that the critics of the *BVerfG* often adhered to a conception of literature that claims absolute poetic autonomy (*aliud*, parallel world, etc.) for literature and instrumentalized this poetical autonomy in order to legitimize institutional autonomy of literature within judicial rulings. In doing so, many of the voices criticizing the *Esra* verdict present poetic preferences as common scholarly knowledge. Not differentiating between autonomy from an institutional and from a poetic perspective and also not differentiating between poetics and scholarly knowledge lead to what can be called the poetical fallacy of many debates on the judicial dealings with literature in Germany since the 1960s, a fallacy not only literary but also legal scholars have fallen into. It seems to me that the academic and societal debate in Germany on legal trials dealing with literature might profit if scholars in both disciplines – law and literature – would take into account these conceptual differentiations more systematically and if they would do so from a historical perspective.

Notes

1 For a general international comparison of personality right and artistic freedom see Ohly, Lucas-Schloetter and Beverley-Smith (2008).

2 Research into this period would be especially interesting though, since in 1938 the *Reichsgericht* still argues in tune with the *exceptio artis* when it bans Josef Winckler's novel *Der Großschieber*. The juridical reason for the ban was that the

name and the 'Dr. h.c.' title of the hero coincide with that of a living person. But the judges do not want to make a rule out of this name-based banning because otherwise the freedom of the writer would be restricted in an unacceptable way, they held (cf. Seiler 1983: 243).

3 This is what most juridical experts seem to think of the 2007 verdict, too, (cf. Helle 2013: 473, 479), including the dissenting Hoffmann-Riem (cf. *BVerfG* 2007, 125).

4 The same disguising of poetics as scholarly consensus can be observed in the criticism of some libel cases by the legal experts Ladeur and Gostomzyk (2004: 431f.). After having asked a poetic question ('What is specific for literature?') they answer by turning to 'basic knowledge' of literary scholars (*literaturwissenschaftliche[s] Basiswissen*), though without giving detailed references. But after half a page they illustrate their argument by saying that the same view is articulated by many literary authors, quoting Nabokov ('Literature is always invention .... Who calls a story true, insults art and truth at the same time.' – *my retranslation*). This tendency to take a specific, normative theory of literature for a general definition or even the 'essence' of literature or art (*Wesensmerkmale*) seems to be widespread in legal scholarship (Neumeyer 2010: 115, 206; Riedel 2011: 58, 132; Bülow 2013: 21, 28, 163).

References

Abrams, M. H. (1971), *The Mirror and the Lamp. Romantic Theory and the Critical Tradition*, Oxford: Oxford University Press.

Anschütz, G. (1960), *Die Verfassung des deutschen Reichs vom 11. August 1919.* Nachdruck der Ausgabe von 1933, Darmstadt: Wissenschaftliche Buchgesellschaft.

Bal, M. (1994), *Narratology. Introduction to the Theory of Narrative*, Toronto: University of Toronto Press.

Beekman, K. and R. Grüttemeier (2005), *De wet van de letter. Literatuur en rechtspraak*, Amsterdam: Atheneum-Polak & Van Gennep.

Biller, M. (2003), *Esra.* Roman, Cologne: Kiepenheuer & Witsch.

Borutta, S. K. (2013), *Der realistische Roman*, Baden-Baden: Nomos.

Bourdieu, P. (2011), *The Rules of Art. Genesis and Structure of the Literary Field*, trans. S. Emanuel, Cambridge: Polity Press.

Bülow, K. S. (2013), *Persönlichkeitsverletzungen durch künstlerische Werke*, Berlin: Duncker & Humblot.

Bunia, R. (2007), 'Fingierte Kunst. Der Fall Esra und die Schranken der Kunstfreiheit', *Internationales Archiv für Sozialgeschichte der deutschen Literatur*, 32: 161–82.

Bünnigmann, K. (2013), *Die „Esra"-Entscheidung als Ausgleich zwischen Persönlichkeitsschutz und Kunstfreiheit. Rechtsprechung im Labyrinth der Literatur*, Tübingen: Mohr Siebeck.

Bürger, P. (1983), *Zur Kritik der idealistischen Ästhetik*, Frankfurt/M.: Suhrkamp.

BVerfG, Urteil des Bundesverfassungsgerichts, 24 February 1971, *Neue Juristische Wochenschrift* 1971(37): 1645–55.

BVerfG, Urteil des Bundesverfassungsgerichts, 3 June 1987, *Neue Juristische Wochenschrift* 1987(42): 2661–5.

BVerfG, Urteil des Bundesverfassungsgerichts, 13 June 2007, 1 BvR 1783/05, 1–151, available online: http://www.bverfg.de/entscheidungen/rs20070613 (accessed 23 October 2014).

Eichner, C. and Y.-G. Mix (2007), 'Ein Fehlurteil als Maßstab? Zu Maxim Billers Esra, Klaus Manns Mephisto und dem Problem der Kunstfreiheit in der Bundesrepublik Deutschland', available online: http://www.literaturkritik.de/public/Mix-EichnerLang.pdf (accessed 23 October 2014).

Gadamer, H.-G. (1960), *Wahrheit und Methode: Grundzüge einer philosophischen Hermeneutik*, Tübingen: J.C.B. Mohr (Paul Siebeck).

Grüttemeier, R. (2007), 'Law and the Autonomy of Literature', in G.J. Dorleijn, R. Grüttemeier and L. Korthals Altes (eds), *The Autonomy of Literature at the* fins de siècles *(1900 and 2000)*, 175–92, Leuven: Peeters.

Helle, J. (2013), 'Der Schlüsselroman und „Esra"', *AfP. Zeitschrift für Medien- und Kommunikationsrecht*, 44: 470–9.

Hütt, W. (ed.) (1990), *Mit den Unzüchtigkeits- und Gotteslästerungsparagraphen des Strafgesetzbuches gegen Kunst und Künstler 1900–1933*, Berlin: Henschel.

Knies, W. (1967), *Schranken der Kunstfreiheit als verfassungsrechtliches Problem*, München: Beck.

Ladeur, K.-H. and T. Gostomzyk (2004), 'Ein Roman ist ein Roman ist ein Roman?', *Zeitschrift für Urheber- und Medienrecht*, 48: 426–36.

Lenski, S.-Ch. (2008), 'Grundrechtsschutz zwischen Fiktionalität und Wirklichkeit – Zum "Esra"-Beschluss des BVerfG', *Neue Zeitschrift für Verwaltungsrecht*, 27: 281–3.

Lukács, G. (1971), *The Theory of the Novel*, trans. A. Bostock, Cambridge, MA: MIT Press.

Neumeyer, J. (2010), *Person-Fiktion-Recht. Verletzungen des Persönlichkeitsrechts durch Werke der fiktionalen Kunst*, Baden-Baden: Nomos.

Nickel-Bacon, I., N. Groeben and M. Schreier (2000), 'Fiktionssignale pragmatisch. Ein medienübergreifendes Modell zur Unterscheidung von Fiktion(en) und Realität(en)', *Poetica*, 32(3–4): 267–99.

Oettinger, K. (1981), 'Kunst ohne Schranken? Zur juristischen Interpretation der Kunstfreiheitsgarantie des Grundgesetzes', in M. Fuhrmann, H. R. Jauß and W. Pannenberg (eds), *Text und Applikation. Theologie, Jurisprudenz und Literaturwissenschaft im hermeneutischen Gespräch*, 179–98, München: Fink.

Ohly, A., A. Lucas-Schloetter and H. Beverley-Smith (2008), 'Artistic Freedom versus Privacy – A Delicate Balance. The *Esra* Case Analysed from a Comparative Law Perspective', *IIC* 39(5): 526–57.

Petersen, K. (1995), *Zensur in der Weimarer Republik*, Stuttgart and Weimar: Metzler.
Riedel, M. (2011), *Vermutung des Künstlerischen. Der Esra-Beschluss des Bundesverfassungsgerichts – eine rechts- und literaturwissenschaftliche Untersuchung*,Tübingen: Mohr Siebeck.
Sapiro, G. (2003), 'The Literary Field between the State and the Market', *Poetics*, 31: 441–61.
Seiler, B. W. (1983), *Die leidigen Tatsachen. Von den Grenzen der Wahrscheinlichkeit in der deutschen Literatur seit dem 18. Jahrhundert*, Stuttgart: Klett-Cotta.
Siegle, M. (2012), *Das Spannungsverhältnis von Kunstfreiheit und Persönlichkeitsrecht. Zur Problematik der Darstellung realer Personen in Kunstwerken*, Baden-Baden: Nomos.
Von Becker, B. (2006), *Fiktion und Wirklichkeit im Roman. Der Schlüsselprozess um das Buch „Esra". Ein Essay*, Würzburg: Königshausen & Neumann.
Weidermann, V. (2006), *Lichtjahre. Eine kurze Geschichte der deutschen Literatur von 1945 bis heute*, Köln: Kiepenheuer & Witsch.
Wittstock, U. (2012), *Der Fall Esra. Ein Roman vor Gericht. Über die neuen Grenzen der Literaturfreiheit*, Köln: Kiepenheuer & Witsch.

8

Defamation Trials in Belgium – The Case of Herman Brusselmans's Novel *Uitgeverij Guggenheimer*

Katharina Hupe

In December 2000, the Belgian author Herman Brusselmans was ordered by an Antwerp Court (*Rechtbank van Eerste Aanleg*) to pay damages to the sum of 100,000 Belgian Francs (about 3,000 US dollars) for defamation of the renowned Belgian fashion designer Ann Demeulemeester through his novel *Uitgeverij Guggenheimer* (Publisher Guggenheimer). This verdict brought to an end legal proceedings that had started more than one year previously when Demeulemeester successfully applied for a preliminary injunction banning the novel by the Appeal Court of Antwerp (*Hof van Beroep van Antwerpen*).

The novel had been published on 17 September 1999, constituting the third volume of a series about the fictitious media tycoon Guggenheimer. In the first two volumes – *De Terugkeer van Bonanza* (The Return of Bonanza, 1995) and *Guggenheimer wast witter* (Guggenheimer Washes Whiter, 1996) – Guggenheimer had already gained fabulous wealth in the movie and advertising business, respectively. In the third volume he decides to enter into the publishing business with the declared objective to establish the most successful publishing house in Belgium and to fill the first three places of the bestseller list with books from his own house. To this end, he starts with quite drastically getting the most successful writers of rival publishers out of his way: Hugo Claus, Monika van Paemel and Jef Geeraerts – all names used in the novel are identical with those of the most prominent writers of the time in Flanders – followed by promoting his own writers in very unorthodox ways. In no time, Guggenheimer manages to found the most successful publisher in Belgium. Along the way, he has enough time for sex with all the women he desires, as all women desire Guggenheimer – among them beautiful young Belgian VIPs who share the names of real Belgian celebrities such as Katia Alens, Joyce de Troch and Sabine de Vos.

Likewise the plaintiff, Ann Demeulemeester, is called by her real name in the novel four times. Two of the relevant passages led to the claim. In the first one, Guggenheimer derogatorily talks about Ann Demeulemeester with his driver and casual killer Jules:

> The bitch that has fitted these rags with cut and seam, she should be executed by firing squad. What's her name again? Damn, her name slips my mind, how is that possible, I was in bed with that chick someday. Such a dwarf gnome with frog eyes and hairs from her twat to her back. I would call her name a thousand times if I wouldn't have forgotten it. Hold on a minute, I remember! Ann Demeulemeester! Yes, indeed .... Of course, buddy. Brown stripes. And her tongue full of holes from swallowing needles by accident when edging and sewing the hems. That's not good for giving blowjobs, I can assure to you. Gee, this Ann Demeulemeester. (Brusselmans 1999: 42)[1]

A similar combination of disdain for Demeulemeester's professional qualities and her physical and sexual attractiveness also characterizes the second incriminated passage in which Guggenheimer, after having had sex with the ex-Miss Belgium Ilse de Meulemeester, wonders:

> 'So, so... Meulemeester... so, so,... Actually, are you related to this other bunch of bones, what's her name... Ann Demeulemeester? This skyrocketing fashion designer of coutureless black rags, for which chichi women pay usury prices without any valid reason? Is that your aunt, even if she looks like your uncle with a carnival wig? Or is she your sister?' 'Eh... no... we are not family.' 'Suppose you are right. You don't resemble her at all. Your tits are in front and Demeulemeester's tits are on the back. Now for something completely different. Do you read a lot?' (Brusselmans 1999: 54–5)

The fashion designer felt personally insulted through these passages and filed a lawsuit against Brusselmans. The fact that the established writer Brusselmans, who had launched his novel as a satire, was convicted in the end is remarkable, especially since literature seems to have been granted a relatively high degree of judicial protection in Belgium (compared to France or the Netherlands for example) since the end of the nineteenth century. The trials in 1900 against the famous writers Camille Lemonnier (the so-called 'Marshall' of Belgian literature) and Georges Eekhoud on grounds of violation of morality had both ended with an acquittal. Lemonnier had been prosecuted for his novel *L'Homme en amour*

(Man in Love, 1897) which contains realistic descriptions of the protagonist's sexual life. Eekhoud had taken issue with homosexuality in his novel *Escal-Vigor* (1900) as one of the first Belgian writers. Not only were they acquitted: Eekhoud and Lemonnier even were the last authors prosecuted at a Belgian Court for violation of morality in their literary writings (cf. Fredericq 1951: 85; De Zegher 1973: 7).

This borderline of institutional literary autonomy was in fact not crossed by several judicial obscenity proceedings at the end of the 1960s. For example, the well-known trial against Hugo Claus – mentioned above as one of the figures Guggenheimer had to get rid of – was not about his text *Masscheroen* but about staging three naked men (impersonating, by the way, the Holy Trinity) in a theatre performance. This trial ended with the confirmation by the highest Belgian Court (*Hof van Cassatie*) of a four-month prison sentence for Claus on conditional discharge (Hupe and Grüttemeier 2014). In the same period, the novel *Gangreen I. Black Venus* by Jef Geeraerts was confiscated. Later, this measure turned out to be a mistake in the course of a proceeding against a dubious bookseller and Geeraerts's novel was quickly put back onto the shelves (cf. Grüttemeier 2013). Therefore, one can hold that concerning the offence of violation of morality, there have not been any trials incriminating literature for more than 100 years. From an institutional perspective, this indicates a relatively stable *exceptio artis* in the sense of a relative institutional autonomy (*sensu* Bourdieu) for literature in Belgium.

However, concluding from the Brusselmans case, one might wonder whether something has changed in recent years, at least concerning the offence of defamation, since this case was not the only one of its kind. Around the same time, literature was subjected to court proceedings when Dimitri Verhulst's mother felt offended by the description of an 'incredibly fat mother' in Verhulst's autobiographical debut novel *De kamer hiernaast* (1999, The Room Next Door) and filed – in this case: unsuccessfully – a lawsuit against her son (*Gazet van Antwerpen*, 28 August 1999).[2] Are these defamation trials an indication for a rollback concerning the degree of institutional autonomy of literature in Belgium? In what follows, the Brusselmans trial shall serve as a case study to answer this question, especially since it can be regarded as representative and since it is relatively well documented. More specifically, the degree of institutional autonomy acknowledged by judges and lawyers in relation to the Brusselmans case will be explored and to what extent different theories of literature had an impact on the proceedings.

The ban on the novel

Brusselmans's friend and fellow author Tom Lanoye found plain words concerning the action against Brusselmans: 'If the argument is that Ann Demeulemeester felt harmed commercially by the book, we cross a border. Then I could likewise take legal action against any negative review of my books' (*De Standaard*, 2 November 1999). Obviously, Lanoye supposed that Demeulemeester simply was afraid of negative publicity and initiated the proceedings against Brusselmans only for this reason. In addition, he suggests that legal action like that initiated by Demeulemeester would result in a flood of complaints and, implicitly, that the freedom of literature as such would be at stake.

Demeulemeester stated that she did not intend to restrict the right of artistic freedom (cf. Buelens e.a. 2000: 201). Nevertheless, she felt that her personal rights were violated in an unacceptable manner, since artistic freedom may not be used to violate the rights of third parties, regardless of the identity of that party: 'Imagine that a novel's author uses such a language for homosexual or coloured peoples, Jews or immigrants. Would the progressive Flanders in this case still talk about artistic freedom?' (*De Standaard*, 3 November 1999) One might wonder at this point whether the plaintiff actually had read the novel as a whole, as there is a large number of minorities in *Uitgeverij Guggenheimer* not exempted from the rants of the central character. For instance, Guggenheimer employs, mainly for purposes of his own sexual interest, an African servant girl forced to wear a mini-skirt during working hours and prohibited to wear underpants at any time (Brusselmans 1999: 16). Guggenheimer sends away two migrant children with the words 'Go away… to your… mother. She is baking camel. Shoo, away!' (236) and feels disgusted by a homosexual waiter: '"Have you seen," said Guggenheimer, "what in God's name, what kind of gay he is? For bringing his mouth in such a form of glance, he must suck dicks more than daily. My blood freezes in my veins when I think about it"' (81). And although the main character Guggenheimer is himself Jewish, this group is not spared either: 'If I was not a Jew myself, I could easily apply for the Gestapo. Or rather for the SS, because I do look enormously good in uniforms. SS member or Jew, the difference is small' (112). Against the background of these examples and other offensive comments in the novel, it seems not unlikely that other people would also have felt insulted by the tirades of the main character. However, apart from Demeulemeester, no other plaintiffs appeared, although the writer Monika van Paemel at least seems to have considered taking legal action (*De Morgen*, 2 November 1999).[3]

On 28 October 1999, two days prior to the commencement of the annual Antwerp Book Fair (*Boekenbeurs*), Ann Demeulemeester filed an application for a preliminary injunction to prohibit publication of *Uitgeverij Guggenheimer*. The very next day, the judges Snelders, Vanstraelen and Wouters formally granted the injunction and justified the necessity of the prohibition by referring to the upcoming book fair that would lead to a broad and very harmful distribution and publicity of the novel. Therefore, they prohibited the defendant Brusselmans, his publishing houses *Prometheus* and *Standaard Uitgeverij*, the wholesaler *Libridis* and the bookshop *Standaard* from distributing the novel in Belgium 'in today's shape, with the passages which are relevant for this lawsuit and which are related to the plaintiff'. In addition to the prohibition of sales, the judges imposed a fine of 10,000 Belgian Francs for each book that was still available on the Belgian market after the verdict (*HvBA* 1999a: 88).

In their reasoning for the injunction, the judges argued that this case required weighing up the right of free expression (Article 25 Belgian Constitution and Article 10 European Convention on Human Rights)[4] claimed by Brusselmans and the right of privacy (Art. 22 Belgian Constitution and Art. 8 ECHR) of Demeulemeester. The relevant passages on pages 42 and 55 of the novel were, according to the judges, 'very... defamatory' with regard to the plaintiff and formed an offence against the plaintiff's privacy. Therefore, the right of free expression must be subordinated until a verdict was given in main proceedings (*HvBA* 1999a: 88). In other words: in a democratic society, the guaranteed right of free expression is not granted absolutely but, according to the judges, subject to necessary restrictions, such as the protection of the rights of others. In the present case, the judges decided that the right of expression has to give way to 'the protection of the private life of the plaintiff' (*HvBA* 1999a: 87).

After the publication ban not only the judgement but also the proceedings as such were sharply criticized by parts of the press. For example Dirk Voorhoof, professor at the Institute of Communication at the University of Gent, described the trial as a 'dangerous precedent' since the opponent party did not have the opportunity to defend its point of view. Furthermore, he criticized the fact that the judges 'did not have the time to read the book and to consider the passages in the context of the novel in question'. Further, according to Voorhoof, the prohibition of preventive censorship, which is legally established in the Belgian Constitution, had been disregarded (Voorhoof 1999: 10).

Another fundamental criticism of the verdict emphasized that the named characters in the novel were part of a fictional world and thus must not be identified or considered as persons existing in reality. Eric Willems, director of the *Standaard* publisher at that time, stated: 'What is surprising is that this is about fiction. The world of the media is criticized, but no people are attacked. The characters are fictitious .... For us, it is about freedom of writing satire and thereby also about freedom of expression' (*De Morgen*, 2 November 1999). This quote reflects two classic arguments of modern literary defence strategies against lawsuits, especially when defamation is at stake. The first argument refers to the impossibility of identifying characters within fictional worlds with real existing individuals. From that perspective, the character Ann Demeulemeester in the novel does not refer to the real fashion designer and, consequently, the character Guggenheimer does not insult her, but a fictitious character with the same name within a fictional narrative world.[5] The second argument emphasizes the specific genre of the text: satire. According to the publisher, it is usual for satirical texts to imply remarks that could be understood as an insult. But such an interpretation would mean misunderstanding the genre and its specific stylistic features. Seen from an institutional point of view, the publisher claimed an absolute institutional autonomy for insulting expressions in satirical literary texts – a postulation that goes far beyond the relative *exceptio artis* granted in the past.

This defence, by the way, was in line with the image of Brusselmans's texts created by criticism. Brusselmans, who is known as a writing maniac and who had already published twenty-six novels and stories prior to the publication of *Uitgeverij Guggenheimer*, is usually quoted in connection with his colleague Tom Lanoye – 'a versatile Flemish poet, playwright, and prose writer' with an 'undeniable talent as a polemicist and public performer'. Both are denoted as 'rebellious young Flemings' and 'angry young Belgians' whose narratives are harsh social critiques of Flemish reality, often using real names for their fictional characters (cf. Brems 2006: 431, 548; Hermans 2009: 651). But at this point, this was only the literary perspective which was not the one of the judges.

Appeal against the injunction

Following the issue of the ban, Brusselmans and his lawyer immediately appealed against the injunction so the proceedings continued at the Antwerp *Hof van Beroep* (Appeal Court) on 4 November 1999. In this trial, the same judges who had decided on the preliminary injunction were appointed again, and based their considerations on the same premises: the conflict between the freedom of expression and Demeulemeester's right of privacy. To begin with, they stated that Demeulemeester would have 'an indisputable right of protection of her privacy' (guaranteed by Art. 22 of the Belgian Constitution and Art. 8 ECHR). On the other side was Brusselmans's right of expression. But the latter right was 'bound to specific formalities, conditions and sanctions which are necessary in a democratic society, *inter alia* to protect the good name and the rights of others' (*HvBA* 1999b: 91). Against this background, the judges concluded that an 'unscrupulous defamation of people's privacy and their own person… must not be tolerated' (*HvBA* 1999b: 89).

In making their balance, the judges explicitly recognized that they were dealing with a novel that displays 'literary forms' and, for that reason, could be classified as a literary work. However, the judges declared the 'literary forms' of the novel as 'irrelevant… in this specific case, considering the fact that the party Demeulemeester is not a fictitious but an existing person who is named with her full personal and professional identity' (*HvBA* 1999b: 91). The main issue identified by the court was that Brusselmans had not taken any steps to alienate the character and separate it from the identity of the real person. This argumentation suggests that the court's judgement might have been different if the persons were less recognizable. According to the judges, people who exist in reality and appear in fictional texts do not automatically become fictive persons – an argument that is not restricted to legal professionals but also can be found in literary scholarship (Seiler 1983: 206–59). The judges corroborated their view with the argument that Brusselmans himself had declared in interviews that 'everything he wrote about the party Demeulemeester is true' (*HvBA* 1999b: 91).

Against this background, the judges assessed the incriminated passages as 'strongly insulting, offending, scathing and absolutely derogatory towards the person… Demeulemeester' (*HvBA* 1999b: 91). They left no room for doubt that the incriminated passages were not protected by freedom of expression: 'the question can be posed if an author has the right to publicly… violate the personal integrity and privacy of an individual… under the pretext of freedom of expression'. Such violations, '*prima facie* exceed the borderline of what is socially tolerable'. However, the confirmation of the injunction by the judges was explicitly declared as provisional 'in expectation of a judgement in the main proceedings' (*HvBA* 1999b: 91). As a result, the novel remained banned in Belgium for the time being.

Van Overloop and Beeusaert, Demeulemeester's lawyers, expressed their satisfaction with regard to the verdict: 'this is a balancing of interests. One may be in favour of freedom of expression, but at the same time not in favour of letting a bulldozer steamroll oneself' (*De Standaard*, 6 November 1999). Not surprisingly, Brusselmans's lawyer Eric van der Mussele criticized the verdict and did so with heavy fire. According to him, a literary genre such as the polemic of satire was obviously no longer allowed in Flanders: 'Polemic exists since the Middle Ages. However, the truth does not play any role in it.... Polemic is the artistic form by which my client expresses himself' (*De Standaard*, 6 November 1999). He stated, just as Brusselmans's publisher after the injunction, that what may be misunderstood as insults were for someone with knowledge of literary traditions a specific feature of the genre. In sum, the lawyer criticized that neither the context nor the literary character of the text had sufficiently been considered by the court.

Likewise, Brusselmans criticized this fact after the trial. He called the publication ban a 'dangerous precedent' and pointed out that the novel belongs to a genre of fiction: 'It's about literature. About fiction' (*De Nieuwe Gazet*, 5 November 1999). Accordingly, literature could not be compared with reality at all, and hence, literature could not violate existing laws. On the basis of that point of view, Brusselmans and his lawyer implicitly advocate an absolute kind of freedom of expression as they obviously do not consider literature as justiciable – and consequently, no balancing of rights is needed.

A number of artists supported Brusselmans, especially his friend Tom Lanoye, who initiated the petition 'Citizens against censorship' and collected signatures at the Antwerp Book Fair. Among them were famous Belgian and Dutch authors, for example Gerrit Komrij, Remco Campert, Bart Moeyaert and Hafid Bouazza. Even two celebrities who had been referred to by their real names in *Uitgeverij Guggenheimer*, Sabine de Vos and Joyce de Troch, signed the petition and were opposed to the verdict, which they considered a 'serious restriction of the freedom of expression', according to the petition's text (*De Standaard*, 9 November 1999). Generally speaking, many artists presented the verdict to be a threat to artistic freedom.

But even though the publication ban partly caused strong criticism in literary circles, at the same time doubts were expressed about the purely artistic intentions of the author. For example, Fernand Auwera assumed that Brusselmans's intention by using names of famous people was to 'cause a scandal in his own interest because this stimulates the sales of the book'. In addition to these financial interests, Brusselmans was also assumed to have had a personal interest in the use of the name of Ann Demeulemeester. Jef Rademakers held that the only reason why Demeulemeester appeared in the novel was that she had rejected a job application filed by Brusselmans's girlfriend at the time, Tania de Metsenaere. Rademakers assessed the use of Demeulemeester's name as 'very poor revenge' (*De Standaard*, 6/7 November 1999). Actually Brusselmans himself had admitted this private connection some days later in an interview:

> I write while the TV is on, and if I need a host in my book, I simply choose the host who is by chance on the screen. It was the same with Demeulemeester: I was working on around page 40 of *Uitgeverij Guggenheimer* when the news came in that Tania did not get the job. Perhaps this is the reason why I mentioned Ann Demeulemeester. That's just the way it is, chance often plays a role in such things. (*Humo*, 9 November 1999)

Also the aforementioned Hugo Claus had expressed doubts on the pure artistic intention of Brusselmans. Claus – who was also a character in *Uitgeverij Guggenheimer* in which he was brutally beaten up to eliminate him as a competitor of Guggenheimer's publishing house, resulting in Claus's subsequent death in hospital – turned against the ban of the novel. But this did not imply a positive attitude towards Brusselmans's novel: 'To ban books does not make sense. It is stupid and may not be done. But do I thus have to show solidarity with Brusselmans? What Brusselmans has done is easy and idiotic. It cannot be justified' (*De Standaard*, 8 November 1999).

The reactions to the verdicts show that all literary parties, including Brusselmans's lawyer, agreed that literature should not be banned. From a literary institutional perspective, the major part of the protest came down to a plea for an absolute freedom of literature and satire with regard to legal prosecution – an absolute *exceptio artis*. However, even in literary circles, doubts had been raised about the question if the specific book *Uitgeverij Guggenheimer* deserves such protection due to the possibly non-literary motives of the author when writing the incriminated passages (cf. *De Standaard*, 7/8 November 1999). As we will see, this point will play a major role in the main proceedings that still were to come at that moment.

Main proceedings

Some weeks before the main proceedings at the Local Court of Antwerp (*Rechtbank van Eerste Aanleg*), Brusselmans did not sound too optimistic: 'I have a fifty percent chance. If I lose the case, I will leave it at that. In God's name, what the fuck can I still do? But I hope that I will win. For myself. And for literature.' (*De Nieuwe Gazet*, 17 November 2000) The presiding judge I. Schoeters and the judges N. Verschuren and B. Bullynck had to decide on 21 December 2000 about the claim of the plaintiff Ann Demeulemeester who wanted to achieve a definitive ban on the novel *Uitgeverij Guggenheimer* as long as it included the passages she felt were insulting. In addition to the publication ban, Demeulemeester claimed a repeating prohibition so that Brusselmans would not be allowed to insult her in any future works. Each further violation should be levied with a fine of 20,000 Belgian Francs (*RA* 2000: 4). Furthermore, she asked, *inter alia*, for compensation to the sum of 100,000 Belgian Francs from Brusselmans for the damages suffered.

In dealing with this claim, the judges not only considered the formal conditions for the legal action as given – the public availability of the incriminated text – but also the insulting character of the incriminated expressions. This necessary condition for criminal liability was fulfilled since Brusselmans admitted the insulting character himself, as the judges argued: 'Brusselmans does not deny that the accusations with which he expresses a description of the plaintiff through his protagonist Guggenheimer, would be deeply violating and insulting to her. Brusselmans explicitly confesses the insulting nature of his accusations' (*RA* 2000: 7). By this, the judges referred to TV interviews with Brusselmans broadcasted on 31 October 1999 on *tv nieuws Canvas* and on 4 January 2000 on *Programma Spiegels Radio 5 Nederland* in which Brusselmans said regarding the legal action: 'It is about a… fictitious character Guggenheimer who says some unpleasant things about Ann Demeulemeester, which are by the way true…. I mean, she feels insulted, I can… understand it… well, but… the last thing you should do is that kind of thing [i.e. take legal action, K.H.]. That is robbery, you know?'

However, the 'insulting nature' of the incriminated passages was not enough for a conviction. As a further condition for the criminal liability of Brusselmans the judges brought the so-called moral part into play – what one might call with Fauconnet the subjective responsibility or the intent (cf. Sapiro, *infra*). The question was whether the defendant consciously, that means in full knowledge, wanted to insult. The judges considered this condition as fulfilled. They quoted Brusselmans, stating on 4 January 2000 on *Programma Spiegels Radio 5 Nederland* about the lawsuit: 'It is not that simple to insult somebody… to do it well, to do it, firstly, in a way that is beautiful to read and, secondly, to insult in a way that it really hurts…. It really must hurt, yes.' (*RA* 2000: 8)

The judges also referred to an article published in the Belgian weekly *Humo* on 25 April 2000 for their argumentation. In this article Brusselmans had stated: 'I like to insult people in my books. I am also good in blustering, insulting, parodying and polemicizing; it is a literary genre, which I like to practise with some intensity. I will not have lived if I did not hurt, both in reality as well as in writing' (*RA* 2000: 8). In the eyes of the judges, this was a substantial proof that Brusselmans indeed intended to insult Demeulmeester personally. On the other hand, the judges left no doubt that they saw *Uitgeverij Guggenheimer* as a novel and thus as a literary work. They even felt obliged to stress explicitly that 'a literary genre, like polemic or satire, is not a charter to commit a crime' (*RA* 2000: 8) – making explicitly clear that an absolute autonomy is not at stake in Belgium, but confirming at the same time implicitly that they are aware of the literariness of the incriminated text. But did they take this into account in their verdict?

At first sight, there are no indications for an *exceptio artis* in the weighing of private rights and the freedom of expression. The court saw a violation of Art. 448 as proven because 'the formulations used [are] strongly insulting and, according to the first defendant [Brusselmans], used with the intention of really hurting and insulting the plaintiff, it can thus be assumed that the plaintiff suffered a significant moral damage' (*RA* 2000: 9). The court convicted Brusselmans to pay 100,000 Belgian Francs to Demeulemeester, following the claim of her lawyers.

But there was also another side to the judgement. To start with, the court did not follow Demeulemeester's demand to prohibit Brusselmans from insulting her in any further publications because this would constitute 'a prohibited preventive measure', and such censorship would be in conflict with the constitutionally guaranteed freedom of expression (*RA* 2000: 10; De Prins 2001: 1454). While this part of the verdict is no reason to imply an *exceptio artis*, a third dimension of the verdict is at least worth some reflection from this perspective: the judges refused to continue the ban on the novel.

The court's main legal argument on this point is known in Belgian Law as 'cascading accountability' (*getrapte verantwoordelijkheid*, Art. 25 Belgian Constitution). Basically, this means that if the author of an incriminated text is known and if he lives in Belgium, he bears the sole responsibility so that the publisher and distributors of the text cannot be prosecuted. So firstly the author, then the publisher (in the case that the author is unknown or not living in Belgium) and, lastly, the distributor (in that case that the publisher is also unknown or not resident in Belgian) are liable for the text. Thereby, complicity is not ruled out. But usually, only the author is prosecuted (cf. De Prins 2001: 1453; Delbecke 2012: 458).

In this case – and remarkable also for legal scholars (Voorhoof 2000: 4) – the judges turned the argument around. Since Brusselmans had transferred the rights on his novel completely to his publishers, they had to be acquitted because of the 'gradual accountability', and a publication ban could only be imposed on Brusselmans. This specific ban, however, would have very little effect in the given situation, the court held: 'Considering the concrete information from the file, the Court supposes that no publication ban and thus no order to return from sale can be imposed in this case' (*RA* 2000: 11).

What seems contradictory – an insult is judicially proven, but the convicted person is allowed to keep on earning money with his insult – is less so when it is placed into the context of a historically deeply rooted benevolence towards literature in the Belgian judiciary. From this perspective, gradual accountability seems to have been the legal instrument with which the judges could give way to the acknowledged fact that they were dealing here with a literary text from an established literary writer.

There is no explicit confirmation in the verdict for this relatively high degree of protection of literature, but the complementarity of this part of the verdict and the main target of societal criticism articulated concerning the injunction (Claus: 'To ban books does not make sense. It is stupid and may not be done.') is telling.

Furthermore, the reactions to the verdict point in the same direction. While Demeulemeester's lawyer termed the verdict after the main proceedings 'inconsistent' because the judges had not prohibited the relevant passages (*De Standaard*, 22 December 2000), Brusselmans's lawyer Eric van de Mussele expressed satisfaction: 'The verdict is reasoned. The court is of the opinion that Demeulemeester really got insulted. But the claim, that the relevant passages should be deleted, did not make any sense. They had already been published in several newspapers' (*De Standaard*, 22 December 2000).

The Belgian legal scholar Dirk Voorhoof, who had criticized the publication ban after the provisional injunction, also spoke about a 'reasoned judgement', because Brusselmans has liberated his insults from their context by himself. Thereby, the court did not even have to consider the novel's literary context and the fact that the insults were spoken by a literary character (Voorhoof 2001: 4).

Conclusion

Looking over the Brusselmans trial, the conflict between the freedom of expression regarding literature – the *exceptio artis* – and the legal protection from insult, referred to by all the judges involved in the legal actions, can be described as a complex balancing act that shows no signs of a principled turn away from the relative *exceptio artis* in the Belgian judiciary.

First of all, the judges continue to consider literature as societally valuable and deserving a special legal protection, which in principle also applies for *Uitgeverij Guggenheimer*. On the other hand, the judges are not willing to accept insulting statements 'under the cloak of freedom of expression' or of art (*HvBA* 1999b: 91). In this case, they had doubts about the pure artistic intention of the author, to say the least (and not only the court had these doubts). However, that does not at all imply a rollback of the existing institutional autonomy of literature in general. That the high degree of protection for literature – literature's relative autonomy within the judiciary, if you like – is still stable becomes clear from the fact that the judges lifted the publication ban after the main proceedings.

The same conclusion can be drawn from the controversial reactions to the legal proceedings. They can be divided into two levels. From an institutional point of view it can be seen that almost all Belgian artists protested against the proceedings in principle and that many artists considered the legal intervention a danger to their artistic autonomy. According to Bourdieu, the fierceness of these protests can be taken as an indication for a high degree of institutional autonomy of the literary field at that time: the stronger the protests, the higher the degree of institutional autonomy of a field (Bourdieu 1999: 349). In this case, the protests against the ban were indeed massive and widespread, as we have seen.

On a second, individual level, the reactions were more ambivalent and the support for Brusselmans was much lower. The same principled protesters against any threat to artistic freedom expressed doubts whether the poetics of Brusselmans in general and especially *Uitgeverij Guggenheimer* was what they wanted to fight for. Hugo Claus was already quoted as exemplary in that regard, but one might also refer to Dimitri Verhulst: 'Of course, censorship is unacceptable… but the book by Brusselmans is an unfortunate occasion to hold a successful debate' (*De Morgen*, 9 November 1999; Meuleman 2000: 83).

Concluding, there is no sign of a rollback of institutional autonomy for literature within the Belgian judiciary at the turn of the last century. This autonomy basically seems solid over the whole twentieth century, leaving aside the times of occupation 1914–18 and 1940–45. However, while obscenity is no longer an opponent that can remind literature of the relativity of its autonomy, defamation is, at least for the time being. Still, the relatively small number of literary defamation trials and the generally careful handling of these cases by the courts structurally indicate mainly one thing from my perspective: a relatively high degree of institutional autonomy for literature in Belgium, independent from the form of accusation.

Notes

1 All translations are mine, except indicated otherwise.

2 For reasons of clarity of presentation, the articles from dailies and weeklies – often anonymous and with very similar titles – are not integrated in the references section. They are traceable by the reference to the name of the periodical and the date given after the quote.

3 There also has been a complaint of the television host and ex-Miss Belgium Lynn Wesenbeek (and her husband), which was apparently discontinued in the further course of the proceedings. Information about this legal action is rare (cf. *De Standaard*, 2 November 1999). After the trial in 1999, the former *Libelle*-editor Suzanne Mastbroek also accused Brusselmans, because he would have called her a 'moronic bitch' (cf. *De Standaard*, 5 October 2000; *Gazet van Antwerpen*, 5 October 2000), but without juridical consequences.

4 Artistic freedom in Belgium is not explicitly mentioned in Belgian law but is subsumed under the freedom of expression, as in a number of countries as the Netherlands, France or the US (Schmidt 2012: 195).

5 Consequently, this view implied that Brusselmans couldn't be judged at all for statements within his fictional worlds. Georges Eekhoud used such an argument in the trial around his novel *Escal-Vigor* in 1900. There, he required that 'the author is not responsible for the speech and actions, which he gives to his characters.' In 1952, also the Dutch writer W.F. Hermans used this argument in his personal statement during his trial because of insulting passages in his novel *Ik heb altijd gelijk* (I am always right). Both claims did not have any juridical success (Beekman and Grüttemeier 2005: 101).

References

Beekman, K. and R. Grüttemeier (2005), *De wet van de letter*, Amsterdam: Athenaeum – Polak & Van Gennep.

Bourdieu, P. (1999), *Die Regeln der Kunst*, Frankfurt: Suhrkamp.

Brems, H. (2006), *Altijd weer vogels die nesten beginnen*, Amsterdam: Bakker.

Brusselmans, H. (1999), *Uitgeverij Guggenheimer*, Amsterdam: Prometheus.

Buelens, G. e.a. (eds) (2000), *De militanten van de limiet. Over censuur en vrije meningsuiting*, Leuven: Uitgeverij van Halewyck.

Delbecke, B. (2012), *De lange schaduw van de grondwetgever. Perswetgeving en persmisdrijven in België (1831–1914)*, Gent: Academia Press.

Fredericq, S. (1951), 'L'art devant le droit pénal', *Journal des Tribunaux*, 82–5.

Grüttemeier, R. (2013), 'De omgang van de rechtspraak met literatuur in België aan de hand van Jef Geeraerts' Black Venus', *Spiegel der Letteren* 55: 35–49.

Hermans, T. (2009), *A Literary History of the Low Countries*, Rochester, NY: Camden House.

Hupe, K. and R. Grüttemeier (2014), 'Vier maanden gevangenis voor de Drievuldigheid bloot. Hugo Claus' toneelstuk *Masscheroen*', in R. Honings, L. Jensen and O. van Marion (eds), *Schokkende boeken!*, 73–80, Hilversum: Uitgeverij Verloren.

HvBA (1999a), Hof van beroep te Antwerpen, eerste kamer, 29 October 1999 (1999/EV/74), *Auteurs & Media* 1: 87–9. Available online: www.brusselmans.be (accessed 23 July 2014).

HvBA (1999b), Hof van beroep te Antwerpen, eerste kamer, 4 November 1999 (1999/AR2890), *Auteurs & Media* 1: 89–92. Available online: www.brusselmans.be (accessed 23 July 2014).

Meuleman, B. (2000), 'De zelfkruisiging der kunsten', in G. Buelens e.a. (eds), *De militanten van de limiet*, 77–83, Leuven: Uitgeverij van Halewyck.

Prins, Dajo de (2001), 'De burgerlijke rechter en de persvrijheid', *Rechtskundig Weekblad* 39: 1445–56.

RA (2000), Rechtbank van eerste aanleg te Antwerpen, 21 December 2000, De Meulemeester t/Brusselmans A.R. (1999/6.882/A), *Auteurs & Media* 1 (2000): 271–6. Available online: www.brusselmans.be/2000_12_21_Brusselmans.pdf (accessed 23 July 2014).

Schmidt, C. (2012), *Rechtsnatur und Verpflichtungsdichte der Europäischen Grundrechte*. München: Herbert Utz Verlag.

Seiler, B. W. (1983), *Die leidigen Tatsachen. Von den Grenzen der Wahrscheinlichkeit in der deutschen Literatur seit dem 18. Jahrhundert*, Stuttgart: Klett-Cotta.

Voorhoof, D. (1999), 'Brusselmans en de rechter', *De Standaard*, 2 November: 10.

Voorhoof, D. (2000), 'Wat na het verspreidingsverbod van „Uitgeverij Guggenheimer"?' *Samenleving en politiek* 7(4): 36–40.

Voorhoof, D. (2001), 'Vonnis Brusselmans beter dan boek', *Juristenkrant* 22: 4–5.

Zegher, J. de (1973), *Openbare Zedenschennis*, Gent: E. Story Scientia P.V.B.A.

9

Libellous Literature: Elton John and the Perils of Close Reading

Peter D. McDonald

There are many reasons for studying literature's entanglements with the law. The most engaging, in my view, has to do with the fact that there is no way of telling how to distinguish literature from other kinds of writing either *a priori* or *a posteriori*. Like many artefacts of human endeavour – democracy, say, or Europe – literature does not constitute an object of knowledge as such. It is not a relatively stable *thing*, which we can learn to identify in the way we learn to distinguish Porsche 911s from other cars or African from Indian elephants. This is not news. The idea that literature cannot be defined once and for all had become a theoretical orthodoxy by the 1970s and 1980s, though, as I have argued elsewhere, the emphasis then tended to be placed on the problems associated with *a priori* definitions (McDonald 2006). The philosopher of art Arthur C. Danto summarized the mainstream view in the following characteristic terms: 'the concept of art [or literature] is not like the concept, say, of cat, where the class of cats do pretty largely resemble one another, and can be recognized as cats more or less by the same criteria' (1999: 7). Few theorists had much to say about the potentially greater challenges of *a posteriori* definition. On this account, literature is not simply an object of theoretical *debate*, perhaps even a quarrel, which, as a matter of principle, can never be resolved. In its most ambitious modes, it is also a self-reflexive, protean cultural *practice*, which often puts established protocols of understanding under extreme pressure, calling for different ways of thinking and new kinds of reader. Whether seen from an *a priori* or an *a posteriori* perspective, these definitional problems create acute difficulties for the law at the level of codification and judicial procedure.

The history of state censorship, which details the repeated failures of the state and its officials to have the last word on literary matters, is essentially an archive of these problems. In the late 1980s, towards the end of the censorship era in apartheid South Africa, the writer J.M. Coetzee put it this way: censors have been 'so ineffectual, century after century', he said, 'because, in laying down rules that stories may not transgress, and enforcing these rules, they fail to recognise that the offensiveness of stories lies not in their transgressing particular rules but in their faculty for making and changing their own rules' (1988: 3). This is a rare statement of the *a posteriori* quandary. Yet it is not only censors, the traditional enemies of literature, for whom this more radical offensiveness creates difficulties. As a peculiarly disruptive form of public writing literature is no less of a problem for its defenders, particularly those who turn to the law for help. The challenges they face were well articulated in the late 1970s during a UK government enquiry into the effectiveness of the Obscene Publications Act, 1959, the legislation that explicitly incorporated an *exceptio artis*, or literary defence, into the Westminster statute book for the first time. Among other things, it afforded literature protection as a public good and authorized courts to call upon literary experts to testify on its behalf. Here, the state is no longer the 'bad' censor but the 'good' guardian of the literary. To put it in the Bourdieuian terms Ralf Grüttemeier and Ted Laros have recently used, we could say that the 1959 Act constituted an important landmark in the 'institutional autonomy' of literature in England and Wales in so far as it reflected a high degree of 'societal acceptance of the literary field within the field of power' and recognized that 'only literary specialists could evaluate literature' (2013: 205, 210). This is broadly true, though, as my own study of the original Victorian statute of 1857 and its initial implementation shows, the possibility of a literary defence was built into UK obscenity law from the start (McDonald 2008). The 1959 Act simply made that largely dormant defence more explicit and robust.

The problems associated with the state's well-meaning intervention on behalf of literature were soon apparent, however. The product of a concerted campaign in the 1950s, the new defence itself became the focal point of a further protest in the 1960s and 1970s, which eventually prompted the government to establish the commission of enquiry led by the philosopher Bernard Williams. Bearing in mind the temporary ban under the 1959 Act of Hubert Selby's controversial novel *Last Exit to Brooklyn* (1966), the commission remarked about the literary defence:

> It is not surprising that [the Act] has been criticised as elitist in conception, and as saying in effect that corrupting books are to be permitted so long as they are

> admired by professors. This criticism is largely unjust, but it hits at a basic fault in the Act, its absurd model of the role of expert opinion with regard to artistic or literary merit. The model is not so much elitist, as scholastic: it implies an informed consensus about merit which, for each work, already exists. In the real world, new works have to find their own way, and see whether they elicit appreciation or not. No one may know, for some time, what to think about them. It is not just a matter of the *avant-garde*: works in some despised medium or style may subsequently turn out to have had more meaning than most experts would have originally supposed (Williams 1979: 110).

The underlying scholasticism of the 1959 Act was exacerbated by the fact that it required the experts to establish, *as a matter of evidential proof*, whether a particular work might warrant exemption on the grounds of merit or, indeed, literariness. Given that such questions inevitably involve a long, uncertain process of cultural debate, which, from the theorists' point of view, would be inconclusive in principle, the commission argued that the 'public good' defence was 'misconceived' and recommended lifting all restrictions on the 'printed word' (Williams 1979: 126, 160). Books with illustrations were another matter. The only viable way of protecting the 'institutional autonomy' of literature was, it concluded, for the courts to play no part in the unavoidably contentious 'Republic of Letters'.

This recommendation, which successive UK governments have continued to ignore, has a number of significant implications. At the most general level, it obliges us to think again about an important further claim Grüttemeier and Laros make, namely, that 'judicial practice can be taken to manifest a kind of crystallisation of ideas on poetics within non-literary elites' (2013: 205). As the Williams commission suggested, and as I argued *The Literature Police* (2009), my own study of literary censorship under apartheid, this process of 'crystallisation' is inevitably fraught. I am not even sure that the metaphor is appropriate, particularly if it implies that 'ideas on poetics' are not just solidified but somehow clarified in the judicial process. Muddying is perhaps a more plausible figure. Besides, my own inclination is to turn the argument around: given the difficulties literature creates for judicial practice, what we tend to see when 'ideas on poetics' enter the courtroom is a muddying not just of those ideas but of the authority and protocols of the court itself. To demonstrate this, and to show that these concerns are not merely historical, nor, indeed, limited to obscenity trials, I shall focus on a recent UK libel case that addresses the particular problem of what happens when ideas of the literary are deployed not by literary experts in the context of the law but by 'non-literary elites', in this instance, an Oxford-educated English High Court judge.

Before I turn to the details of the case, it will be worth briefly describing the legal background, especially as my example dates from 2008, that is, five years before the Defamation Act (2013) was passed. This was the first major reform of UK libel law since the 1950s. Historically libel has both an extensive meaning in UK law, covering blasphemy, sedition, obscenity and defamation, and a peculiarly precise designation where, in cases of defamation, it is contrasted to slander. Crudely stated, libel is defamatory writing, slander is defamatory speech. This reflects the etymology of the word, which derives from the Latin *libellous*, the diminutive for book. This curious distinction is unknown in most modern jurisdictions. In Scots law, for instance, both libel and slander are treated as 'verbal injury'. Unsurprisingly, the distinction generated problems of its own in the changing media environment of the twentieth century from the advent of radio in the 1920s to the spread of the internet in the 1990s. In response to these developments, 'written' came to be understood, in the words of one English judgement from the 1930s, as 'permanent matter to be seen by the eye' (Deakin 2013: 637). Yet it was not only the medium of expression that created problems. Perhaps most significantly, unlike slander, libel did not historically require proof of damage from the plaintiff. Once the libel is proved, serious damage is assumed; whereas, in most cases, victims of slander are required to demonstrate actual damage relating to, say, loss of earnings. This idiosyncrasy, which created an opening for trivial or vexatious actions, was readily construed as a bias in favour of plaintiffs, particularly rich or powerful ones who could buy silence by threatening or instituting legal proceedings. The still controversial reforms introduced in 2013 were intended in part to close this loophole, requiring plaintiffs in libel cases to submit evidence of serious harm as they had been obliged to do in cases of slander. A further key feature of UK libel law is its anti-intentionalism. 'Liability for libel does not depend on the intention of the defamer,' one judge noted in the 1920s, 'but on the fact of defamation' (Deakin 2013: 633). Seen from the perspective of literary studies, this kind of anti-intentionalism may look like US New Criticism *avant la lettre*, but, unlike the New Critics of the 1940s, UK law did not substitute the vague and debatable intentions of the author/defamer for the apparently more objective 'words on the page', the text of the libel. It shifted the burden on to its reception, which, as we shall see, only created a new set of quandaries with literary and legal consequences.

Unlike obscenity, and to a lesser extent blasphemy and sedition, libel rarely features in the cultural histories of literature and the law in the English-speaking world. Indeed, as Sean Latham comments in *The Scandal of Art* (2009), 'our understanding of the intersection between literature and the law' since the nineteenth century 'has been severely distorted by an almost obsessive focus on the famous obscenity trials of *Ulysses* and *Lady Chatterley's Lover*' (2009: 72). Yet the case history for this period is there. We need only recall Oscar Wilde's libel trials in the 1890s. Wilde's failure to clear his name was largely a consequence of the changes introduced under the Libel Act (1843), which held that in a criminal case the truth of an allegedly libellous claim constituted a legitimate defence, so long as its publication was also in the public interest. Wilde's own aesthetics, and some of the more dramatic moments of the trial, all turned on the question of art's claims to truth. For Latham, the fact that libel has been left out of the story is not surprising. The more famous obscenity trials, he argues, 'have become part of a liberal romance of art's ever-expanding freedom', one of literary history's most cherished grand narratives (2009: 72). By contrast, the various libel cases he discusses, all of which relate the genre of the *roman à clef*, oblige us to consider the extent to which 'literary modernism', or, for that matter, Wildean aestheticism, 'failed in what Pierre Bourdieu calls its "conquest of autonomy"' (2009: 73). Noting that his concerns lie as much with the gaps in literary history as with the orthodoxies of literary criticism, Latham opens his study with this playful gesture: 'Be warned: this book commits one of literary criticism's deadliest sins by treating seemingly fictional works from the early twentieth century as if they contained real facts about real people and events' (2009: 3). He then goes on to show how various writers in the course of the early twentieth century, including Joyce, Aldus Huxley, D.H. Lawrence, Wyndham Lewis, Osbert Sitwell and Jean Rhys, experimented with the *roman à clef*, testing and sometimes falling foul of, English libel law, while at the same time questioning the institutional and aesthetic autonomy of fiction. It is, however, not only the *roman à clef*, or, indeed, genres of writing that are generally considered to be literary, that probe the limits of libel law and oblige us to revisit the grand narrative of literature's conquest of freedom. As my own more contemporary example suggests, cases involving apparently more mundane forms of writing, which seldom feature in conventional literary histories, also have a bearing on these issues. Here, too, 'ideas on poetics' and 'judicial practice' confront each other with equally unpredictable consequences.

The case

In late September 2008, Sir Elton John sued the *Guardian* newspaper in the UK for libel. This is not especially remarkable. Elton John has been suing newspapers for the past thirty years on a fairly regular basis, often successfully. On this occasion, however, things proved less straightforward, mainly because of the nature of the public comments to which he took exception. The offending text, which first appeared in the *Guardian* on 5 July 2008, is worth citing in full, partly because it is a libel in the original etymological sense. It has the virtue of being short. The speaker is Sir Elton himself, and the text is a diary entry, covering two days in late June 2008. Sir Elton records his thoughts about attending Nelson Mandela's 90th birthday celebrations on the 25th and about a charity ball he held the following day at his Windsor mansion to raise funds for his Aids Foundation.

> What a few days it's been. First I sang Happy Birthday to my dear, dear friend Nelson Mandela – I like to think I'm one of the few people privileged enough to call him Madiba – at a party specially organised to provide white celebrities with a chance to be photographed cuddling him, wearing that patronisingly awestruck smile they all have. It says: 'I love you, you adorable, apartheid-fighting teddy bear.'
>
> The next night I welcomed the exact same crowd to my place for my annual White Tie & Tiaras ball. Lulu, Kelly Osbourne, Agyness Deyn, Richard Desmond, Liz Hurley, Bill Clinton – I met most of them 10 minutes ago, but we have something very special and magical in common: we're all members of the entertainment industry. You can't manufacture a connection like that.
>
> Naturally, everyone could afford just to hand over the money if they gave that much of a toss about Aids research – as could the sponsors. But we like to give guests a preposterously lavish evening, because they're the kind of people who wouldn't turn up for anything less. They fork out small fortunes for new dresses and so on, the sponsors blow hundreds of thousands on creating what convention demands we call a 'magical world', and everyone wears immensely smug 'My diamonds are by Chopard' grins in the newspapers and OK. Once we've subtracted all these costs, the leftovers go to my foundation. I call this care-o-nomics. (Hyde 2008a: 16)

As I said, Sir Elton did sing at Mandela's 90th on 25 June 2008 and his White Tie and Tiara ball did take place on the 26th, but, as you will have by now guessed, this is not really a diary entry, and the speaker is not really Elton John. Following a well-established journalistic tradition in England, which can be traced back to the seventeenth century at least, it is a spoof involving an act of rhetorical ventriloquism in which Marina Hyde, a *Guardian* staffer, does the smug but also acerbic voice of the celebrity prima donna for satirical purposes by purporting to quote from his diary. The regular column, to which Hyde often contributed, was called 'A Peek at the Diary of'.

This is not how Sir Elton saw it. On his reading Hyde's text was neither a diary entry nor a satirical parody of one. It was a libellous attack on his moral integrity. In a writ issued against the *Guardian* on 7 August 2008, suing the paper for £150,000 damages, he called it a 'gratuitously offensive, nasty and snide' slur, which damaged his reputation as a public-spirited philanthropist and Aids campaigner by falsely accusing him of being an insincere, uncaring self-promoter (Limbrick 2008). It is important to stress that, given the terms of English libel law and the level of compensation he sought, Sir Elton accused Hyde of knowingly making false claims with malicious intent. In earlier correspondence with the *Guardian*, he also said she had branded him a racist, a charge he subsequently dropped from the formal writ. The *Guardian* accepted none of this and, in an effort to get the matter sorted out as quickly and as cheaply as possible, it made an application for a judicial ruling on Hyde's words and their meaning. The hearing eventually took place in early December 2008 with the Hon Mr Justice Tugendhat presiding. Given the unpredictability of High Court appointment processes, the *Guardian* was lucky to get him. Unlike some of his esteemed colleagues, Tugendhat, then the most senior media judge in England and Wales, earned a reputation for being an especially robust defender of press freedom. William McCormack, instructed by Carter-Ruck, the UK's leading media law firm, represented Elton John; while Gavin Millar QC and Anthony Hudson, both defamation specialists of Doughty Street Chambers, represented Guardian News & Media Limited.

The hearing turned out to be an oddly academic affair, which has an unexpected bearing on the question of literature's status as an object of knowledge. Not for the first time, and no doubt not for the last, the Royal Courts of Justice in London's Strand became a forum for heated debate not just about the unique intricacies of UK libel law, the right to freedom of expression or, for that matter, the meaning of words but about how meaning is understood to be made and what role publishers, readers and ideas of the literary play in the process. Tellingly, though there were a number of avenues open to the *Guardian's* lawyers – they could, for instance, have argued that Hyde was justified in making her claims by proving them to be true, following the provisions of the Libel Act (1843) – they chose to focus primarily on the defence of fair (now honest) comment in the public interest, which, somewhat surprisingly, turned on the even more subtle question of literariness. In their view, the words to which Sir Elton took exception were not actionable as libellous because they could not be 'understood as statements of fact', or even as allegations of fact (Tugendhat 2008: 27). Rather they were part of a specifically literary mode of writing. In making this argument, which is a particular version of the fair comment defence, they did not appeal to any supposedly inherent idea or unique property of literariness, say, that a literary text is always and only fictional (although, as we shall see, much turned on a particular understanding of irony). They focused on the question of how words might be taken to be literary depending on the context in which they appear. As Justice Tugendhat put it in his summing up, 'it is common ground that the meaning of words, in law as in life, depends on their context,' though, as he noted, following the arguments put forward by the defence, the term 'context' could be construed in two ways (2008: 20). In the first, the context referred to the larger 'circumstances under which the words were published', which, in this case, included the two key events, Nelson Mandela's birthday and the White Tie and Tiara Ball (20). This has a particular bearing on the truth or falsity of Hyde's claims. The second 'narrower sense', which Tugendhat took to be especially significant from a legal point of view, referred to the material context in which Hyde's words were first published. This has a special pertinence to their literariness (20).

Drawing attention to the details of this narrower context was the burden of Tugendhat's first lesson in the perils of close reading. By focusing exclusively on some of Hyde's words, he argued, Elton John had made the fatal mistake of failing to give due weight to their precise provenance in the *Weekend* section of the Saturday *Guardian* for 5 July 2008. Adopting the pose of a careful descriptive bibliographer, Tugendhat explained perhaps a little too pedantically:

> This section is made up of 104 pages (including advertisements), illustrated in full colour, and is itself divided into sections headed Starters, Fashion, Food & Drink, Features and so on. Like the Saturday editions of a number of other English newspapers aimed at an educated readership, *The Guardian* is made up of separate or pull out sections, of which Weekend is only one. While different types of speech can appear in any of these sections, the designation of the section assists in understanding the extent to which particular speech is to be understood as factual or not. Weekend is not the news section of the paper (2008: 23).

It is worth noting that Tugendhat did not mention the online version of the piece, which displays none of these print-based bibliographical features, making such fine discriminations between factual reportage and other 'types of speech' (strictly writing) much trickier in a digital context, a point to which I shall return (2008: 22).

Having established that the immediate print context constituted the first legally noteworthy frame for Hyde's words, Tugendhat then turned to the article itself, and more particularly to its title, which, he argued, functioned as another key framing device, albeit one that was more difficult to read. By presenting the words under the heading 'A Peek at the Diary of Sir Elton John', 'that is, as if they are an extract from a diary written by the Claimant "as seen" by the journalist', the editors, according to Tugendhat, chose not to indicate 'what statement the reader is to expect, as title [*sic*] to news articles generally do' (2008: 23). By contrast, the headline on page 2 of the main paper, which appeared under the running header 'News', reads: 'Johnson forced to remove his deputy mayor after magistrate claim proves false' (Taylor 2008: 2). The report that follows then gives an account of Boris Johnson's embarrassments over one of his first mayoral appointees who was obliged to resign amid allegations of financial misconduct. In this case, then, the title constitutes a précis of the factual report, helpfully guiding the reader's expectations; whereas 'A Peek at the Diary of' plays all sorts of rhetorical games, setting a trap for unwary readers, especially those like Sir Elton who choose to read too closely.

Yet, as Tugendhat recognized, the argument from bibliographical provenance, though necessary for a literary defence, was not sufficient. After all, despite its location in the *Weekend* section, he noted that Hyde's article contained 'a number of statements of fact attributed to the Claimant [Sir Elton] which are true, and obviously intended to be understood as true' (2008: 27). As everyone in the High Court acknowledged, these included the reference to Mandela's birthday party, to the ball and to the photographs that did actually appear in the celebrity magazine *OK!* Tugendhat added that there were also some 'statements of both fact and opinion', citing as an example the spoof Sir Elton's reference to the photographs in *OK!* (fact) and his comments on his fellow celebrities wearing their 'immensely smug' grins (opinion) (2008: 28). For Sir Elton's lawyers, these complexities made it unclear which interpretative protocols applied, especially when it came to what they took to be the most offensive statement in the piece, the penultimate sentence: 'Once we've subtracted all these costs, the leftovers go to my foundation' (Hyde 2008a: 16).

In their view, the implications (specifically 'innuendo') of this sentence were clear, unliterary and so libellous: it meant that Sir Elton and the organizers of the Ball deducted 'all the costs of providing the lavish evening, including the costs incurred by the guests for new dresses and diamonds, and that it was only the balance that went to the charitable foundation' (Tugendhat 2008: 29).

At this point Tugendhat offered his second lesson in the perils of close reading, shifting the terms of his argument from bibliography to reception theory, from the materiality of the print *Guardian* to what he took to be the interrelated questions of readership and literariness. Having noted that the Saturday *Guardian*, with its various supplements like *Weekend*, was 'aimed at an educated readership' – the typical *Guardian* reader is popularly regarded as being a left-leaning member of the comfortable middle classes – he focused on what he termed, following legal precedent, the figure of the 'reasonable reader' (2008: 22, 28). When it came to deciding which interpretative protocols applied to the penultimate sentence, he was in no doubt that this particular reader would understand that 'the words complained of are obviously written by the journalist, who has attributed them to the Claimant as a literary device', and that the 'transparently false attribution is irony', which, he explained, is 'a figure of speech in which the intended meaning is the opposite of what is expressed by the words used' (2008: 24). For this reader, then, the fictionality of the entire piece was obvious. Irony, one of the subtlest, socially coded rhetorical devices, also applied more specifically to the key penultimate sentence, which, Tugendhat noted, is presented not as fact but 'as an allegation that the Claimant is making against himself' (24). Bringing together the two strands of his reading lesson, he suggested that no 'reasonable reader' would understand the sentence in the way Sir Elton had because she would 'expect so serious an allegation to be made without humour, and explicitly, in a part of the newspaper devoted to news' (32). By mistaking a piece of light-hearted, even 'teasing', literary satire for serious reportage, Sir Elton had, he concluded, suffered a sense of humour failure complicated by a bad case of hermeneutic myopia (31). Hyde's article was therefore not actionable under UK libel law, and, consequently, Sir Elton's claim for damages had to be struck out. Tugendhat also ordered him to pay costs, despite the fact that the *Guardian* had applied for the hearing.

Not content with this outcome, Sir Elton's lawyers then took their case to the Court of Appeal, only to have it rejected once again. On 26 March 2009, over eight months after Hyde's piece first appeared, they finally conceded defeat and gave up. No doubt the vanity of celebrities – who can also afford the fees – helps to explain their persistence. Yet, since it is unlikely that an established and very successful firm such as Carter-Ruck would put its professional standing on the line without good reason, the tenacity of Elton John's team also says something about the legal niceties of the case.

The conclusion

This is where the legal story of Sir Elton's lessons in the perils of close reading ended. Yet, for anyone concerned about 'Literature in Law', I would argue that it is at this point that the real interest of the case starts. Seen from a literary rather than a legal perspective, the closure Justice Tugendhat brought to the proceedings, which was subsequently confirmed by the Court of Appeal, looks more pragmatic than principled. This is in part because, as I have already suggested, he chose to stabilize the process of meaning making by privileging the original print version of Hyde's piece, ignoring the complications any mention of the online version might introduce, an issue both legal teams also overlooked. Online publication, whether on the internet or via social media sites like Twitter, is especially testing for UK libel law not just because it raises new questions about the 'written' word, authorship and ownership, which the Defamation Act (2013) has attempted to address but because it does not necessarily bring with it the extrinsic markers of status and provenance associated with the traditional medium of print, which played such a central part in Tugendhat's determination. As the case history develops, however, the particular ways in which digital media create new forms of context for 'permanent matter to be seen by the eye' are being taken seriously (Deakin 2013: 637). In one noteworthy case from 2010, for instance, which relates to an allegedly libellous online article, the hyperlinks inserted in some of the words were deemed to constitute a part of the relevant meaning-making context (Deakin 2013: 633). In its online version Hyde's piece contains no hyperlinks, though it directs the reader to a number of related categories via a sidebar, including 'music', 'celebrity', 'life and style' and more from 'The Peek at' series, which it also describes as 'a glimpse inside the celebrity mind'. These arguably ensure that the online reader does not mistake the piece for factual reportage, albeit not as clearly as the contextual markers in the print *Weekend* supplement.

Tugendhat's ruling also looks more pragmatic than principled because he cut the interpretative uncertainties short by invoking the legal fiction of the 'reasonable reader'. In so doing he was following sound legal precedents, though, as Markesinis and Deakin point out in their magisterial textbook *Tort Law* (2013), precedents that are a source of much legal contention. Setting out the key issues, they explain: 'Courts treat the meaning of words as a matter of construction rather than evidence, to be interpreted objectively in their context, with reference to the opinion of right-thinking members of society' (2013: 633).

This is why Tugendhat expressly made no mention of Hyde's intentions in his ruling and why he focused exclusively on the effects her words might have on what he called the 'reasonable reader', given the precise bibliographical provenance. Yet, as a test, this anti-intentionalist legal convention is, as Markesinis and Deakin observe, 'vague and unsatisfactory', not least because it begs a series of large questions about who the 'reasonable' or 'right-thinking members of society' might actually be (2013: 633). Given the emphasis Tugendhat placed on irony in his ruling, this has a particular bearing on the Elton John case. Did Tugendhat have a particular theory of irony? On the basis of what he says in his ruling, this is highly unlikely. At best, he was working with a very rudimentary critical lexicon, concerning irony, fiction and satire as literary devices, though, as I have suggested, one that none the less has some theoretical implications. His arguments assumed that irony cannot, for instance, be understood in purely structural terms, since its effects depend on what linguists call its pragmatic context. For Tugendhat, this was defined in part via the legal fiction of the 'reasonable reader', but, as I have already noted, irony is among the most precarious and socially charged rhetorical devices, relying as it does on easily missed (often veiled) markers, subtle inference and implied background knowledge, which only some readers might possess. It is, in fact, often used precisely to separate a narrow circle of those in the know (one version of the 'right-thinking') from a wider audience who cannot pick up the signals. As such, it is a consciously disruptive mode that courts misreading and cannot be understood independently of the complex, never wholly assured social contexts of its use.

As Tugendhat noted at various points in his ruling, such intricate interpretative issues would be a matter for the jury if the case actually went to court. This was written into UK law with 'Fox's Libel Act' (1792), which made juries the ultimate arbiters of whether or not a text is libellous. Until that point, judges had decided, and juries were required only to determine if the defendant had published the text. In the absence of a jury, Tugendhat was obliged to invoke the 'reasonable reader', which opened up other uncertainties. As the shifting legal terminology during the latter half of the twentieth century shows, deciding who the 'right-thinking' or 'reasonable' might be is far from obvious. In the 1960s these readers were deemed to be 'ordinary' rather than 'logical' men; in the slightly less sexist 1980s, the 'hypothetical reader who is not unduly suspicious but who can read between the lines'; and, a decade later, the 'substantial and respectable proportion of society' (2013: 633–4). The terminological challenges are relatively minor, however. As Markesinis and Deakin note, the more pressing question is: 'Is the test of defamation what right-thinking persons belonging to the class to which the statement is published think? Or right-thinking persons *generally*?' (2013: 634). The case history since the 1930s indicates that the latter view has prevailed in UK courts, but, as we have seen, Tugendhat focussed on the 'reasonable reader' of the Saturday *Guardian* rather than reasonable readers in general. As a challenging recent case suggests, this judgement has particularly fraught implications in contemporary inter- or multicultural societies. Echoing the kinds of argument associated with the literary theorist Stanley Fish, who championed the idea of 'interpretative community' as the arbiter of meaning in the 1970s, a UK court of appeal in 2000 respected the particular construction members of the Muslim community might give to certain statements about women and sexuality. As Markesinis and Deakin then comment, this opens up the worrying possibility of 'the same statement having certain consequences for one section of the population of one state but not for other citizens of the very same state'. 'In an increasingly pluralistic society', they add in their rather bland textbook prose, 'the designation of one or more sections as "right-thinking" [or "reasonable"] results in difficulties' (2013: 635).

For the *Guardian* the outcome of the Elton John case was 'A victory for irony', but, in her own reflections on the whole episode, Marina Hyde, the journalist at the centre of it all, registered some mordant disquiet: 'We British have a rich tradition of irony and satire but there is very little case law protecting what may well turn out to be one of the few comforts left to us in these darkening times' (Campbell 2008: 1–2; Hyde 2008b: 2). Moreover, she added, 'there is something absurd about a silly little piece of fluff about Elton John's annual White Tie and Tiara ball being used to enshrine such important principles' (2008b: 2). She was none the less pleased that she had helped to defend 'our right to be a tiny bit ironic about a diamond-encrusted celebrity Aids fundraiser' (2). She was also happy to report that, according to the *Guardian's* 'head of legal', 'we made good law' (2). I am not so sure. Seen against the broader background I have been sketching, Justice Tugendhat's appeal to the 'reasonable reader', coupled with his decision to restrict himself to the print version of Hyde's article, begins to look less like an assured 'victory' and the Royal Courts of Justice, for all their Victorian Gothic magnificence, start to lose some of their comfortingly impressive institutional solidity. They begin to seem less like authoritative bastions of interpretive clarity and more like vulnerable, because always questionable, sites of hermeneutic closure.

From a legal and journalistic point of view, Tugendhat may have determined the saving literariness of Hyde's 'piece of fluff' by accepting the *Guardian's* defence, thereby bringing the meaning of Hyde's words to a judicially defensible end and making 'good law'. From a literary point of view, it is clear that he could do so only by relying on a restricted conception of their public context, on the legal fiction of the 'reasonable reader', and on a socially laden and inescapably precarious idea of irony as a 'literary device'. Far from manifesting 'a kind of crystallisation of ideas on poetics' in the context of 'judicial practice' as exemplified by a member of a 'non-literary elite', then, this case reflects the challenges courts and other tribunals face when they attempt to treat literature as a clearly identifiable object of knowledge or to apply secure tests for literariness, exposing the gulf between literary and legal approaches to language, cultural value and meaning. As I have argued, it also suggests that the problem of scholasticism, which Bernard Williams's enquiry identified as one of the main faults of the British Obscene Publications Act, 1959, may be more pervasive than we like to think and may, in fact, be impossible to eradicate from the courtroom, given the particular, and ultimately pragmatic, imperatives of the law and the protean qualities of the literary. Since no one is safe from the perils of reading, whether closely or not, the Elton John case offers little assurance about the future of 'irony and satire' in England and Wales, and every assurance about the ongoing trouble literature will bring when it gets entangled with the law. And so the 'liberal romance' of literature's autonomy or 'art's ever-expanding freedom' remains as alluring and as unworkable as ever.

References

Campbell, D. (2008), 'A Victory for Irony as Elton John Loses Guardian Libel Case', *Guardian*, 13 December: 1–2.

Coetzee, J. M. (1988), 'The Novel Today', *Upstream*, 6(1): 2–5.

Danto, A. C. (1999), *Philosophizing Art*, Berkeley, CA: University of California Press.

Deakin, S. et al. (2013), *Tort Law*, Oxford: Oxford University Press.

Grüttemeier, R. and T. Laros (2013), 'Literature in Law: Exceptio Artis and the Emergence of Literary Fields', *Law and Humanities*, 7(2): 204–17.

Hyde, M. (2008a), 'A Peek at the Diary of Sir Elton John', *Guardian Weekend*, 5 July: 16. Available online: http://www.theguardian.com/music/2008/jul/05/popandrock (accessed 10 September 2014).

Hyde, M. (2008b), 'Comment', *Guardian*, 13 December: 2.

Latham, S. (2009), *The Art of Scandal*, Oxford: Oxford University Press.

Limbrick, S. (2008), 'Elton John Demands £150k Over "Offensive, Nasty and Snide" Article', *Press Gazette*, 26 September. Available online: http://www.pressgazette.co.uk/node/42118 (accessed 10 September 2014).

McDonald, P. (2006), 'Ideas of the Book and Histories of Literature: After Theory?', *PMLA*, 121(1): 214–28.

McDonald, P. (2008), 'Old Phrases and Great Obscenities: The Strange Afterlife of Two Victorian Anxieties', *Journal of Victorian Culture*, 13(2): 294–302.

McDonald, P. (2009), *The Literature Police*, Oxford: Oxford University Press.

Taylor, M. and D. Hill (2008), 'Johnson Forced to Remove His Deputy Mayor After Magistrate Claim Proves False', *Guardian*, 5 July: 2.

Tugendhat, J. (2008), *Sir Elton John v. Guardian News and Media Limited*, EWHC 3066 (QB), 5 December: 1–47. Available online: http://www.bailii.org/ew/cases/EWHC/QB/2008/3066.html (accessed 10 September 2014).

Williams, B. et al. (1979), *Report of the Committee on Obscenity and Film Censorship*, London: Her Majesty's Stationary Office.

10

'The Law Is a Ass': Obscenity, Blasphemy and Other Literary Offences after Lady Chatterley

Martin A. Kayman

A ban on a play which was claimed to be blasphemous has been lifted by a council in Northern Ireland. Members of the artistic board at Newtownabbey, Co Antrim reversed an earlier vote, allowing the Reduced Shakespeare Company to now stage The Bible: The Complete Word of God *at Theatre at the Mill, which is run by Newtownabbey borough council. The artistic board voted last week to ban the play when some Unionist members, including the mayor …, claimed it mocked Christianity. Councillors who backed the play claimed the ban made them look like a laughing stock.*
*(*The Guardian, *28 January 2014)*

In memoriam Stuart Hall (1932–2014), Terry Hawkes (1932–2014) and Richard Hoggart (1918–2014)

In an article explaining the theoretical background to this volume, Ralf Grüttemeier and Ted Laros (2013: 205) argue that 'literary trials can be taken to register the acceptance of certain poetical standpoints in non-literary circles. Given the central function of the law and the courts in the field of power as Bourdieu sees it, judicial practice can be taken to manifest a kind of crystallisation of ideas on poetics within non-literary elites'. In particular, they claim, the application of a doctrine of *exceptio artis* can be viewed as 'a decisive step towards the formation of a relative autonomous literary field'. My contribution will address the *dearth* of literary trials for either obscenity or blasphemy in the half-century or so since the Lady Chatterley trial. What does this tell us, not only about attitudes to literature but equally about the pressures on, and preoccupations of, law in postmodernity?

The essay will articulate a number of claims. First, I shall challenge the dominant view of the Lady Chatterley case by arguing that if, in one sense, it did consecrate the autonomy of literature, it at the same time presaged transformations in its constitution that undermined the robustness of that position. The narrative of changes in the contours of literature opened up by this account, and the implications for its role in law, lead to the second claim. Here, the decline in trials is read against the background of the criminalization of new forms of literary offensiveness in the multicultural UK of the late twentieth century. In this context, I argue, the sort of concerns that the courts had negotiated in their dealings with literature have been displaced by issues which address contemporary law's relationship with religion. In doing so, these issues bring into question the foundations of law's claims to a monopoly of jurisdiction in a multicultural and globalized world. In examining how a liberal conception of law has been reasserted in response to these challenges in Britain (as in the episode recounted in my epigraph), my final claim, then, will be to uncover the fragility and divisiveness behind the apparent confidence of that position, and to point to the persistence of fundamental issues of the sacred at the heart of law.

In making its way to these conclusions, the essay will necessarily take a different approach to relations between law and literature to that articulated by Grüttemeier and Laros. Thinking historically, the struggles in the English courts to define the legal concept of literary property initially created by the first legislation on copyright (1709) were certainly an important contribution to the establishment of the modern concept of literature (cf. Rose 1993). However, as the excerpt above from Grüttemeier and Laros reminds us, in Pierre Bourdieu's account the pre-eminence of the law is a given. In 18th-century Britain, on the other hand, the traffic was not only one-way: the incipient autonomy of literature was relative to that of a legal regime which was itself engaged in consolidating the ideological supremacy of the rule of law that characterizes modernity. As I have argued elsewhere (Kayman 1996: 795), at this point of expansion in parliamentary statute as the primary source of law-making, the courts' demarcation of literature as original, imaginative and subjective expression implicitly constructed the written law as immune from such 'literary' qualities, and hence supported its modern character as the impersonal source of sovereign justice.

Today too, the 'force of law' (Derrida 1990) continues to rely on aesthetics, as well as violence, to renew and sustain its position (cf. Douzinas and Nead 1999; Sherwin 2011); and it needs constantly to disavow both in order to maintain its consensual authority. By 'aesthetics' here I am referring not simply to the literary qualities, imagery, ceremony and fictions of law but to what Jean Rancière theorizes as 'the distribution of the sensible' achieved by such means. Such 'common sense' involves both 'the system of self-evident facts of sense perception that ... establishes at one and the same time something in common that is shared and exclusive parts' (Rancière 2004: 12), and 'a distribution of what is visible and what not, of what can be heard and what cannot' (Rancière 2010: 36). I start, then, with a focus on the crime of obscene libel because it plays a fulcral role in separating a concept of literature as aesthetic writing from law which, in this way, maintains its distance from aesthetics. Thus, the preamble to the 1959 Obscene Publications Act declares a double purpose: both 'to strengthen the law concerning pornography' and 'to provide for the protection of literature'. When, twenty years later, the Committee on Obscenity and Film Censorship chaired by Bernard Williams recommended that all written material be excluded from the act (Williams 1979: 102), the home secretary firmly reasserted the privileges of a strictly aesthetic understanding of the literary. Sir Patrick Mayhew rejected Williams's recommendation on the grounds that not all published writing was 'literature'; the committee's blanket exclusion ignored 'pornographic novelettes, with no literary pretensions, known to the police as "readers"' (Hansard 1981: 492). In abandoning any legal distinction between literary and pornographic reading materials, Williams's proposal threatened to dismantle the conceptual barrier that separated the corrupting sensuousness of pornography not just from literature but from all other bodies of writing. On the other hand, designated as the lawful space for the improving pleasures of reading, literature acts here as a buffer between pornography and other writing that, while not literary itself, was thereby protected from being 'obscene', that is, likely to have a harmful aesthetic influence. It is the business of the obscenity laws, then, to police the borders of the sensuous aesthetic.[1]

By making literary merit a defence against obscenity and admitting the expert testimony of literary critics in court, the Obscene Publication Act can be seen as the legislative embodiment of Bourdieu's relative autonomy of the literary field (cf. Kirchhofer, *infra*), and the trial of *Lady Chatterley's Lover* (*R. v. Penguin Books* 1961) as its triumphant enactment. The failure of the prosecution has been followed by what Paul Kearns (2007: 667) has called an 'ineluctable decline of obscene libel' and, consequently, of the use of the literary defence. Although the law has resisted proposals to abolish the statutory distinction that relies on an exceptional field of aesthetic writing, literary authors are nowadays more likely to risk condemnation by the judges of the *Literary Review*'s 'bad sex award' than prosecution for obscenity in a court of law.[2] So, why, while maintaining the legislation in place, has the law all but ceased to engage in trials of the literary over the lawful limits of the aesthetic? My response has two components. In the first place, as indicated above, I shall read the Lady Chatterley trial not as the triumph of the autonomy of literature but as the announcement of an imminent destabilization of the ideological and social structures which had supported this status. Both a radical opening up of the boundaries of the literary and changes in its critical readership have weakened the utility of literature in policing the aesthetics of language. In the second place, we will find that the pressure on law from aesthetics that had been managed hitherto through obscenity has been displaced by the emergence of another issue at the intersection of literature and law, that of religious belief.

The first movement I shall be describing can be illustrated through the stark contrast between the high legal concepts of obscenity and literature mobilized in 1961 and the issues at stake in the most dramatic obscenity trial since the turn of the century, *R. v. Peacock* (2012). The sensational nature of the depictions of violent gay sadomasochistic practices purveyed over the internet by Michael Peacock ensured wide publicity for the case. Although the Crown Prosecution Service's criteria clearly mandated prosecution, Peacock was acquitted by the jury. Like many others, Nichi Hodgson's report (2012) invoked the precedent of *Lady Chatterley's Lover*, but there is little relation between the literary heterosexual buggery of Lawrence's artistic novel and the graphic fisting of Peacock's commercial DVDs. Indeed, the defence here did not rely on aesthetic value at all. The aesthetic appeared only in the more fundamental terms of the difference between the practice of consensual violence and its depiction on screen – in Rancière's terms, what may be visible and shared. When literature did make its appearance at the trial, it was emphatically in a minor key. According to one observer:

> Whilst the prosecution had turned to a Woody Allen quote in their summing up, the defence referred to the book and film *The Da Vinci Code*. The Dan Brown story features scenes of flagellation, and the prosecution rhetorically asked whether this suggested it was OK for religion, but not sex. Then – and to the delight of academics and theorists following the trial on Twitter – the defence quoted the French postmodern theorist, Foucault: 'if you are not like everybody else, then you are abnormal, if you are abnormal, then you are sick', but these terms are mistakenly conflated when they are in fact three different

things – different, abnormal and sick. To be merely different does not denote 'sickness'. (Ashford 2012)

Neither argument seems particularly substantial, but the choice of literary exempla from the realms of popular culture, the references to the interface of writing and film and to social media, and the citation from critical theory point to exactly the sort of transformations that I shall be tracking from the Lady Chatterley trial and which have undermined the capacity of literature to support the law in configuring the boundaries of the aesthetic.

The prosecution's question contrasting sex and religion will prove equally apposite. Bourdieu's critique of taste – an influential contribution to the changes I am alluding to – mobilizes a metaphor that denounces 'culture' as the 'present incarnation of the sacred' (1984: xiii). However, this figure was to be challenged by the eruption of the sacred in its literal sense within the trials of literature. In 1977, the writ of blasphemous libel – unused since 1922 – was resurrected against *Gay News* for publishing James Kirkup's 'The Love that Dares to Speak its Name' (*Whitehouse v. Lemon* 1979). While this case may have felt to most contemporaries like a reactionary hangover, the demands of the sacred arose more problematically in the most notable literary trial *not* to take place in Britain, *in re* Salman Rushdie's *The Satanic Verses* (1988). If obscenity trials implicitly settle issues of law's relation to sensuous aesthetics, then blasphemy trials address the ethos of the two kinds of law, state and religious. While one strain in the law-and-literature movement stressed the literary as the exemplum of the imbrication of aesthetics and ethics (cf., White 1985; Nussbaum 1995), the law avoided trying this issue on the ground of literature. As we shall see in the last section of the essay, in the absence of literary merit as a robust buffer, English law has hitherto responded somewhat nervously to the challenge from religion, pointing to what I shall conclude is an as-yet unresolved crisis in the authority of modern law in a postmodern, globalized environment.

Unsettling the contours of literature: The rise of cultural studies

I am proposing, then, that the prosecution of *Lady Chatterley's Lover* remains key to the British narrative of law and literature not because, in Bourdieu's terms, it confirmed the autonomy of the latter – which, in jurisprudential terms it clearly did – but because it simultaneously signalled the erosion of the boundaries which had secured the consensus about the nature and value of literature required to support its exceptional status in law. In particular, the new law brought professional literary critics into the courtroom to testify to the nature and quality of the literary text at the very point that the authority and views of the professional reader were to undergo a period of significant change which was radically to diminish the capacity of literature to play its confident aesthetic function in court.

The most frequently mentioned witness here is Richard Hoggart, himself a representative of a new style of working-class academic from a recently founded university (Leicester), which was part of a sector that was to gain twenty-five institutions in the course of the 1960s. Reflecting on the trial in his autobiography, Hoggart (1992: 52) commented that 'one might have expected that it would attract today no more than a footnote... Instead, it has echoed loudly down the decades.' The repercussions of the case have however had little to do with the legal recognition of the integrity of the literary work, the aesthetic merit defence, or the role of literary critics as expert witnesses. Rather, what echoes in the cultural memory is the question – 'quoted in every discussion of the trial I know' (Hoggart 1992: 55) – posed to the jury by Melvin Griffith-Jones QC: 'Is it a book that you would even wish your wife or your servants to read?' (Rolph 1961: 17) Anachronistic as the question appeared in the 1960s, Christopher Hilliard (2013) has pointed out that the potential reader had been at the heart of obscenity law since *R. v. Hicklin* (1867) established that the key issue in obscene libel was the effect on those 'into whose hands a publication of this sort may fall'. According to Hilliard (2013: 654): 'The *Lady Chatterley's Lover* trial was the last sortie of a convention that had held since the nineteenth century: that material the authorities would ban if it were produced for a mass audience did not necessarily warrant prohibition if it was directed toward a privileged readership in whose judgment the courts could have more faith.' In this sense, the cultural legacy of the trial has had less to do with literary aesthetics than with democracy: the universe of 'persons likely to read' literature, in the words of the statute.

The crucial consideration in the case was hence the fact that *Lady Chatterley's Lover* (Lawrence 1928, 1932, 1933, 1956) had been issued as a Penguin paperback (1960). Founded by Allan Lane in 1935, the Penguin project was to put modern fiction into the hands of the public at large, priced at the same level as 'a packet of cigarettes' (*About Penguin: Company History*). The trial of *R. v. Penguin Books* thus reflected the profound changes underway in access to the literary and to a literary education and, consequently, in the attitudes and practices of reading, both professional and popular, associated with literature by witnesses and jurors. In that sense, something like *The Dark Sun* (1956), an acclaimed study of Lawrence's novels by the first witness for the defence, Graham Hough, is of less use in understanding the cultural significance of the trial than Hoggart's *The Uses of Literacy* (1958) – which, the author later claimed, Allan Lane had regarded as 'exactly the kind of book he had hoped to publish when he founded the Pelican list' for non-fiction two years after Penguin (Hoggart 1992: 5). Hoggart's study of 'aspects of working-class life, with special reference to publications and entertainments' (to cite the sub-title) was a foundational document for that transformation of the study of English Literature in the UK that is signalled by the name 'cultural studies'. Hoggart's text asked the reader to attend critically not, as F.R. Leavis argued, to the complex moral vitality of a literary canon but to that of the popular culture of the working classes. The first half of the book used a literary-critical approach to document and analyse the persistent features of traditional working-class life, while the second discussed changes to that culture resulting from the expanding industries of popular literature and music. In this way, the literary and its methodologies became embedded in the popular and the multimodal and, as with Hoggart's equally influential contemporary, Raymond Williams (cf. 1961), within a holistic notion of culture.

The Centre for Contemporary Cultural Studies (CCCS) founded by Hoggart at the University of Birmingham in 1964 was designed as the academic embodiment of this project. Penguin Books provided a grant to help establish the Centre, funding Hoggart's research assistant and successor, Stuart Hall. In his inaugural lecture as Professor of English Literature at Birmingham, Hoggart had made 'the case for widening the boundaries of English as it was offered at universities' (Hoggart 1992: 93). The Centre would achieve this by drawing on sociology and social psychology alongside literary criticism in a way that, in the words of its first report, 'will … fall into line with the best critical work done in schools of literature, while at the same time extending this work in scope' (1964: 3–4). As CCCS developed after 1968 under Hall, its methodological focus engaged with and contributed to the broader theoretical turn occurring in English and other subjects in Britain – as represented, for example, by the Essex Sociology of Literature conferences that ran between 1976 and 2001, the 'New Accents' monograph series (1977–2003), under the general editorship of Terence Hawkes (2007), and *Textual Practice*, the journal Hawkes established in 1987.

Although Hoggart's project was originally conceived within the discipline of English Literature, English and Cultural Studies drifted apart, in large part over the balance of literary and sociological approaches. Nonetheless, a dynamic had been firmly established: thus, while the CCCS was transferred from the Department of English to Birmingham's Faculty of Social Science in 1988, the institutional impetus continued the following year with the founding, by a group including Hawkes, of the Centre for Critical and Cultural Theory (CCCT) within the Cardiff School of English, Communication and Philosophy. In sum, while the experiment started by Hoggart led to the emergence of distinct disciplines in the study of popular culture and media, it had still played a central role in a process that has transformed understandings of what is included within English Literature and literary criticism. Without documenting the debates that have taken place over the last half-century, one can, I believe, state with confidence that the landscape within which even traditional approaches to English are carried out has been transformed. Most of all, one might say, the assumed boundaries and contours of English Literature have been questioned and opened up in terms not only of the canon of strictly literary texts and genres but equally in relation to the media, histories, geographies, and subjects within its purview, with especial attention to the disempowered and subaltern – what used to be regarded as 'wives and servants', if one likes. Assumptions regarding aesthetic value and institutional autonomies have been challenged by a holistic view of culture and an awareness of the intricate interdependencies of expression, representation, and power – as reflected, for example, in the law-and-literature movement in which this essay situates itself.

Changes in critical readership: The rise of the book club

A key insight from cultural studies and critical theory has been the active contribution of the reader/viewer to the work. The opening up of the theoretical and methodological constitution of literature in the UK is one side of a process that, as I indicated above, included changes in the structure of its critical readership. Here, arguably the most interesting symptom of change has been the growth of the book club or reading group. I am not referring to the commercial book club but to the appropriation of the model by social enterprises, like public libraries, or, most commonly, by informal groups of friends who get together regularly to socialize by talking about books which they select for discussion themselves. Having started in the United States, informal, non-commercial book clubs have burgeoned in the UK since the late 1990s.[3]

In her pioneering survey of the phenomenon, Jenny Hartley estimated in 2001 that some 50,000 groups existed in the UK at that point, and growing (Hartley 2001: vii). Hartley notes the role of campaigns by the Orange telecommunications company (1997) and the *Mail on Sunday* (1998), and the creation of BBC Radio 4's 'Bookclub' (1998) as important impulses for the revival and expansion, in modern form, of what is in fact a long-standing social practice. Informal reading clubs have existed throughout the modern period, be they circles of aristocratic women, aspirational Dissenters in the provinces, or political reading groups formed by working men in industrial cities. The revival at the turn of the twenty-first century is, as one would expect, more heterogeneous. Membership of a reading group would appear to be connected with the expansion of the university sector from the 1960s, with Hartley (2001: 33–4) reporting the majority of members, particularly among younger readers, having had some form of tertiary education. The groups are predominantly constituted by women, although mixed groups made up over a quarter of the 350 clubs studied (Hartley 2001: 25–6). Notably, though, some 80 per cent of respondents met in members' homes (2001: 15). Such feminized, domestic, neighbourly communities (as Hartley [2001: 14] puts it: 'The group is itself a micro-neighbourhood') do not replace professional literary criticism, but they have the capacity to reconfigure the practices and objects of literary reading.[4] For the producers of Radio 4's 'Bookclub', '[a] reading group is a halfway house between' solitary reading and the way professional critics read (Flynn and Guttridge). More broadly, Wendy Griswold, Terry McDonnell and Nathan Wright (2005: 134) have argued that book clubs offer a praxis that embodies the contemporary theoretical recognition of reading as a social, rather than individual, activity. In their numbers, the book clubs collectively exert influence on publishers' lists; moreover, they generate and disseminate their own reading practices and understandings of literature which do not necessarily see themselves in alignment with professional literary criticism.

While only a limited amount of sociological research on reading groups is, as yet, available in relation to the United Kingdom, they are a sufficiently recognizable and significant feature of everyday life to have themselves become the object of fiction. The first novel to employ the reading group as a setting was ... *And Ladies of the Club* (1982) by the 87-year-old Helen Hooven Santmyer. The 1,334-page novel used the book club as a social focus and a narrative mechanism through which to chronicle the changes in a fictional mid-American town between 1864 and 1932. Santmyer's work had only moderate success on publication by the Ohio State University Press, but its adoption by the Book-of-the-Month Club two years later turned it into a best-seller. The first appearance in British popular culture was the comic Channel 4 television series *The Book Group* (2002). Appropriately for a practice imported from the United States, the protagonist who founds the group is a recent arrival from Cincinnati. During the second half of the decade, book clubs became enough of a social reality to be introduced into the popular soap operas *Coronation Street* (in 2005) and *EastEnders* (2009). In fiction, book clubs are not merely a device for bringing diverse characters together and creating social communities around reading; by thematizing their reading practice, they provide a metacommentary on literature in people's personal and social lives. By taking the form of the genres they mainly read – romantic comedy and crime fiction – book club novels engage reflectively with the role of popular narratives of love and death in their characters' lives; a creative mode of cultural study, one might say.[5]

Julie Highmore's enticingly named novel, *Pure Fiction* (2003), celebrates a full emancipation of the book club by affirming the capacity of 'reader power' to actually control the social narrative. Stylistically, the novel presents itself as a romantic comedy in which the characters' membership of the club saves them from their individual plots of adultery, abandonment and sexual exploitation by providing a new network of sentiment and solidarity. Zoe's narrative is both functionally and ideologically central. Zoe is a highly-strung, lonely and attractive 31-year-old who commutes to London for her office work and to see her lover, Ross Kershaw. An MP and also a popular novelist, Kershaw is a representative of 'law-and-literature' – in his case, one with a taste for troilism and drug-taking. After Zoe has been abandoned by him, another member of the group, Donna, an aspiring working-class single mother of two, takes her place and suffers the same treatment. This precipitates the denouement in which the other members of the group, learning of his behaviour towards their fellow-readers, re-name their book club 'The North Oxford Literary Society' and invite the MP to give a talk to them on his novel, *Out for the Count*. When Kershaw appears, they literally knock him out and use the threat of exposure to force him to resign from Parliament. The Club hence serves as the comic mechanism which allows a narrative of isolation and abjection to be transformed into a fantasy of popular revenge by a group united by reading against the corrupt male legislator and author.

At the same time, *Pure Fiction* asserts the value of its own conventions, as life comically follows art. Thus, while Zoe's romance with Kershaw ends sordidly, her motivation for joining the club – the fact that she has 'lots of time to read on trains and couldn't bear another God-I-really-want-a-husband book' (Highmore 2003: 78) – becomes her own 'rom com' plot. It is precisely her gift to a fellow commuter of a copy of *Middlemarch*, which she has just finished reading for the Club's next meeting, that brings them together and leads to their marriage.[6] The novel thus thematizes the role of reading and of fiction in the sexual and social lives of the individuals and, within the modalities of a romantic comedy, asserts the potential of a community built around reading literature as a social, rather than individual, act.

If reader power here has only the confidence of comedy, it is nonetheless firmly asserted at the expense not only of the corrupt legislator/author but of the professional critic. In many ways, besides Kershaw, the most significant male character in the novel is not the principal narrator and struggling author of genre fiction, Ed, but Gideon, the lower-middle-class, middle-aged lecturer in English Literature. As a member of the club, Gideon's pretentious, facile, second-hand 'lit. crit.' views render him a ridiculous and uncooperative reader.[7] At the same time, his presence alerts us to the fact that, while the novel is set in Oxford and the club's reading list would not disgrace an undergraduate course in English Literature, the University is all but absent from the narrative.[8] Gideon is a lecturer in a second-rate technical college and the only literary scholar to be mentioned in the text other than the famous authority on Dylan Thomas, Professor Thomas Thomas, who dies in the course of the narrative. On the other hand, the uneducated Donna joined the group because she saw it as a way of getting 'some practice' to help her realize her 'ambition ... to get an English degree' (Highmore 2003: 122–3) and the novel ends with her on her way to her desire, a star student in her evening class, evidenced by her ability to identify George Eliot as an 'omniscient narrator' (239).

While Donna embodies a democratic vision of an English degree that includes students of her own class, Gideon's professional life also reflects the changing understanding of literature that I have been referring to. At the start of the novel, Gideon is responsible for the college's nineteenth-century novel course, which he prides himself on delivering in a traditional manner, 'rather than the all-encompassing, let's-deconstruct-sauce-bottle-labels "English Studies"' (Highmore 2003: 133).[9] However, later in the novel he finds himself required to teach 'a course that encompasses African, African-American, Afro-Caribbean and Asian writers' (201), so as to reflect the cultural mixture of the college's students. This is not a demographic that has other than a marginal presence in *Pure Fiction*. But it is here that the changing readership of literature in Britain signified by the prosecution's anachronistic question in the *Lady Chatterley* trial was to meet the theoretical transformations discussed above, with a hard edge.

The obituary for Stuart Hall in the *Guardian* reminded readers that he was known as 'the godfather of multiculturalism' (Butler 2014). This is not a term that Hall favoured but the appellation links the change in the ethnic and racial make-up of the UK population over the period and the consequent expansion in the visibility of diverse cultural and aesthetic forms with an ideological response based on respect for cultural difference. The latter of course owed much to the defamiliarizing and queering of the 'proper' and 'normal' and the valuing of alterity that had been a central theme in the work pioneered in the UK by CCCS, CCCT and many others. It was, then, within the dynamic of multiculturalism that the encounter between the democratic opening of literature and its readers, and the return of the sacred in a literal sense, gave rise to what I have been pointing towards as a new fault-line for law.

Taking offence: Race, ethnicity and religion

The fault-line manifested itself through something common to the subjective experience of both obscenity and blasphemy and which, in its literal sense, is at the very heart of crime: offence. While prosecutions for obscenity are frequently motivated by a sense of outrage, offensiveness *per se* is not the test for obscenity but the tendency to 'deprave and corrupt'. Remedy against offensiveness relies rather on the common-law writ of 'outraging public decency'. The parameters of this writ were also reviewed in the early 1970s, driven, as was to be the case with Peacock and Kirkup, by gay sexuality. In upholding an appeal by the publishers of a magazine against a conviction for publishing adverts for gay prostitutes, Lord Reid defined the offence as covering any display 'which an ordinary decent man or woman would find to be shocking, disgusting and revolting' (*Knuller v. DPP* 1973: 458); however, he insisted, the display in question had to be open to the public gaze. Material contained within the closed pages of a magazine, the court held, did not constitute a 'public exhibition'. Hence, besides benefiting from its privileged standing in relation to obscenity, literature also enjoyed the protection against offensiveness granted to all material published under covers. Nonetheless, the capacity of literature to cause (an) offence did become a challenge in the late twentieth century in a way that, as we shall see, left law problematically exposed to the issue of the sacredness not of culture but of religion, and hence, I shall argue, of itself.

Reid's ruling on public decency shared the liberal spirit informing legal attitudes to obscenity post-*Lady Chatterley*. However, at the turn of the 1990s, the prosecution of Michael Butterworth and David Britton introduced a new dimension at the margins of obscenity and offensiveness. In one sense, this is just a story of the crude use of the powers granted to magistrates under section 3 of the Obscenity Act to confiscate obscene material without the benefit of jury trial. The case is important, however, not just because it was the last occasion (at the time of writing) on which a book was banned under the statute but because the ultimate failure of the prosecution focused attention on a new territory of offence beyond the established parameters of obscenity and public decency.

The straightforward account is as follows. As a centre for avant-garde culture, the bookshops founded in Manchester in 1976 by Butterworth and Britton soon became a target for a moral campaign led by the new Chief Constable, James Anderton, a militant Christian and renowned homophobe (see Weeks 2012: 382). First charged with selling obscene material in 1982, the owners of Savoy Books were convicted in 1991 for publishing an obscene novel entitled *Lord Horror* (Britton 1989) and a related comic book, *Meng and Ecker No.1* (Britton and Guidio 1989). Savoy's cause was taken up by the campaigning group, Article 19, and the following year the verdict was overturned in the Crown Court (*R. v. Britton & Butterworth* 1992). If, in *Lady Chatterley*, readership was the subtext, here it was the key issue, explicitly outweighing considerations of literary value. As reported by Julian Petley (1996: 165), although the court did not concede any 'approval' to the content of *Lord Horror*, it felt that the novel presented little risk since, as the judge put it, 'no-one is prepared to read this work unless they are willing to digest large amounts of philosophy and complex argument'. On the other hand, the court upheld the conviction of the comic book on the grounds that it was 'luridly bound' and far more likely than the novel 'to attract attention from the less literate' (Petley 1996: 166). The judge concluded that the comic presented 'a glorification of racism and violence. It contains pictures that will be repulsive to right-thinking people, and could be read – and possibly gloated over – by people who enjoy viciousness and violence.'

However, the overturning of the conviction for obscenity on the grounds of the likely readership does not disarm the novel's capacity to offend in ways that may not be protected by law. Be it in the form of prose, graphic novel, or, indeed, 'talking book', this is, frankly, difficult material.[10] The figure of Lord Horror is based on the executed Nazi collaborator 'Lord Haw Haw' (William Joyce), while *Meng and Ecker* refer to Auschwitz's 'angel of death', Josef Mengele, and the co-founder of the Nazi party, Dietrich Eckart. More than the explicit depictions of sex and violence, it was the anti-Semitic content of Britton's work that disturbed both the court (see Kerekes 1995) and the press (cf., e.g., the leader in the *Independent*, 31 July 1992). Finding Anderton's widely publicized comments on gays spoken by a character called Anderson, with 'Jews' replacing the word 'homosexuals' (Petley 1996: 164), no doubt makes for uncomfortable reading; however, readers are likely to find the articulation of Nazi ideology, the stylish presentation of its imagery, and the virulent anti-Semitic passages in the novel, like the one in which Lord Horror dismembers and eats a Jew (Britton 1989: 94), even more disturbing. In the appeal, Geoffrey Robertson QC argued that *Lord Horror*'s offensiveness was aimed at shocking readers into repulsion towards Nazism and its contemporary manifestations (Anthony-Woods and Mitchell 1995). However, this classic realist defence does not do justice to the aesthetic challenge of the texts and their images.

Indeed, as Benjamin Noys argues, *Lord Horror* presents a 'profoundly ambiguous and profoundly disturbing' engagement with what Susan Sontag had diagnosed in 1974 as the contemporary resurgence of 'fascinating fascism' (Sontag 1996; Noys 2002: 309). Through their treatment of Nazism as carnival and their attack on the traditional narrative of British resistance to Hitler, the texts deliberately undermine 'the political positions that have formed around our ability to distribute collective actors into the categories of perpetrators, bystanders and victims' (Noys 2002: 316). In sum, 'the *Lord Horror* graphic novels…force us to face the question of fascinating fascism without any possibility of evasion' (Noys 2002: 307); their potential offensiveness derives from the absence of a position from which we can sit comfortably in judgement on the Nazi culture presented in the works.[11] Here, then, the common conflation of 'obscene' and 'offensive' takes on the particular colour of racism. As Joylon Jenkins (1991: 37) was not alone in pointing out, if the predominant character of the offensive material was its anti-Semitism, then it should be prosecuted not under the Obscene Publications Act but under the Race Relations Act.

Whether a prosecution under the latter for publishing 'threatening, abusive or insulting' words likely to stir up racial hatred (Race Relations Act 1976: IX. 70 [5A]) would have succeeded is moot. In any case, it is possible that recent events weighed on the failure of the Director of Public Prosecution to proceed against Britton on these grounds. The publication of *Lord Horror* had come a year after Rushdie's *The Satanic Verses* (1988), the most notorious literary prosecution that 'did not bark in the night'. Together, the cases link the decline of obscenity and blasphemy trials to the emergence of new classes of offence in multicultural Britain. While, with *Lord Horror*, there was at least a possibility of addressing the offensiveness of anti-Semitism within a legal framework, the Rushdie affair revealed the existence of a legal aporia regarding offences to religious belief.

The aporia arises for two reasons which reflect the problematic legal position of religion in a multicultural society. In the first place, although *The Satanic Verses* did cause offence among many members of specific ethnic and racial groups in Britain, recourse to the Race Relations Act was not an option since the law did not include religion amongst the protected classes: 'colour, race, nationality or ethnic or national origins' (Race Relations Act 1976: I. 3 [1]). The Act had been a theoretical option with *Lord Horror* only because Judaism, like Sikhism but unlike Islam, is seen as mapping onto ethnicity. Secondly, the traditional legal framework for criminalizing offences to religion – blasphemous libel – also proved to be inapplicable. The recent history of blasphemy trials in the UK is even more conspicuously a history of absence and decline than the stuttering series of obscenity cases since *R. v. Penguin*. As I have already noted, no public prosecutions for blasphemous libel have taken place since 1922, and the verdict in the private prosecution against *Gay News* was overturned on appeal in 1979. When Christian Voice sought to bring another private prosecution in 2007 against *Jerry Springer: the Opera*, the judge refused to issue a summons. The blasphemy laws were repealed the following year.

Abdul Hussain Choudhury's attempt to have Rushdie and Viking Penguin prosecuted for blasphemous libel was an important contribution to abolition. The key factor in the appeal court's decision to uphold the magistrate's refusal to issue a summons was the recognition that the offence applied only to blasphemies against Christianity. The court agreed that 'There can be little doubt that the contents of the book have deeply offended many law-abiding Muslims who are United Kingdom citizens' (*R. v. Chief Metropolitan Stipendiary Magistrate* 1991: 309); but its review of 'the long history of blasphemy in our criminal law' (311) concluded that it was only legally possible to blaspheme against the established religion of the country. Lord Scarman had already suggested in the *Gay News* trial that 'there is a case for legislation extending [the libel] to protect the religious beliefs and feelings of non-Christians.... In an increasingly plural society such as that of modern Britain it is necessary not only to respect the differing religious beliefs, feelings and practices of all but also to protect them from scurrility, vilification, ridicule and contempt' (*Whitehouse v. Lemon* 1979: 658). However, the judges in the case brought by Choudhury declared that they supported the recommendation made in 1985 by the Law Commission to abolish the blasphemy laws. Although the court ruled that, under existing jurisprudence, fiction was no defence against blasphemy (*R. v. Chief Metropolitan Stipendiary Magistrate* 1991: 310), Robertson had again argued for the freedom of the literary work to be offensive. But the law did not need to adjudicate between the rival claims of literature and religion since it declared that it had no jurisdiction over alleged offensiveness to Islam and wished to have none in any case. In a sense, then, the bullet was dodged.

Nonetheless, for theoretical as much as social reasons, the law cannot simply disclaim any jurisdiction over offences to religion. Here was a conflict not between two distinct institutions like law and literature but between two institutions each claiming the violent force of law – in Robert Cover's sense, two rival *nomoi* (Minow, Ryan and Sarat 1992: 95–113) – each of which were offensive to the other here. Although *The Satanic Verses* did not undergo a trial in the UK, Rushdie was, notoriously, the object of a judicial ruling which effectively constituted an incitement to a serious offence under British law. The fatwa issued by the Ayatollah Khomeini drew attention to how globalization had opened up the national borders which had previously constrained the existence of plural *nomoi* and jurisdictions in the world. Resolution of tensions had hitherto worked in one direction only: through imperial law and, since the Second World War, the globalization of human rights legislation including, of course, the right to freedom of expression. The Rushdie affair precipitated a confrontation between the universal values modern Western law ascribes to itself and the global assertion of a religiously-based jurisprudence, a sacred law. In this case, secular law asserted its pre-eminence by avoiding bringing the matter to trial and using the agent of lawful violence, the police, to protect the author from violence sanctioned by the religious ruling.

Literature can only operate as a buffer between law and religion so long as culture remains 'the incarnation of the sacred', as Bourdieu put it. When the sacred re-asserts itself in its literal, religious sense, law is faced directly with the question of its claim to pre-eminence as the guardian and enforcer of norms – its own sacredness, in fact. *The Satanic Verses* had precipitated a confrontation, as John Berger (1989) put it, between 'Two Books and Two Notions of the

Sacred' – the sanctity of holy writ and what he referred to as the 'sacred cause to the European world' of 'freedom of expression'. Whichever notion was more worthy of legal protection (Berger and Rushdie took opposite positions), it was less difficult for literature to draw a line than it was for law. When Rushdie addressed the issue in a lecture entitled 'Is Nothing Sacred?' (Rushdie 1990), he distinguished the mode of reading implied by fiction from that mandated by the religious word, between, as one might say, the 'willing suspension of disbelief' and the will of belief. But what of law? If we believe in freedom of expression as a 'sacred' principle, it can only be as a sacred *juridical* principle. Law could not mark its difference from religion here on the ground of fiction v. devotion but only on the contested terrain of belief in, and allegiance to, what Cover called 'the sacred narratives of jurisdiction' that 'ground judicial commitments' and justify the law's violence (Minow, Ryan and Sarat 1992: 177–8). When confronted by a sentence based in Koranic law – or, for that matter, Old Testament (cf. Kayman 2011) – secular law is obliged to distinguish the grounds and nature of the commitment it demands from individuals to its scripture from that of religious belief – lest law indeed reveal itself as the new 'incarnation of the sacred' rather than the positive democratic consensus of reasonable people it claims to embody.

As with literature, the 'common sense' of the pre-eminence of law is normally achieved by its offering protection to religion. Although the Human Rights Act (1998) declared a commitment to the freedom to manifest and practise one's religion, the abolition of the blasphemy laws in 2008 would have left religious belief outside legal protection from offensive words afforded to other characteristics of difference in a multicultural society, were it not for the introduction of the Racial and Religious Hatred Act in 2006. However, the incorporation of religion into this legislative framework was far from untroubled and involved a compromise that, as I shall now argue, is the focus for secular law's nervous negotiation of its relations with the sacredness of religious belief in multicultural Britain, and hence of its own status relative to religion.

Taking a joke

The problem with the inclusion of religious alongside racial hatred was played out in terms of the parameters of offensiveness: what sorts of hateful words might constitute an offence in these cases? The original proposal was simply to insert 'or religious hatred' into the clause regarding 'threatening, abusive or insulting' words that defined incitement to hatred on the grounds of race, colour, ethnicity or national origin in the existing law. However, following a two-year campaign in the media, the terms 'abusive or insulting' were removed from the offence of stirring up religious hatred, which became a distinct article, limited to 'threatening' words only (Racial and Religious Hatred Act 2006: 29B). The matter did not rest there. The expression 'threatening, abusive or insulting' originated in the Public Order Act of 1936 as a generic offence relating to breaches of the peace in the light of demonstrations by the British Union of Fascists and was retained when a new general offence of 'harassment, alarm or distress' was introduced into the act in 1986. Nonetheless, in 2012, a second campaign led to the removal of the word 'insulting' here too. In the cases of religion and sexual orientation (added to hatred legislation in 2008), insult and abuse have been exempted from the offence of inciting hatred, and insult from the general offences of harassment and causing distress to someone. On what grounds?

The campaigns to decriminalize insults united religious organizations and secularists, liberal lawyers and right-wing conservatives in the cause of freedom of speech. But, as I indicated earlier, the issue was not played out now on the traditional terrain of high literature. Rather, Rowan Atkinson, the comedian who had gained fame as 'Mr Bean' and 'Blackadder', emerged from the start as the popular face of both campaigns. He became the leading spokesperson for a case that relied on two distinctions. In the first place, as he put it: 'To criticize a person for their race is manifestly irrational and ridiculous, but to criticize their religion, that is a right' (Hall and Branigan 2004). Additionally, he maintained that 'the right to offend is far more important than any right not to be offended'. Both campaigns were successful, and, while 'insulting and abusive' was removed from the category of offending words or behaviour, the conflation of criticism and offensiveness was consecrated in a clause explicitly exempting 'discussion, criticism or expressions of antipathy, dislike, ridicule, insult or abuse' of particular religions or belief systems from the terms of the act (Racial and Religious Hatred Act 2006: 29J).

Atkinson was a member of a generation of stand-up comedians that came to public notice following the first 'Secret Policeman's Ball' in 1979 and the start of the more abrasive 'alternative' stand-up scene at the London Comedy Store in the same year. A key effect produced by his prominence was that words that might be abusive or insulting about religion became, essentially, a joking matter. Headlines reporting Atkinson's launch of the campaign on 7 December 2004 included: 'Comedian stands up for right to joke about religion' (*Guardian*); 'Blackadder backs right to poke fun' (*Express*); 'Mr Bean defends the right to laugh' (*Daily Mail*). Po-faced and pious objections raised in 1979 to Monty Python's *Life of Brian* were likewise resurrected. Casting the issue in terms of humour took the sting out of 'insult' and 'abuse' – and entirely begged the question of the ethics of critical debate. In the 2012 campaign, where examples of religious satire were joined by anecdotes involving views on sexual orientation and personal ridicule in general, an association was forged in the media, as in debates in Parliament, between the criminalization of insults and abuse, and the lack of a sense of humour. Typically for discussions in the UK to do with 'political correctness', the 'evidence' overwhelmingly featured a small set of examples of the ridiculous over-zealous application of the legislation – such as the much-cited case of the English Literature graduate arrested in 2005 for suggesting that a police horse was gay.[12]

In that spirit, consider the epigraph to this essay: the attempt of members of a faith group to block the performance of a comedy based on the Bible by a theatrical company which made its reputation through their 90-minute comic cut-down of the complete works of Shakespeare. The councillors' inability to take a joke has made them join Shakespeare and the Bible as 'laughing stock'. In the same way, in the campaigns around 'insulting words', the exemplary case for freedom of expression became the (offensive) joke and hence, by failing to show that it had a sense of humour, the law risked exposing itself to ridicule. On the other hand, by decriminalizing insults of a non-racial character, including religious and homophobic ridicule, the law demonstrated that it shared the national 'common sense' in these matters, as expressed in the robust register of popular comedy.

Thus, by aligning with a culture of comedy, the law humanizes itself, distinguishing its good-humoured ethos from that of a religion that might challenge it, by casting those offended by criticism of their beliefs as humourless zealots – in the same way that feminists and gay rights campaigners are often described in quasi-religious terms as 'puritanical'.[13] The law thereby disavows any proximity between its texts and institutions and the dogmatic modalities of religion and assures its pre-eminence in the global stakes of competing *nomoi* on the basis of its embrace of the comic and popular. I nonetheless characterized this resolution above as 'nervous'. The characterization does not rely simply on the notion that the comic is often a sign of temporarily unresolved tension. While law must not take itself too seriously, it is of course, no laughing matter. An anxiety about humour is hence fundamental to its negotiations with aesthetics.

The anxiety becomes visible if we return not to trials of literature in the courts but to the representation of trials in literary works. Comedy looms large in the best-known examples. The most famous would no doubt be *The Merchant of Venice* – where the Jew confronts the Christian in a comedy about ethnicity, gender, sexual orientation and cross-dressing. Both Mr Pickwick's trial for breach of promise (Dickens 1836) and *Jarndyce v. Jarndyce* in *Bleak House* (Dickens 1853) remain in the popular imagination as by-words for the absurdities, comic or not, of the law. However, perhaps the reference to legal proceedings in English literature that most reverberates here is Mr Bumble's response to Mr Brownlow's explanation of the technicalities of the legal fiction of marriage from that other novel which courts anti-Semitism, *Oliver Twist* (1838). At the denouement, when the destruction of the evidence linking Oliver to his true origins is revealed, Mr Bumble claims that it had been his wife's fault:

> 'That is no excuse,' replied Mr. Brownlow. 'You were present on the occasion of the destruction of these trinkets, and indeed are the more guilty of the two, in the eye of the law; for the law supposes that your wife acts under your direction.'
>
> 'If the law supposes that,' said Mr. Bumble, squeezing his hat emphatically in both hands, 'the law is a ass – a idiot. If that's the eye of the law, the law is a bachelor …' (Dickens 1838: 279)

On the one hand, this may be read as just a moment of harmless English music-hall misogyny providing light relief from the dreadful narrative that Brownlow is reconstructing. On the other hand, 'If the law supposes that … the law is a ass' is, I suggest, a charge that haunts the law in the UK – supplemented, as here, by the fear that it will at the same time be revealed to be a 'bachelor' – a man ignorant of women.

This is what makes the present accommodation of law and religion fragile. Law has articulated its pre-eminence in relation to religion and at the same time avoided becoming a laughing stock, like the good counsellors of Newtonabbey, by allowing religious belief, along with homosexuality, to be objects of insult and abuse, covered by the deployment of the aesthetics of comedy. The pressure has emerged from the claims of multiculturalism in the context of a globalized rule of law, but, as we all know, there are few things harder to translate – and, therefore, to share – than a joke.[14]

Notes

1 The law underwrites the same argument, *mutatis mutandis*, for the legitimation of knowledge by science.

2 The 'Bad Sex Award' has run annually since 1993, and appears to have gained increasing ribald exposure on mainstream news media.

3 The Book-of-the-Month Club was founded in the USA in 1926 as part of a strategy to promote bookselling through mail order. The television-based Oprah Winfrey club was founded in 1996 and imitated in the UK by Richard and Judy in 2004. By 2006, the *Observer*'s literary editor, Robert McCrum (2006), had made the latter first in his list of 'Our top 50 players in the world of books'.

4 For a curmudgeonly response to the phenomenon from a writer and critic, see Will Self's comments in the *Guardian* (3 October 2014).

5 Examples of the first are the *Jane Austen Book Club* (Fowler 2004), where each of Austen's novels in turn provides the background for the sentimental adventures of the group's members, and the *Dirty Girls' Book Club* (Fox 2013), where an erotic novel provides a parallel narrative to the sexual education of a young widow. An example of the crime genre is Paul Bryers' *The Used Women's Book Club* (2003) – the title resulting from a mistyped invitation to join a 'women's used book club'.

6 Ironically, *The Middle Class Handbook* website identifies *Middlemarch* as one of the '5 Ways to Kill Your Book Club' ('Sharon T.' 2012).

7 Cf. the tiresome graduate student, Barney, to whom no one listens in C4's *The Book Group*: 'God, an expert!', as Kenny says at the first meeting.

8 The club reads (or fails to read) *Ulysses*, *Jane Eyre*, *Middlemarch*, *Heart of Darkness*, and *Crime and Punishment*; also *The Unbearable Lightness of Being*, *White Teeth*, *The Color Purple*, *The Shipping News*, *The Beach*, *The Accidental Tourist*, *The Collected Short Stories of Roald Dahl*, and a non-fiction work, *Never Cry Woolf*.

9 The reference is no doubt to Roland Barthes' *Mythologies* (1972), but it could just as well gesture to a scandal in the popular press in the 1990s about the practice in the Cardiff English department of teaching students to analyse a package of Kellogg's Corn Flakes (Masters 1995).

10 *Lord Horror* was the first of an on-going series of publications: the novels *Motherfuckers: The Auschwitz of Oz* (1996), *Baptised in the Blood of Millions* (2001), and *Invictus Horror* (2013); the comics collected as the *Lord Horror* series (1–7) (1989–90) and *Reverbstorm* 8-14 (1994–2000) (2012). Besides Meng & Ecker, Lord Horror also spawned *La Squab* (2012). The 'Talking Book' version of the first, difficult to obtain, novel, was performed by the disgraced pop singer, P.J. Proby (Britton 1999).

11 For an updated account of Britton's work, see Noys (2013).

12 See the examples given of 'victims' of legislation on the movement's 'Feel Free to Insult Me' website, http://reformsection5.org.uk.

13 By permitting insults and abuse of sexual orientation, the law also of course reasserts its heterosexual normativity and disavows its own homosocial tendencies. The essay does not seek to minimise this aspect of the debate, which it is not difficult to correlate with the issue of religious authority.

14 The essay was written before the attacks on the offices of *Charlie Hebdo* on 7 January 2015 and on the café in Copenhagen where Lars Vilks was to speak on 15 February. It would be glib and improper to shoe-horn these atrocities into this essay, so close to the events, and without due regard to the different cultural and jurisprudential traditions of France and the UK. I nonetheless feel bound to balance the opening 'in memoriam' for the literary and cultural critics who passed away in the course of composing the text by remembering here the victims of the murderous violence ostensibly provoked by the cartoons. Without compromising this expression of respect, I would, however, also register concern at the strident assertion of the unconditional pre-eminence of the law of freedom of comic expression that has dominated responses to the events across the West. The emotional force of the internationally adopted slogan 'Je suis Charlie' has threatened to smother the position of others whose deep offence at such cartoons does not become a pretext for murder. Furthermore, it has also diminished the visibility of the victims and causes of the anti-Semitic attacks on the supermarket and the synagogue that followed the assaults on the cartoonists in each case. They too should be remembered here.

References

About Penguin: Company History, available online: http://www.penguin.co.uk/static/cs/uk/0/aboutus/aboutpenguin_companyhistory.html (accessed 6 February 2014).

Anthony-Woods, P. and D.M. Mitchell (1995), 'Black Easter: The Trials of Savoy Books', *Rapid Eye*, 2, available online: http://www.savoy.abel.co.uk/HTML/beast.html (accessed 21 February 2014).

Ashford, C. (2012), *Making a Fist of It: The Law and Obscenity (UK Human Rights Blog)*, 9 January, available online: http://ukhumanrightsblog.com/2012/01/09/making-a-fist-of-it-the-law-and-obscenity/ (accessed 24 February 2014).

Barthes, R. (1972), *Mythologies*, trans. A. Lavers, London: Granada.

Berger, J. (1989), 'Two Books and Two Notions of the Sacred', *The Guardian*, 25 February: 23.

Bourdieu, P. ([1979] 1984), *Distinction: A Social Critique of the Judgement of Taste [La Distinction]*, trans. R. Nice, London: Routledge & Kegan Paul.

Britton, D. (1989), *Lord Horror*. Manchester: Savoy.

Britton, D. (1999), [CD] *Lord Horror Read by PJ Proby*, Manchester: Savoy; PJ Proby.
Britton, D. and K. Guidio (1989), *David Britton's Meng & Ecker*, vol. 1, Manchester: Savoy.
Bryers, P. (2003), *The Used Women's Book Club*. London: Bloomsbury.
Butler, P. (2014), '"Godfather of Multiculturalism" Stuart Hall Dies Aged 82', *Guardian*, 10 February.
Centre for Contemporary Cultural Studies (1964), *First Report*, University of Birmingham, available online: http://www.birmingham.ac.uk/Documents/college-artslaw/history/cccs/annual-reports/1964.pdf (accessed 20 January 2014).
'Culture of Sleaze' (1992), Editorial. *The Independent*, Friday, 31 July.
Derrida, J. (1990), 'Force of Law: The "Mystical Foundation of Authority"', *Cardozo Law Review* 11: 920–1045.
Dickens, C. (1836), *The Posthumous Papers of the Pickwick Club*, London: Chapman & Hall.
Dickens, C. (1838), *Oliver Twist; or, the Parish Boy's Progress*, London: Richard Bentley.
Dickens, C. (1853), *Bleak House*, London: Bradbury & Evans.
Douzinas, C. and L. Nead (eds) (1999), *Law and the Image: The Authority of Art and the Aesthetics of Law*, Chicago, IL: University of Chicago Press.
Flynn, D. and P. Guttridge *Running a Bookclub*, BBC Radio 4, available online: http://www.bbc.co.uk/radio4/features/book-club/running-a-club/ (accessed 16 February 2014).
Fowler, K.J. (2004), *The Jane Austen Book Club*, Harmondsworth: Penguin Books.
Fox, S. (2013), *The Dirty Girls Book Club*, Harmondsworth: Penguin.
Griswold, W., T. McDonnell and N. Wright (2005), 'Reading and the Reading Class in the Twenty-First Century', *Annual Review of Sociology* 31: 127–41.
Grüttemeier, R. and T. Laros (2013), 'Literature in Law: *Exceptio Artis* and the Emergence of Literary Fields', *Law and Humanities* 7(2): 204–17.
Hall, S. and T. Branigan (2004), 'Comedian Stands up for Right to Joke About Religion: Measure to Protect Muslims Puts Free Speech in Jeopardy, MPs Told', *The Guardian*, 7 December: 10.
Hansard (1981), 'House of Commons Debates', vol. 7, 26 June: cc 491–55.
Hartley, J. (2001), *Reading Groups: A Survey Conducted in Association with Sarah Turvey*, Oxford: Oxford University Press.
Hawkes, T., ed. (2007), *New Accents Library Collection* [1977–2003], 41 vols., London & New York, NY: Routledge.
Highmore, J. (2003), *Pure Fiction*, London: Review.
Hilliard, C. (2013), '"Is It a Book That You Would Even Wish Your Wife or Your Servants to Read?" Obscenity Law and the Politics of Reading in Modern England', *The American Historical Review* 118(3): 653–78.
Hodgson, N. (2012), 'Obscenity Trial Shows up Outdated Law', *The Law Society Gazette*, 9 January, available online: http://www.lawgazette.co.uk/63682.article (accessed 5 February 2014).

Hoggart, R. (1958), *The Uses of Literacy: Aspects of Working-Class Life, with Special Reference to Publications and Entertainments* [1957], Harmondsworth: Pelican.
Hoggart, R. ([1992] 1993), *An Imagined Life*, Oxford: Oxford University.
Hough, G. (1956), *The Dark Sun: A Study of D H Lawrence*, London: Duckworth.
Jenkins, J. (1991), 'The Trial of Lord Horror', *New Statesman & Society*, 27 September: 37.
Kayman, M.A. (1996), 'Lawful Writing: Common Law, Statute and the Properties of Literature', *New Literary History* 27(4): 761–83.
Kayman, M.A. (2011), 'The Bill of Rights: "Icons" of Liberty and Law in the Early Twenty-First Century', *Law and Humanities* 5(2): 323–48.
Kearns, P. (2007), 'The Ineluctable Decline of Obscene Libel: Exculpation and Abolition', *Criminal Law Review* 667–76.
Kerekes, D. (1995), 'Banned, Torn and Quartered: The Story of Savoy', *Critical Vision*, available online: http://www.savoy.abel.co.uk/HTML/hdprss.html (accessed 8 February 2014).
Knuller v. DPP (1973), AC 436.
Lawrence, D.H. (1928), *Lady Chatterley's Lover*, Florence: Privately Printed.
Lawrence, D.H. (1932), *Lady Chatterley's Lover*, London: Martin Secker.
Lawrence, D.H. (1933), *Lady Chatterley's Lover*, Paris: Odyssey Press.
Lawrence, D.H. (1956), *Lady Chatterley's Lover*, Complete unexpurgated ed., The Hague: William Heinemann.
Lawrence, D.H. (1960), *Lady Chatterley's Lover*, Harmondsworth: Penguin Books.
Masters, B. (1995), 'Weekly Column', *Sunday Mail: Night & Day*, 5 March: 6–8.
McCrum, R. (2006), 'Our Top 50 Players in the World of Books', *Observer*, 5 March.
Minow, M., M. Ryan and A. Sarat, eds (1992), *Narrative, Violence, and the Law: The Essays of Robert Cover*, Ann Arbor, MI: University of Michigan Press.
Noys, B. (2002), 'Fascinating (British) Fascism: David Britton's Lord Horror', *Rethinking History: The Journal of Theory and Practice* 6(3): 305–18.
Noys, B. (2013), *Full Spectrum Offence: Savoy's Neo-Weird*, available online: http://leniency.blogspot.co.uk/2013/11/full-spectrum-offence-savoys-neo-weird.html (accessed 9 November 2013).
Nussbaum, M. Craven (1995), *Poetic Justice: The Literary Imagination and Public Life*, Boston, MA: Beacon Press.
Petley, J. (1996), 'Savoy Scrapbook', *Index on Censorship* 25(1): 162–6.
R. v. Britton & Butterworth (1992), unreported 30 July, Manchester Crown Court.
R. v. Chief Metropolitan Stipendiary Magistrate, Ex P Choudhury (1991), 1 All ER 306.
R. v. Hicklin (1867), 3 QB 360.
R. v. Peacock (2012), unreported 6 January, Southwark Crown Court.
R. v. Penguin Books (1961), Crim LR 176.
Race Relations Act (1976), c. 74.
Racial and Religious Hatred Act (2006), c1.

Rancière, J. (2004), 'The Distribution of the Sensible: Politics and Aesthetics', ed. and trans. G. Rockhill, *The Politics of Aesthetics: The Distribution of the Sensible*, 12–19, London: Continuum.

Rancière, J. (2010), *Dissensus: On Politics and Aesthetics*, London: Continuum.

Reform Section 5: Feel Free to Insult Me, available online: http://reformsection5.org.uk/ (accessed 20 January 2014).

Rolph, C.H. (1961), *The Trial of Lady Chatterley: Regina v. Penguin Books, Ltd.*, Harmondsworth: Penguin Books.

Rose, M. (1993), *Authors and Owners: The Invention of Copyright*, Cambridge etc.: Harvard University Press.

Rushdie, S. (1988), *The Satanic Verses*, Harmondsworth: Penguin.

Rushdie, S. (1990), 'Is Nothing Sacred? The Herbert Read Memorial Lecture', *Granta*, 31: 98–101.

Santmyer, H. Hooven (1982), *... And Ladies of the Club*, Columbus, OH: Ohio State UP.

Self, W. (2014), 'The Fate of Our Literary Culture Is Sealed', *Guardian*, 3 October.

'Sharon T.' (2012), '5 Ways to Kill Your Book Club', *The Middle Class Handbook*, 8 May, available online: http://www.middleclasshandbook.co.uk/journal/2012/5/8/5-ways-to-kill-your-book-club.html (accessed 15 February 2014).

Sherwin, R.K. (2011), *Visualizing Law in the Age of the Digital Baroque: Arabesques & Entanglements*, London: Routledge.

Sontag, S. (1996), 'Fascinating Fascism', in *Under the Sign of Saturn*, 73–105, London: Vintage.

The Book Group (2002), [Series] Dir. A. Griffin, Channel 4.

Weeks, J. (2012), *Sex, Politics and Society: The Regulations of Sexuality since 1800*, 3rd ed., Harlow: Longman.

White, J.B. (1985), *The Legal Imagination*, abrid. ed., Chicago, IL etc.: University of Chicago Press.

Whitehouse v. Lemon (1979), AC 617.

Williams, B. (1979), *Report of the Committee on Obscenity and Film Censorship*, London: H.M.S.O.

Williams, R. ([1958] 1961), *Culture and Society 1780–1950*, Harmondsworth: Penguin.

Index